KNOW YOUR FAITH

Know Your Faith

BY NELS F. S. FERRÉ

ABBOT PROFESSOR OF CHRISTIAN THEOLOGY

ANDOVER NEWTON THEOLOGICAL SCHOOL

HARPER & BROTHERS, PUBLISHERS | NEW YORK

FOR MRS. AXEL OLSON
WHO, WHEN I WAS AN IMMIGRANT BOY,
SICK, PENNILESS AND WITHOUT FAMILY,
NURSED ME BACK TO HEALTH

CONTENTS

7

PREFACE

Popular books on religion keep pouring from our presses. Professional tomes on theology crowd one another. But the former usually are not solid, while the latter are seldom intelligible to the general public. The Marcia E. Wertsch Lectureship, of which this volume was the opening series, was dedicated to fill the gap between popular and professional theology. Its purpose is to make solid theology generally available. I have made a prayerful attempt to do so, especially in view of the fact that the money for the lectureship was given by a laywoman who cared for the intellectual welfare of the Church.

I feel deep gratitude to President Lewis B. Carpenter, and to the faculty and students of the National College for Christian Workers in Kansas City, Missouri, where the lectures were given. I am indebted, too, to my wife, who has listened to the reading of the manuscript and who has made innumerable suggestions as to its improvement. Few occasions have offered more delight than this working together on the final draft of a book. Dr. Everett Tilson of Vanderbilt University Divinity School has made constructive suggestions on the second draft of Chapter Four. The successive drafts have been typed by Mrs. Harold Kieler of Vanderbilt University, and Mrs. Richard Olson and Mrs. Wayne Johnson of Andover Newton Theological School. To them, thanks!

No book has caused me more pain of authorship than this one. Those who heard the lectures perhaps will not recognize them! But the substance of thought is the same, only radically rewritten to make the thought more readily available to the larger circle of readers. If harder writing makes for easier reading, without forfeit of content, the pain is worth while. As with all my books, I now leave this one in the hands of the final Judge to be used as is needed.

N. F. S. F.

Newton Centre, Massachusetts
January, 1959

KNOW YOUR FAITH

I | By What Authority?

Some moments of life are peculiarly luminous. Suddenly some truth strikes us with irresistible vividness and compelling conviction. What was vague becomes focused. What is secondary falls into place. Life itself takes on new meaning and our work, a more urgent purpose.

The New England Inter-Seminary Conference, dealing with "Authority in the Christian Faith," was such a luminous occasion for me.

The situation itself was simple. Several speakers had been asked to develop different views on the subject. It fell to my lot to summarize the results, to suggest a final focus, and generally to draw together the truths in the various views into "the extreme center," into "the harmony in contrariety," which is no compromise, but consummation.

Because this Conference helped me in trying to help the students, I am going to use it as a framework in the discussion of this topic. A concrete occasion often best illumines a general truth.

What does constitute authority in the Christian faith?

Our age in particular needs a straight answer to the problem of authority. If we meet this demand we shall also have done something essential to provide an answer to that other basic need of our age: motivation. We say that we know what is right, but do not do it. However, this is not the whole story. If there were more certainty as to what has the final authority to command our lives, would there not be a far smaller gap between knowledge of the right and the incentive to do it? Uncertainty and confusion drain the emotional springs for action. Clarity of faith increases the command of faith.

For decades the World Council of Churches, especially the Faith and Order Commission, has been studying the nature of authority in the Christian faith. Since its beginning, it has asked the various denominations to examine their own history to find at what point their particular strands of confession became unraveled from the total rope of Christian faith. Whenever a denomination made

14

such examination, the general result of its findings was the insistence that its confession was the original rope!

Recognizing scant hope in this approach, the Faith and Order Commission meeting in Lund, in 1952, decided to appoint a new commission, "Christ and His Church in the Light of the Holy Spirit." Its task would be, not first of all to look back to find the original rope, but, rather, in the light and power of the Holy Spirit to gather both past and present into a creative Christian future in order to twist together again the various strands into a firmly spliced rope. Those of us who have worked on this Commission have come to see, beyond every denial, how central the problem of authority is for Christian people today. It was obvious, therefore, that the New England Inter-Seminary Movement had undertaken no small task in discussing this topic in one conference.

What the program committee decided to do was to have one speaker be the advocate for *Christian experience* as determinative for faith; another as advocate for *the Bible*; two more to discuss *the Church* as final authority. My own task, after these presentations, was to discuss all these standards and to evaluate them. All the candidates for authority were represented by distinguished scholars and church leaders who believed their respective approaches to be basic. In following the sequence of the Conference as a framework for our chapter, let us foot-light the stage with a few observations.

In the final analysis, of course, God alone is authority. God is the final source of creation, the final power in control of all happenings, the final agent of man's redemption, and the final determiner of destinies. The Koran (Ch. IV) states that "God is a sufficient witness unto himself." Barth thunders that nothing in history can take the place of God, that ultimately God is his own message and method. Tillich insists that since God cannot be known directly, all symbols that point to God must be "broken." This means that no creature can ever know as God knows; therefore, all knowledge of God is mixed with human imperfection.

Although God is infinite, the historic channels for his self-revelation and the human interpretation of this self-disclosure are both finite. For this reason, it is not enough for us to say: "God is his own authority. Let God be God." It is not enough for us to say: "The Christian faith is its own authority." The question is, rather, how can we recognize the human and historical channels of God's authority? Granted that God alone is the authority of the Christian faith, how can we choose among conflicting claims to historic authority?

Before we proceed to discuss candidates for authority in the Christian faith, it is well to keep two facts in mind. The first is that Christian authority is not domineering. Jesus himself said that the kind of authority the Gentiles sought after, the disciples should shun. God never violates our freedom. He never makes us do his will. Bernard of

Clairvaux, in writing to the Pope, stressed that "love has no lord." If God is Love, his representative on earth can never "lord it over" anyone. Therefore Eric Fromm's accusation that Christianity represents an authoritarian character structure is false. The Christian faith is authoritative, but never authoritarian. Jesus calls his disciples not servants, but friends. Christian authority frees the person for fulfillment in fellowship. St. Augustine long ago defined the nature of Christian authority in saying that the service of God is perfect freedom.

The second fact to keep in mind about Christian authority is that it can never become so much a matter of sight that it no longer remains the occasion for faith. We are bid to live not by sight, but by faith. If the authority which commands us can become so clear and definite that faith is no longer required, that authority is no longer Christian. Authority in the Christian faith must speak to the inner man in such a way that the more solution is offered the more faith is demanded. Only he who is justified by faith shall live, writes St. Paul in Romans, but we often forget that justification is not only of life but of knowledge as well. In discussing experience, the Bible, and the church as candidates for authority in the Christian faith we know at the outset that Christian experience cannot be communicated except by being shared, that the law of the Bible is not of the letter but of the Spirit, and that the church cannot be an institution that compels, but a community that frees.

17

I

The first candidate is experience. Let it present its credentials! The immediate claim of this aspirant is that no one can get outside or beyond his own experience. What is not real for us in experience is accordingly not real. The final judge, therefore, is experience. Besides, every clinching of conviction is within ourselves. The click of conviction is unexceptionally a matter of personal experience. How else can the Christian faith be real to us except as we know it, feel it, or do it? But knowing, feeling, and doing are all matters of experience. Even faith is a response, a commitment, or a trusting, all of which are kinds of experience. Thus we can never get outside our experience, in the first place; and, in the second, whatever convinces us must gain the assent of our experience.

If, moreover, we try to go beyond our own experience, we ascertain what others believe the authority of the Christian faith to be. As John Dewey used to say, we affirm what we believe can be confirmed. But such appeal beyond our own experience is recourse to the experience of others. What they have experienced as real they communicate to us, and thereby is opened to us a larger experience. As far as we can, of course, we ought to seek authority as widely as possible. In theory, at least, or in intention, we ought to collect man's total experience both in the past and in the present. The systematic interpretation of this total experience—what the speaker on this subject called "comprehensive coherence"—should then become the best standard for the authority of the Christian faith. One of the other speakers at the New England Inter-Seminary Conference appealed also to Jesus' frequent employment of experience as witness to his message. Faith for Jesus, for that matter, seemed to be a matter of trusting the power of God in one's own experience.

Experience as a candidate for authority in the Christian faith makes a strong case for itself. No interpretation that leaves out experience can be wholly valid. All the reasons introduced for the importance of experience are authentic and inescapable. Nevertheless, experience is not the main or primary channel in human history for authority in the Christian faith. The main grounds for rejecting it as the chief channel are two:

First, experience cannot be the criterion for authority in the Christian faith since experience is itself under judgment. It is our experience that needs authority. It is our experience that needs judgment. It is our experience that needs to be changed. We who have the experience are in need of salvation. How then can the experience we have be the authority for our faith?

But suppose that we do not speak of experience in general, but of Christian experience. What then?

Secondly, then, it is no longer our experience as such, but our Christian experience which becomes our authority. Our Christian experience is of Christ. Therefore, it is not our *experience* of Christ, but our experience of *Christ* that counts. Authority then does not lie *in* experience, but comes *through* experience. Experience is the channel, of course, no matter what the content. Religion has to become personal in order to be real. There has to be experience of Christ for genuine convictions to conquer our lives. But Christian authority is not *in* experience but *for* experience; it is not of experience but *through* experience.

II

The Bible as a candidate for authority in the Christian faith is also strong and should be listened to with respect. In the first place, Christianity is a historic religion, and the Bible is the only record it has of its historic foundation. What other authority can there be for a historic religion than its original title deed? In the second place, the Bible is the most open, public, and objective standard possible. It is written once for all. Besides, the Bible does not vary from age to age as do the nature of personal experience and the interpretations of the Church. In the third place, the Bible is the authority that all Protestant denominations accept. Why not utilize the fact of this practical source of unity? In the fourth place, the Bible has proved itself capable of inspiring endless creative variety. To accept the Bible as the authority of the Christian faith, therefore, is not to accept merely some static dogma that lays the dead hand of the past on the fresh life of the present.

20

Nevertheless, in spite of the place and power of the Bible in Christian authority, we must reject this candidate, too, as the main channel of authority of the Christian faith. We do so for the following reasons:

The Bible is not meant to be a textbook for Christian theology, but a source book for living faith. Barth is right in teaching that the Bible becomes the Word of God only for faith. The Bible itself maintains that the letter kills while the spirit gives life. If the Bible were a textbook we could now live by sight; since it is a source book we must keep living by faith.

Even before we started examining our candidates we pointed out that any authority that makes for sight instead of faith is wrong by the very nature of the Christian kind of authority. The Bible plays a leading role necessarily in the authority of the Christian faith. When it is used as a source book, it becomes the means of the Spirit that gives life, but when it is used as a textbook, it can become the letter that kills.

Jesus asked: How can you understand my words when you do not hear my Word? Only when Christ as the living Word of God's love is accepted, can the words of the Bible find their proper context.

Furthermore, there is, in fact, no developed doctrinal unity in the Bible. The Bible is the record of God's great deeds in raising up a people unto himself. It is the story of a people who were called by God and the response they made to God—good, bad, and indifferent. It is the recitation of the lives and teachings of great prophets; and, in the fullness of time, of the Son of Man. But there is no one doctrinally developed system in the Bible. If we ask about man, even a specific question concerning man, such as what precisely is the image of God in man, the Bible has many answers. If we ask about the very heart of orthodoxy, the doctrine of the Trinity, there is no doctrine of it in the Bible. If we seek to find one interpretation of Christ, doctrinally developed and clear, we shall be profoundly disappointed. Theologians read back their own versions and distort or disregard the other material, but honest competence will know that while the Bible is universally accepted within the Christian churches, the churches do not in fact interpret the Bible in the same way.

Therefore, whenever the Bible has been made the final authority in the literal sense, or in the sense of the open, public appeal to it as objective authority, there has arisen in the church division upon division. Human nature is such that when a strong leader becomes convinced of the supreme importance of one teaching or of one strand, he makes that one the most important; and since such definiteness and such focus as act to differentiate certain believers from others are very dear to human nature, one new sect after another is founded. Thus the Bible in becoming the basis for endless creative variety also becomes the occasion for endless conflicting difference. The Bible therefore needs within it a pattern and a spirit of unity that goes beyond its objective use in merely being available to be read and interpreted.

Thus the function of the Bible is to be a mirror both for the individual Christian and for the people of God. In it we see our ordinary world in the light of a new world. We see our common words and deeds in the light of the living Word. We see ourselves, at the same time, both as we are and as we ought to be. The reason for this double vision is the presence of God in Christ showing up life in general. Christ is the love of God come to full fruition in man. He is, as the New Testament calls him, "mature manhood." Therefore it is not any specific documentation in the Bible that is authoritative, nor even the Bible in general, but rather human experience and human history interpreted in the light of Christ. Therefore, it is still Christ who constitutes the authority of the Bible. Is it anything less than the full picture of the universal love of God the Father in the face of Jesus Christ that is the authority of the Bible? The Bible is itself under the authority of the pattern of God who is the personal Spirit who is holy Love. The Scriptures tell of him as they point forward and backward to their own fulfillment in the Incarnate Word.

Even so, it is not the biblical Christ of the past that is the standard, but the living Christ who bids us look less back to Jesus than up to God. Christ is the pattern and the power of God's love drawing all men unto himself only when he is lifted up. The historic figure of Christ "after

the flesh" is fulfilled by the "Lord who is the Spirit." The
Christ of love who once came in the fullness of time is
now the Living Lord who comes fulfillingly to each and
all as we press forward into the endless future.

We never catch up with the Christ. While he walks
with us as God's presence in our lives, he also walks before
us as the eternal resource of God for our lives. The authority of the Christian faith is Christ before and beyond
our experience through the Book that testifies to him. The
Book is a powerful means giving us the picture of the
Christ. The Bible provides the pattern of God's love. The
picture, however, needs the power of Christ's presence.
The pattern needs the reality of the Person.

Thus again we have as authority not the Christ of the
Bible nor in the Bible, but the Christ who has come to us
through the Bible and still can come to us through the
Bible. Christ is God's love enmanned. He is God as Love
become flesh. He is a human being fulfilled by the presence and power of God.

III

The third candidate for authority in the Christian faith is
the church. At our Inter-Seminary Conference two outstanding churchmen, Roman Catholic and Episcopal respectively, espoused the cause of the Church as the main
channel of authority of the Christian faith. The Catholic
position is that an authoritative revelation of Christ re-

24

quires an authoritative organ of interpretation and application. The final heresy then becomes the refusal to submit to the official voice of the church in matters of faith and morals. The Catholic representative, in his great outgoing spirit, spent most of his time showing that the Roman church does respect and guard the individual conscience. Protestants should therefore be careful not to caricature the official position of the church with regard to authority.

The Anglican scholar gave large credit both to experience and to the Bible, but stressed that in actual churchmanship, decisions become, in the last analysis, either a matter of thin individualism or of listening to the long wisdom of the mature church and of co-operating with the total community in its faithfulness to the inner heart of the Gospel. The church therefore represents the corporate judgment of the believers, not *infallibly*, but *authoritatively*.

For the church as authority it should be said that the church at the heart of its being is the embodiment of the eternal purpose of God in human history. God created the world so that we might learn to become mature members of the kind of community that Christ offers us, the open, creative, inclusive community of love.

The church is the building for which the Bible offers the blueprint. The Bible exists for the sake of the building—which is Christian community. Therefore, although in one sense the blueprint is the authority for the kind of building to be constructed, in another sense, the actual needs of the building in its concrete situation must govern the decisions in the erection of it. The Bible gives general directions; the church needs specific instructions as to the application of these directions. Authority is needed for the specific decisions.

Perhaps the best way of stating this truth of need for concrete authority is that the church is the actual locus of corporate decisions. The church faces necessarily inescapable choices as to faith, morals, and strategy. Can the Bible make the choice? Who then has the right to make the decisions: the individuals as such; local groups; or the church, which represents the corporate experience both of interpreting and of applying the biblical directions?

The church is also the agent of the Holy Spirit. The church was born when the Spirit came on Pentecost. In a peculiar way the Holy Spirit is the Spirit of the church. The Holy Spirit is that reality in God that is the eternal prototype of perfect community. Therefore the church by its very nature and total function is best able to heed and to carry into effect the biddings of the Holy Spirit.

On the other hand, the reasons that we cannot make the church the main authority of the Christian faith in spite of its obvious, irreducible importance are as follows:

The actual church as corporate judgment has made mistakes. The mistakes of the Greek and the Roman churches resulted in their splitting apart. The mistakes of the Roman church resulted in the birth of the Reformation. The

mistakes of the Anglican church gave rise to the Methodist denomination.

The ground for these mistakes has been lack of flexibility. The church should have a balance between the
corporate and the personal relation to Christ. Schleier-
macher taught that the difference between a Catholic and
a Protestant is that the Catholic comes to Christ through
the church whereas the Protestant comes to the church
through Christ. The fact is, however, that both the church
and the Christian ought to come to Christ. The corporate
cannot be reduced to the personal nor the personal to the
corporate. The figure of the church as the body of Christ,
in which the individual cells have no direct relation to the
head, needs to be complemented by the figure of the people of God, in which the individual persons can have direct access to their Lord.

God wants no freezing of history in any ultimate sense
of authority. Such authority can and does become legalism. It becomes a matter of telling people what to believe
and what to do. Therefore, it becomes a living by sight
and not by faith. The church as final authority in history
takes the place of personal faith and personal decisions.
Either the church exercises such authority concretely or
it does not. If it does, it precludes the fullest opportunity
for personal faith. If it does not, it recognizes in fact an
authority beyond its own decisions. The Roman Catholic
church is more consistent at this point than is the Anglican.

The fact has been demonstrated that the natural conservatism of human authority in religion tends to domesticate the Holy Spirit. When authority is finally vested in any institution, the wielders of power in that institution become institutionalists, generally more concerned with the promotion and defense of the institution than with God's creative will and with men's changing needs. Human history itself shows the need for people who conform not first of all to institutions, but to truth and human needs. Christian history proves abundantly the need for people who relate themselves primarily to the living Christ and to their fellow men.

The church is subject to Christ. It is his body. He as its head is its only authority. It is not the *corporate* nature of the decisions that count, but their *Christian* nature. Sometimes a prophet of the living Christ will have to stand over against the corporate judgment to recall the church to its primary allegiance and to reclaim it to its only Lord. The corporate judgment may very likely be the truer wisdom. It may serve to caution individual enthusiasm. But it may also need the challenge of charismatic personalities, those who have the gift of the Spirit.

The authority needs to be channeled through the church for decency and order within the community. But the authority of the Christian faith is never *of* the church nor *in* the church; it is *for* the church and *through* the church.

28

IV

The upshot of the evaluation of the three contending positions—experience, the Bible, and the church—is as follows:

Christ alone is the authority of the Christian faith. Nor is Christ merely a mystery. He is God's revelation in a person, in a mighty deed of salvation, and in the teachings of the Kingdom of God. To be sure, as a person and as God's mighty deed he can never be reduced to any meaning nor confined within any idea. The great Creator is no system of thought nor any impersonal force. He is the living Lord of love.

On the other hand, all meanings meet in him who himself is God's Word. Christ is God's communication to the world. He is the living Word: *God is faithful!* He is God's Truth from whom all truths flow and on whom all truths depend. To say that the living Lord is "our Father" who is Spirit is to affirm at once the biblical bedrock of the authority of the Christian faith: God is Love; we have seen his presence in the person of Jesus as the Christ.

Granted that this is so, have we not avoided the question of authority *in human history?* Of course, God's Christ is the authority, for he is God's presence and power in human history. But how do we know and receive him authoritatively if not through experience, through the Bible, and through the church? Certainly we need all these channels. They are expressions of the revelation. But they are not the authority. Notice that it is *through* them that the authority comes. *They* are not the authority, any one of them or all of them together. They constitute, rather, a *needed configuration with Christ as their main pattern*. Christ as God's love for the world—the Cross and the Resurrection—is the pattern of Christian authority for and in experience, for and in the Bible, for and in the church. Christ as the *pattern* of God's love, then, is our historic authority.

This pattern is never reducible to the configuration. The pattern is not of the configuration, but shapes the configuration. Christ is always more than experience, the Bible, and the church. The configuration changes necessarily with history. Our ways of entertaining the experience, of interpreting the Bible, of living in the community change, but the pattern itself is exhaustlessly both beyond change and yet present for change. Christ is the same yesterday, today, and forever, for he is the enmanned image of God's changeless love. Yet, as real and relevant for every change in time, Christ is also the most changeable, who is always more than all change and ever ready for it. Although changeless as Love, as Love he is sensitive to every change and relates himself appropriately to it.

Professor Gustaf Wingren of Lund University in Sweden has written in his profound book *Skapelsen och Lagen* (*Creation and Law*) that the constant task of the church is to interpret the world in terms of the Bible, and the

Bible in relation to the world. The same truth holds for experience and for the church as well. Thus Christ as God goes *beyond* human history; Christ as man is *in* human history; Christ as the Godman is ever *both beyond and in* human history, the challenge to faith and work.

Experience, the Bible, and the church are all in the world. The Holy Spirit is beyond it. Christ as the God-man is both in and beyond the world. Only when the Holy Spirit can draw from "the things of Christ," using the channels of experience, the Bible, and the church, can we find that authority of the Christian faith which is truly of God, ever beyond the world, and yet also truly in the world for man. We turn therefore to a fuller consideration of the Christ who alone is the authority of the Christian faith.

II | The Son of His Love

One day a Jewish rabbi telephoned me, challenging me to come to hear his sermon: "Why Judaism Does Not Need Christ." The claim of the sermon was that Judaism was more universal in its understanding of the love of God than was Christianity. Instead of Judaism's being an "arrested form" of Christianity, as Toynbee holds, he contended that Christianity was a sect of Judaism that walled people off by its worship of Jesus. Then with great generosity he invited me to take his pulpit some future Sabbath night, at the main service of the week, to answer him. I chose as my sermon topic "Why Judaism Needs Christ."

32

Does it? We have lived with Judaism a long time. In the future we shall have to be in ever closer contact with other living religions. Is Jesus a help or a hindrance to the universal faith the world now needs?

A Muslim girl studying at Southern Methodist University came up after a lecture to ask me about Christ.

"I believe," she said, "that God is universal love. I believe no one will ever know him who does not accept the community of his love. I believe that the world could come together on this basis. But why do you Christians insist on Jesus' being the Son of God? What do you mean by the Son of God? Is the Father older?"

"No," I answered, taken aback.

"Then is he more dignified?"

"Of course not!" I retorted.

"Do you, then, believe in the Father's actual physical generation of the son?"

"Certainly not!" I replied in horror.

"Can you give any dictionary definition of the father-son relation that applies directly to your Christian doctrine?"

"I guess I can't," I admitted.

"Well, then why do you use such language? It only confuses people," was her quick and telling return.

Why do we?

Another Muslim, a professor of philosophy from the Middle East, came to Nashville, Tennessee, to speak. He opened his address as follows:

33

"The Koran begins 'God is love.' If only we could get the Christians to believe this, we could have a new world!"

My copy of the Koran opens "In the name of the most merciful God," but certainly the meaning that God is love is there. Are we, by a narrow and dogmatic interpretation of Jesus, blocking effective communication and spiritual communion in a day when the world's destiny may hang on our finding the world-wide faith?

At Vanderbilt University, in one year, two outstanding students became converts to Bahá'í, one a student in the Divinity School and the other an honor student in mathematics. They both told me, when I reasoned with them, that they had found that the Christian churches suffocated every chance at effective understanding and practice of the universal love of God. They both believed in Jesus devoutly and continued to believe that Christ as God's universal love is the ultimate truth, but they felt that now his truth had to be cut loose from those who smother it, and to be announced through a new Manifestation, the more universally and effectively to serve our age.

The world is waiting for a universal faith that can be believed. God's eternal presence and power, the God who is universal Love, is the truth we need as individuals, as people, and as the world. Exactly—this is Christ. If any religion is in fact more universal than Christ's in love, truth, and law, I will join it. Christ is sinned against, I believe, when anything less than this universal, complete

34

love is made central, either to God's nature and purpose, or to man's nature and destiny.

I

Let us consider Christ under three titles: Son of God, Son of Man, Savior.

What does it mean to call Jesus Son of God? The New Testament has three basic definitions of God. The first calls God "our Father"; the second states that "God is Spirit"; the third says that "God is Love." These three New Testament characterizations of God are central to our discussion of Christ as Son of God. If God is best understood under these three ascriptions, his Son obviously must be interpreted in terms of them. Two other definitions of God in the New Testament, "God is light" and "our God is a consuming fire," indicate not so much who God is as the integrity of his character (light) and his complete opposition to evil (a consuming fire). Biblically, then, God is Father, Spirit, Love.

When we call Christ Son of "our Father" we indicate that personal relations are ultimate. God is personal. We meet God, the eternal Father, in the human, historic Son. God is not to be known basically in terms of ideas, systems, or speculation. The Father God is the eternal Compassion who has created us, controls his creation, and will fulfill what he has started.

While Jesus lived, and when the disciples began to be-

35

lieve that they had met God in him, as the earliest writer, Paul, and the earliest Gospel, Mark, indicate, there was no question in their minds that God was also in heaven. Not all of God came! Jesus prayed to him and worked and spoke for him. Thus God was somehow *in* Jesus, but he was also *beyond* Jesus. Consequently the language of Father and Son was born.

There is nothing sacred about the biblical language as such in relation to God. What the language is trying to convey is that God is personal. He is conscious. He wills, he knows, and he cares. He answers the prayers of individuals, but he also controls the nations. This personal God came into human history fulfillingly in Jesus. God's presence and power came in Jesus in such a way that we beheld "the glory of God in the face of Jesus Christ."

Since God took the initiative in this coming to us, we speak of God *sending* his Son. Since God is personal, we say that God sent his *Son.* The important thing is that we know who God is, that he is personal, and that we can only be in line with reality and fulfilled as persons and as people when we understand and accept the true God, and ourselves and others in him. When we decide to trust this God for what he is, for what he has done for us, and wants to do for us, we "accept Christ." Such is the heart of the meaning of Christ as the "Son of God" with reference to God's being "our Father."

That God is Spirit means that God is not a limited or a localized personality. He is not a glorified man sitting enthroned somewhere. He is everywhere. He is beyond all spatial ideas. The statement that the Lord is Spirit and can be known only in the Spirit, emphasizes the truth that, although God came into human history, he can be confined and contained by none of its forms.

It is the invisible realities that are eternal. Things are what they are. Facts can be handled and controlled. The Spirit, however, is creative. We call the Spirit "he" because we speak of the Spirit who is the personal God. He is free. He goes where he wants.

Things have spatial relations. They have to stand side by side or under and over. Even when material is crushed there are small particles that are next to each other. Even personalities are discrete individuals. They learn from others and live with others. But they are themselves.

Spirit, however, can be invisibly present everywhere and can even penetrate personality into its deepest selfhood. Spirits can interpenetrate, be "one"! Thus even though the personal God is always himself and remains his own inviolate identity, God as Spirit came into Jesus and molded triumphantly the life of Jesus. Therefore, Jesus could pray to the God in heaven, the Father beyond him, even while he knew that the true God who is not only personal but also Spirit was present in him as his deepest personal reality. The Spirit came from the Father, but was truly present in Jesus as the Son of God.

Above all, God is Love. The Bible says that love is of God, and that whoever loves knows God, for God is Love.

37

Jesus is called "the Son of God's love." That God is Love means that he can be perfectly trusted. God is ever faithful, never fickle; God is continuously working in our behalf, never only at times and in part. God loves all, is always doing what is best for each and for all.

Love, says the New Testament, keeps everything going in perfect harmony. Paul's hymn to love in his I Corinthians 13 is indirectly the height of man's description of God. Faith and hope will remain because the greatest of all realities, Love, remains forever without disappearing or failing.

The great parables of Jesus yield their meaning to the key of love. The Sermon on the Mount sings the song of love. The deeds of Jesus express his love. The death of Jesus is the supreme example of love. The Cross of Christ shows us the very heart of God. And Jesus' rising from death is the declaration forever of God's faithfulness toward man.

Mysterious is the full meaning of the Personal. Mystery, too, lies in the unfathomable depths of Spirit. Beyond our fullest imagination lie the endless resources of the love of God. That Jesus is the Son of God means that this personal Love, this eternal Spirit who God is, became present, known, and powerful in human history in Jesus Christ. Anything less than, or contrary to, such assertions is the denial of the Christian faith itself that Jesus is the Son of God.

38

II

Jesus was not only Son of God; he was also Son of Man. The latter was his favorite expression for himself. Those who try to find the meaning of this term in the Old Testament or in noncanonical uses of the word usually go back to Enoch's apocalyptic Son of Man. He was to come on the clouds to deliver his people. The Son of Man is used this way in Mark, for instance, when Jesus warns the Sanhedrin not only that he is Son of Man, but that they will see him sitting at the right hand of Power and coming with the clouds.

Others use the term as in Ezekiel. According to this usage Jesus was man in a corporate sense. He was not a man, but Man, in the sight of both God and men. He was, then, the messianic Man, the deliverer, or Paul's new Adam.

But the simplest way to use the term, if we are to follow Old Testament precedent, is as did Jeremiah, who stressed the individual as representative of man. Jesus himself was using the term in this way when he said that the Sabbath was made for man and not man for the Sabbath; therefore the Son of Man is Lord even of the Sabbath. This seems very likely the original use of the term, since later worshipers would hardly use such a designation for Jesus and the term is quite in line with what is unique and powerful in his spirit.

Scholars have written many learned theses and tomes on the subject, but possibly the most fruitful investigation is that of Dr. Henry Cadman of Mansfield College, Oxford University, who after a learned doctoral dissertation on the subject and a lifetime of devotion to it comes to the conclusion that from mere textual criticism we cannot finally decide among the three. In the light of the whole Gospel, however, we may feel free to use the term in its most natural sense.

What troubles many people about Jesus is that they can believe in God, but not in Christ. Christ for them is a problem and an emotional burden. Somehow they think that they know God enough apart from Jesus and that all this business about Jesus being Christ is something they should force themselves to believe in order to be Christian. The New Testament says that no one comes to the Father except through the Son, that there is no other name by which we must be saved. Therefore many, at least figuratively, hold their noses and gulp down the unpleasant medicine of faith in Christ. When they have managed to keep it down, they become proud of their achievement and call this the narrow way of confession that alone leads to life. They derive a kind of selfish joy out of seeing others choking and retching. The whole Christian doctrine of Jesus as the Christ has putrefied within the consciousness of mankind because of this basic misconception of the meaning of Jesus as the Son of Man as well as the Son of God.

40

Jesus was just as human as anyone else. If anything, Jesus was not less man but more. He was human the way God means us all to become human. We may even say that in a real sense he was the first fully human being.

Man is human in two senses: as a creature rightly related to God and fulfilled by him; and as a creature made to find God in freedom through his own experience. Human nature can be thought of either as "mature manhood" or as a process of maturation. Jesus was human in both senses, but the former understanding of man swallowed up the second effectively. We tend to think of Jesus more as the perfected man than as a man in the process of perfecting.

If we look at Jesus' life *as a whole*, we get the impression that here was a life that overcame man's problems to the point where the whole world has come to know the power of his life. If we look at his life *as a whole*, we get the feel of it as that of a person who was tempted most severely, but who won out over man's sins so basically that he can now be called man's Savior. If we consider his Cross and his Resurrection, and what they have come to mean as a message for mankind, we find that in Jesus we meet the God who is Love, who came to save and who won the victory over man's enemies. We see both God and what God can be and do in a human life. We see the meaning of man's life in the purpose of God's love.

Well-meaning but foolish faith longs to accept Jesus as Son of God, but it dreads Jesus' being fully human. If his humanity has to be admitted, these misguided devotees want him to be Son of Man in no real sense, or else Son of Man only in the sense of a perfect human being.

Ardent but misguided devotion wants to worship the deity at the expense of the humanity. Man's longing is for God, and misled piety therefore wants to subtract, at least from conscious recall, the completely human nature of Jesus.

Misspent adoration wants Jesus to be entirely unique. Otherwise, it is feared, he is not authentically Son of God. This craving is due, not only to the desire to have him really be God, but also to the fear that, if he was like us, God demands that we become like him. And that is intolerable! Thus foolish faith and faithless fear combine to reject his full humanity.

In the same way and for the same reasons many insist that Jesus was completely sinless from the beginning of his life. The ground for their insistence is partly that man wants to be sure that God's saving presence was full in Jesus Christ and that God's work of salvation was effectively completed. But this clamor for complete sinlessness in the human Jesus can also be the result of a Jewish and Neo-Platonic idea that God, the perfect, is too holy to behold sin and certainly too holy actually to identify himself with the sinner. God's identification with the sinner is, however, the very heart of the Christian Gospel.

This longing for complete sinlessness in the human Jesus can also be due to a moralism which feels that God can be pleased with and dwell only with those who are good. Thus in man's relation with God, man's goodness is made determinative, rather than God's forgiving Love and empowering presence.

We know, however, that Jesus was human in all respects, even though the sinless God was victoriously present in his life. In any case, the whole history of the Christian church has witnessed a continuous battle to keep full and real the whole humanity of Jesus. The deeper Christian instincts have always come forward to insist that Jesus was not only Son of God but also Son of Man.

Jesus as Son of Man was not only the conclusive presence of God's perfection in his life as a whole, but through the history of his life he became a perfected man. We recall the New Testament phrase "having been made perfect."

Let us examine other biblical expressions. If Jesus grew in strength, weakness is presupposed. If Jesus asked questions from the rabbis in the temple and learned from them, or did not know when the world's end would come, ignorance is presupposed. If Jesus grew angry, lack of self-control is presupposed. If Jesus groaned in his spirit, lack of peace is presupposed. If Jesus complained of his tensions, lack of freedom from anxiety is presupposed. If Jesus learned obedience through what he suffered and was made perfect so as to become the pioneer or perfecter of our faith, lack of submissiveness is presupposed.

Thus in Jesus as the Son of Man we have not a pre-

43

fabricated human nature, some ready-to-wear suit, but the
Son of Man who was truly a human being both in his
being perfected and in his being the mediator of the perfect Love. We know that Jesus was a real, historic figure,
a human being such as we are, who by God's presence in
him, and by his human acceptance and transformation by
that presence, showed us who God is and what God can
and will do to save us. Jesus was both Son of Man and
Son of God because the life of Jesus became fulfilled by
the love of God.

The sinlessness of Jesus is a complex question. In one
sense, God, the sinless, had to remain sinless in Jesus or
else he would not be God. God cannot sin and God was
truly in Jesus. In another sense, if Jesus had been sinful
the way we are, there would have been no real victory in
his life. Then the power of the Cross over history and the
reality of the Resurrection are basically called in question.
In such a case, it is useless to speak of Jesus as in any effective sense the world's Savior. Therefore the insistence
on the sinlessness of Jesus is not without critical importance.

On the other hand, if Jesus never knew man's sin and
never had to struggle with its power, Jesus was never a
human being in the full sense of the term. He was then
perfect humanity, but never perfected. God then never
identified himself with our deepest plight. The sinless was
then never "made sin," to use the biblical expression, in
order to give us the new righteousness of God. The job

then was at best merely external and mechanical, never the work of a participant, of one who shared our lot, who understood our sinful state, and who demonstrated the power of God to overcome it in actual human life.

But God came to us not merely to overcome our weakness and our ignorance, but precisely to enter into our rebellious and faithless state and to set us free. According to the record, as far as we have it, Jesus never committed any deliberate sins of rebellion against God. He was certainly not sinful, because then he could not have become victor over sin. Dominant love excludes sin. Victorious love conquers it. Perfect love throws it out. Jesus was rather the participant in our common human nature and sinful situation.

The Bible says he feared. He knew our human anxiety. This is the root situation that occasions open sinning. Whatever be the sum and substance of ordinary responses (and it is wrong also to separate Jesus here from humanity), Jesus at least knew our deepest ailment of sin: the effective experience of accepted anxiety was his. For this reason he could even at the end realistically differentiate between his own and the Father's will, crying "not my will but Thine," and feel himself desperately forsaken by the presence of God even on the Cross.

God entered sinlessly and victoriously our full human situation in the life of Jesus in such a way that he can also enter into and become victorious in any human life, if he is understood and accepted. For God was in and with Jesus

45

in life and death and finally raised him up, "declaring him Son of God with power." Such is Paul's basic theology; and it is still the best for the church.

In Jesus, God showed himself to be Love. He did so by being himself present in him. God was truly in Christ reconciling the world unto himself. He did not come first of all to give us knowledge or to show his wisdom and power. He came to set us free from sin; to heal us; to save us; to overcome our alienation from himself; to establish fellowship with us and among men within the presence and the power of Love.

God showed himself to be Love in a real human being. That he could do this without violating, but rather fulfilling, human nature means that when God created man he made him in such a way that man could be right and real only within his true relation to God.

Man is empty at the center of his being. That is why he can grow. But man will never grow to full maturity until he becomes "filled with all the fullness of God." That man can have right relation to God *in* Christ and *with* Christ, to use the biblical expressions that abound, is due to the fact that Christ combines in himself the Son of God and the Son of Man, not artificially, but as the very fullness of time when the purpose of God in creating man is made effective by his coming to be in man. Because such a purposed fulfillment came true in Jesus and can come true in us "until we all come to mature manhood, the measure of the stature of the fullness of Christ," we now turn to the meaning of Jesus as the world's Savior.

46

III

Jesus is not only Son of God and Son of Man; he is also and particularly Savior. Our interest in Jesus is not mostly intellectual, but springs from the crying need of the human heart. Abstract theories or learned theologies can hide from us him whom God sent for our salvation. For this reason Jesus is *particularly* Savior.

If analysis of the life of Jesus prevents our seeing his life as a whole, God's mighty Christ-deed for our salvation, we have indeed exchanged our birthright for a mess of pottage. Analysis should rather show us how God's coming in Christ should be followed by his coming in us; how Christ should dwell in our hearts by faith. We should be perfected by grace until we can become presented, to use the Bible again, "mature in Christ." Only by such "mature manhood" as God achieved in Christ can anyone ever become fulfilled or fully real.

As Savior, Jesus shows us our sin both of self and of society. The light shows up the dark. Unless we can see what is wrong with us, we are unwilling to be made right. How dark sin is, was not seen until Jesus lived.

Sin is not largely wrongdoing. It is not basically a matter of breaking the law. It is not first of all shortcoming or missing the mark. Sin is a kind of life, a quality and direction of living. Before sin becomes sins or acts, it is a state of the self. Sin is a matter of being before it becomes a matter of doing.

Jesus by becoming a true self shows up the false self.

47

Jesus lived the Love that is the light of the world and the law of life. Therefore he lays bare the dark drives of human nature and uncovers the lack of love that causes lawlessness. Before Jesus' time men never had to face the merciless floodlight of God's holy, universal, unfailing love. They did not know how God demanded that they be and act. Therefore Jesus' life took away the excuse for their sin.

The sin of self is, deepest down, the lack of love. In one sense sin, as Richard McCann points out in *Delinquency: Sickness or Sin?* is a deficiency disease as well as a state or act of will. Lack of love engenders fear. Fear occasions hatred of those who threaten the self. Hatred fashions cruelty, deceit, and blindness to others' needs or good points. Thus hatred breeds contempt and strife. Or it smolders until it bursts into tensions that make us ill. Lack of love carries through a program of evil all the way from carelessness to murder. The self that is starved for love fights the world. It alternates between defensiveness and aggressiveness.

Lack of love, surprisingly, is a chosen state. The self isolates itself from love because of a false love for itself. Such rejection of love, as the eminent psychiatrist Clemens Benda reveals in *Der Mensch im Zeitalter der Leiblosigkeit* (Man in the Age of Lovelessness), is due, however, to the experience of false love or the lack of experience of real love. A loveless person needs love, but he fears love.

Love hurts the self not primarily, however, by exposing

the self to rejection or to hurt by others. Love hurts the self mainly because love is death to the loveless. The self that is turned in on self dreads being turned out. Love does just that. Therefore the loveless person hates those who love. Their love threatens him.

The lovers of mankind are often its martyrs; because, as Oscar Wilde said, Jesus was a lover for whom the world was too small, he had to die.

The loveless, nevertheless, need love and crave it. They know that they are hurting themselves in shutting love from their lives. Therefore they hate themselves in their sin as well as those who love them. They have a false love of self that must die at the hand of true love. Only so can the loveless find reality and release.

Lack of love is sin, for it is lack of faith in God. Sin, in biblical thought at its highest, is lack of faith, and faith is the affirmation of love. "Whatsoever is not of faith is sin," says the Letter to the Romans, and "perfect love," adds the First Letter of John, "casts out fear." Therefore, the lack of faith that is the heart of sin is due to a lack of love.

When love comes, faith grows, and fear goes. When Jesus came as the Love of God in human form, he exposed man's sin as never before. From then on, there is New Testament depth in the understanding of sin. The New Testament is merciless in exposing the depth of sin. No one can be Savior of men who does not first show what is wrong with them. Jesus threw the full light of reality on man's sinful existence.

The sin of self is also lack of action. The Letter of James

49

affirms that sin is knowing what is good and not doing it. This understanding of sin does not go so deep as does the interpretation of sin as lack of faith through a refusal to accept the Love that is offered. Nevertheless, when man refuses to affirm Love because of his faithlessness, he also translates this attitude of rejection into inaction. He does not feel like doing good because his heart has become hardened. Soon he may not even see need or genuine sympathy. He will turn increasingly, perhaps, toward himself and toward what he considers to be his own true good.

Oppositely, the loveless and the faithless may compensate in overactivity. Feeling guilty within and coveting being right with God, the sinner may do good things or give to good causes in order to make himself feel that he is really good and truly right with God. The sinner may thus both do and give in order not to have to accept God's love. God's free love costs far too much.

Yet Love *is* free unconditionally. Jesus demonstrated that God loves us completely just because he is God. When we show our lack of trust in him by trying to win his approval by what we do or give, we reveal, however good our intention may be in our own eyes, that we are guilty of sin at its deepest base. We disclose that we dread Love, the Love freely bestowed on us.

By living Love, Jesus showed us by the full floodlight of his personal attitudes and choices that we are sinners precisely in our lack of love. Sin becomes our deepest death when we refuse God and human fellowship in the spirit of Jesus. Overactivity, a guilty restlessness, may be a sign of the refusal of the Spirit of Jesus Christ. Whether sin manifests itself overtly as lack of action or as compensatory action, however, is a matter of secondary consequence. Jesus is the world's Savior in that he reveals the full nature and depth of man's sin.

Jesus Christ as the coming of God's holy, universal, ever-faithful love into a genuine human being also shows us our social sins. God's all-inclusive love condemns as sinful all separation due to pride and faithlessness. Most of such separation is personal or private in nature; then it is personal sin.

But sin is also social. The pitting of nation as ultimate against nation is presently our most terrifying sin. Shutting out persons or peoples in any place where public communication should be unrestricted is another form of social sin. Segregation based on race, for instance, is sin. Segregation based on religion is also sin. Discrimination based on social standing or property, again, is sin.

Love, of course, makes for creative difference and not for flat sameness. Certainly there is place for voluntary groups inviting whom they would. There can be no compulsion of friendship, or prohibition, or even prejudice, against congregating according to interest or kind. But such freedom for variation and intensive community is one thing; compulsory segregation in public places for civil, educational, or religious activity, again, is quite another matter. It is definitely social sin in the light of Christ the Savior.

Christ condemns as sin lack of public concern, lack of

responsible political participation, lack of commitment to ways of peace in public life and concord among the nations. Christ shows up the sin of our indifference when we live in abundance, without basic sharing, while the world, in large part, starves. Christ condemns as sin our walking in the secular ways of the world in our education. We should rather be alert to interpret all things in the light of Christ wherever we have educational opportunity. Often to accept secular knowledge as final fact is to crucify Christ afresh on the tree of knowledge.

To retain sectarian worship, moreover, and consider it Christian is to deny that Christian co-operation is stamped with a cross and that denominational loyalties are fulfilled only in the great glory of a common Christian faith. Local loyalty apart from, and over against, the whole body of Christ, Christ himself condemns as social sin.

For sins of both self and society, however, Christ is the Savior. Christ as God's universal love, if truly accepted, gives us a heart that cares, a mind that considers and co-operates, and a hand that is willing to work in places of need.

The Savior of men must show us in the full light of God's living truth the fact and seriousness of our sin. He does so, however, entirely in order to save us. God sent not his Son to condemn the world, but that the world through him *might be saved!* Christ as the Godman not only shows us our salvation, but effects it.

Salvation depends on light. Sin must be seen in order to be recognized; unless we really face sin, head on, we cannot be convicted of it and repent of it. Christ enables us to see sin and to acknowledge it to ourselves, to others, and to God. God in our hearts, Son and Spirit, or the Personal and Communal aspects of Love, alone can give us the strength to be sorry for our sin and the genuine desire to be rid of it. It takes great grace to repent, to be turned and to turn.

Christ also enables us to receive God's forgiveness. He has himself tasted the power of sin and borne its cost in his own body. He has wrestled with it and won. The Son of God as Son of Man has met sin, law, and death head on and conquered them all. God has assumed our plight, the whole plight, in Jesus Christ, and come off victorious within genuine humanity.

For us, God has done this self-emptying and self-expressing; therefore we can look to him and be saved. We can look to him and accept as penitent sinners his going to death for us. He who forgave those who crucified him, waits to forgive all who keep crucifying him.

The Cross is God's seal and sign that he loves us and craves to forgive us in order to have us enter into the fellowship for which he created us. The Cross is God's work in history whereby he has poked a hole in heaven's floor to let the divine light shine upon earth. The Cross is the outlet from eternity into time of the power of God for salvation that comes with forgiveness. Here God drilled through the partition between eternity and earthly time to admit the highest voltage wire of his love.

God as Man assumed the burden of our sins that we

might know who he is, who we are, and for what he has made us. God as Love walked our weary ways. Fully identified with a human being, he felt hunger and thirst, loneliness and rejection. He suffered the pangs of death within our experience. But he did so to conquer and to give us authentic life. The *victim* became the *victor*.

God in his boundless love could go with man to death and share man's agony of dying; yet the Deathless could not die and he who in the Son of Man was also the Son of God, broke the power of death in man. By so doing he bestowed upon us the power of the resurrection even before and while we share the fellowship of his sufferings.

Jesus Christ enables us to become fully and effectively saved because as God and Man he has gone with man to man's furthest extremity. By God's conquest in man of man's furthest extremity, man became Man; potential man became true Man. Consequently the Mediator is not God or the Son of God as such, but—as the Bible says— "the Man Christ Jesus." God as Son became man that the Son of Man might forever minister to all men. He shared our whole human experience, becoming the summary and summit of man's history, in order that we, seeing him, the Man Christ Jesus, might trust the Son of God not only to convict us of God's truth, of sin in us, but also to convince us of God's fuller truth, the power of salvation for us.

Thus by accepting "Jesus Christ as Lord and Savior" the official formula of the World Council of Churches for world-wide Christendom, we receive the presence of God

54

as universal Love whereby alone we can attain mature manhood. The Godman thus helps us to become God-men. Paul prays not in vain that we all be filled with the fullness of God!

Christ shows us what we can become and empowers us to attain our vision. When God fills the empty centers of our lives we can be made whole. High and holy is the Christian call to newness of life. We are bid to take Jesus Christ as our actual example, "to walk even as he walked," to be perfect even as God is perfect, yes, even to imitate God himself. We are enjoined not only to live in the Spirit but also to walk in the Spirit. To grace we are told to add virtue. Jesus himself bids his disciples take up their cross and follow him.

Not humility, but self-pride causes us to reject our instructions. God came in the flesh in the fullness of time to empower us "to live godly lives." God assumed generic humanity to cure the ills of man's heart. The Son of God, through his generic humanity, comes to us as individuals that we might become new creatures in him and walk in newness of life.

To become Christians, therefore, is to become in some real sense different in our motivation. We do not, of course, escape human moods; most certainly we do not become God; but every genuine Christian life contains a quality of effective Christian witness. In spite of our all too obvious failures and sins, we have so identified our lives with God's will for the common good that we no

55

longer can recognize such failures and sins as willed by our most authentic self. Now we can understand what Paul meant when he wrote, "It is no longer I but sin that works in me."

Something real must also happen in the church. In Christ a new community was started. The community of the universal love of God began a new age in human history. The only full witness to Christ is the power of God's love in his people. Christ is best announced by the effective living of the Christian community and by the leaven of this community's concern for the concrete needs of men.

Christ rightly interpreted is the Word of God's eternal love become historic, of God's universal love become personal. Can anything be more universal; can anything be more needed? Here we have the answer to Judaism, to Islam, to Bahá'í. Christ can be and has been falsely interpreted so as to block communication, but he can and should be understood in such a way that an open, concerned community is created.

III | To Mature Manhood

Our age is man-centered. We are sure of man, but we are not sure of God. Because doubt and despair come more easily than faith, we reinterpret the classical affirmations of faith in terms of man. That, indeed, is what "existentialism" is all about. To some this man-centeredness seems the nadir of faith. We have gone about as low as we can go. Tillich, however, in his Lowell Lectures, has pointed out that the kind of science and the kind of philosophy that made man an object, a thing, was even lower.

Existentialism, even nihilistic existentialism, is *at least* the affirmation that man is free to choose. All roads may equally lead to nothing, as Sartre claims, but *at least* man is free to throw himself into the pursuit of his choice. *At least*, as Hesse maintains, every man is a road unto himself. There is some hope *at least* in the Chinese poet who cried that out of nowhere nothing answered yes!

But the full standard for man is Christ. Christ is the fullness of God in the fullness of man in the fullness of time. He is God as universal, unconditional Love, the reality of eternity fulfilling created time. He is the Godman in whom are joined the nature of God as entire Love and the nature of man as made for that Love. He is God convincingly present in one of us, showing us his heart in the Cross and his arm in the Resurrection.

If we look at man in the light of Christ, how does he appear? If the God who came in Christ created the world, creation is good. To deny this is to deny Christ. On the other hand, when we look at the merciless ravages of nature or at the bestiality, even of religiously educated man —especially as we have seen him in this century—it is impossible to maintain that creation is merely good. It is also somehow terrifyingly evil.

This fact gives ground for the historic doctrine of "the fall" of man. In the history of man as anthropology shows it, however, there is no such fall. But if God is the creator of man and nature, in some way man has "fallen" from his origin. The least that can be said is that evil nature and sinful man are not God's intention in creation.

Therefore, no discussion of the Christian understanding

of man can be right if it so glories in the goodness of creation as to obscure the reality of "the fall," or so grovels in the depravity of "the fall" as to deny the goodness of creation. This double fact concerning man sets the problem of our discussion on this topic.

I

First, we must ask if man is good or bad. This question can have no easy answer. The answer depends upon the meaning of the question. From the point of view of creation, man is good. God cannot make a bad world or a bad man. The Bible says that God saw everything that he had made and that it was good. The God who created man is the same God who came in Christ to save him. How can such a God be guilty of an evil creation? God has all possible power and wisdom. Creation suffers from no defect. Therefore, if we start with God the creator, man is *essentially* good.

He is essentially good because he is from God. The origin of man is perfect. The source out of which he was made is flawless. Besides, if God is the one to and through whom all things are ultimately related, man's chief reference is good. Man's present nature is primarily related to God. Therefore by main reference man is essentially good.

Besides, man's destiny is to be made for God. God made him for himself. When he created, the perfect, all-wise and all-loving God created man for a perfect destiny.

59

Anything short of such an affirmation would be a denial of the reality and nature of God as seen in Christ. Man in the light of Christ is consequently essentially good. This way of looking at man is ultimate. There can therefore be no dispute about the fact that man is essentially good. Such is the view of man from the point of view of creation, reference, and destiny.

Nevertheless, looked at the opposite way, at his *actual* nature, while similarly in the light of Christ, man is undeniably bad. Man, we remember, is made to be all good, as God his Father is. Jesus bids us to be perfect even as our heavenly Father is perfect. The perfection Jesus enjoins is a maturity of love that is universal and indiscriminate. God lets his sun shine on the just and the unjust and we likewise are required to love all people alike. Man appears continually to be selling God short. He falls prey to fears and becomes guilty of accepting anxieties. But perfect love casts out fear, we know, and we are bid to be anxious in nothing, but in everything to be thankful. Being honest with ourselves and unsentimental about others, can we say that in these respects we are predominantly good?

With regard to others, we are told to prefer them in honor and never to measure ourselves by them. As a matter of fact, we are created to be continuously and unexceptionally outgoing in our acceptance of others and in every needful self-involvement in their lives. Who dares to say that, measured by this standard, he is more good than bad?

Who knows his deepest motives and hidden drives enough to say that he has been delivered from self-regard and knows his life to flow like a fountain, full and free, in mature good will to others? And knowing that nothing is impossible for God, if we trust him, who can look at his own life as not only free from distortions but also as a living miracle of world-shaking power for good? Who dares to take literally the biblical promise that greater works of faith than Christ's shall be done because Christ has gone to his Father? When we measure the best of men by Christ's standard, then, not even to mention the full, gross, common sinfulness of man generally, how can we claim even for a moment that man is basically good?

Thus we seem to be up against the fact that either our faith is wrong or our observation of man in the light of it is incorrect. We could conclude that the Christian faith taken at its own best is idealistic and unrealistic, that it is in fact, escapist. Or on the other hand we could conclude that man is not really bad, not really sinful in the Christian sense of being "curved in on himself." But neither choice will do.

We have, then, to find a possible solution of this seemingly impossible dilemma. The Christian faith has its own problems, but it is easier to accept these problems than to deny the central light Christ sheds on existence.

God made man good. This is his essential nature. Man's fallen nature is not his real nature, but only the actual condition of his nature. He is in alien territory but he is still a citizen of heaven. What does this mean?

First of all, we must view all things, especially man, in the light of God. Seen thus, earthly existence is only a small segment of God's preparatory work. If we make this time-space world central to our existence, there is no answer to our dilemma in terms of an adequate faith. The length of time God takes to prepare for free life staggers us. His molding man from "the dust of the ground" is a cosmic process of millions of years. Incomparably long is the time he took to prepare for the coming of life on this planet.

By contrast our little lives here on earth are but a brief bit in his rearing. Decision before God, not the false assumption that our time-space existence is all there is or the only place for choice, makes life important. Unimaginably beyond our lives on earth, God works his way of fostering his children.

God has given man a unique capacity to know and to respond to him. He created him in his own image for eternal life. God offered man the knowledge of good and evil. But such knowledge can be received only by the taking. It comes through the making of choices and the discovering of consequences. By the freedom to make real choices involving good and evil, God let man become real. He did not want puppets. God, being no paternalist, created a world of real risk. On the other hand, in order that man might not be self-sufficient, he left him hollow at the center.

Man, therefore, risks falling either in or out, so to speak, in an attempt either to become secure by filling in his own emptiness or to find safety by leaning on others. Not only is man made precarious within his own nature; he finds precariousness in nature. Hence his insecurity and anxiety.

Consequently, man works to make himself safe. He tries to remake himself by self-improvement. He struggles to conform to what others believe or want. He labors to lay aside means of security, whether in terms of working competence or in terms of cash savings. He invests in friendships, in "connections."

The fact that God also made this world dependable enough for man to plan and to achieve, to sow and to reap, to study and to grow, gives the false hope that he can escape from this hollowness at the center of his being. No planning, doing, or saving can make man secure. Threatened by this God-made insecurity, man sins in his attempt to be self-sufficient and self-important.

What is true for the individual is also true for the group. Groups, too, are threatened by collective insecurity and commit social sin by striving to become collectively self-sufficient and self-important. Although God created us insecure and thus gave the occasion for our sinning, God never causes sin; sin cannot be caused; but he knew at the creation of the world that man would become himself only through his finding in freedom the difference between good and evil.

The very hollowness of man's center, however, God meant for himself. Only when God is truly the center of man's life, can man escape the insecurity that tempts him to curve in on himself, or to lean on others as means to his own safety, and to be faithless toward God.

When God the eternal Spirit fills man's central hollowness, on the contrary, man accepts himself, finds true community, and lives in peace and power with God. Thus man's essential goodness is his potential goodness. His sin is holding God off. The more he knows God, the greater the sin.

If freedom is to be real and God's good freely chosen, man needs this experience. He needs to be alienated from God. To say so is not to make light of sin, but to honor God's way of working. The more and the sooner God is accepted as central, however, the better. It is God's will and man's destiny that God become thus central. Therefore, although man is under the dominion of sin, he is even more made for God. The way nature works is to show man that although he can plan and grow in personal responsibility and in community, there is no permanent or sufficient fulfillment except in relation to God, in whom is man's true life.

Man is made for the Love God is. This Love is man's essential nature. Therefore, although in his immaturity man finds sin easier than love, nevertheless, in the light of God's long-distance plans for man, he is essentially good.

II

The nature of man is best lighted up by a discussion of what it means that man was created in the image of God. This subject has been the occasion for fierce dispute in modern theology. Such sharp disagreement is understandable, since the subject involves man's central relation to God, and since, as we have seen, man's very nature is determined by his relation to God. Emil Brunner has never tired of saying that man can know himself only when he knows God in his Word; and Peter Taylor Forsyth drives home the same fact when he makes the central perspective for the understanding of man not the world, but the Word.

One long and sturdy strand of historic thought has it that the image of God in man is *reason*. Man is a rational animal, a morally responsible creature, because he can think, reflect, evaluate, decide. Man alone, therefore, this position holds, can be like God. In this respect he is unique. As a rational creature, the great amphibian transcending time, man bears the stamp of God's image. The Early Church Fathers usually supported this position. It has, so to speak, been the main line on the subject.

The question we must ask ourselves, however, is this:

65

what view of God is implied if God's image in man is reason? Is God centrally a thinker? Is God like Rodin's famous statue, a static figure contemplating the world? Greek philosophy, in large part, would shout its muted amen (reflective thought shouts only silently and inwardly!). Plato's perfect forms are statically immovable and Aristotle's unmoved mover is unmoved. The passively perfect gives rise to the actively imperfect, seeking the beauty of abiding rest in the undifferentiated unity of the One. Pythagoras' forms underlie even the music of the spheres. Christian thought has been Circe-ed by the endless ocean of unmoved rest beneath the troubled waves on the surface.

Or thought can have its impersonal logic and its history of development as the key to all reality, as in Hegel. Modern mathematicians like Sir James Jeans can find in God, the Thinker, the final explanation of the starry heavens and of man's life; and a modern philosopher like Alfred North Whitehead can find God to be the vision of the whole and of what can be, and the mediating thought between them, as he contemplates or "envisages" the possible beauty of the harmonies among the worlds of flux.

But the Christian who starts with Christ, with the Cross, with God as Love, knows that whatever truth there may be in the image of God as *reason*, it cannot be the full and final truth. It cannot be the "extreme center" where all aspects of truth find their delimitation and fulfillment.

66

Others, like Professor Mowinckel of the University of Oslo, find the image of God to be the Old Testament version of it in the Eighth Psalm: "What is man that thou art mindful of him, and the son of man that thou dost care for him? Yet thou hast made him little less than God . . . thou hast put all things under his feet." In other words, the image is specifically developed by Professor Mowinckel in connection with the Eighth Psalm as man's *power over creation*. In view of man's nearly insatiable drive for power, or as Joseph Haroutunian puts it, man's "Lust for Power," it is easy to believe that this is man's central image.

But what does this do to our view of God? It is no longer Christian. It is pagan. It presents God as basically power in nature. A dictator! But, said Bernard of Clairvaux, "love has no lord!" Great Jewish scholars like President Louis Finkelstein of the Jewish Theological Seminary in New York City are fighting a valiant battle to show that such a view of God is not even the heart of the Old Testament. There is, of course, some truth in this position of the image of God as man's power over creation, but certainly not the truth that fulfills.

Some theologians, notably Reinhold Niebuhr, interpret the image of God in man as man's *capacity for creative self-transcendence.* This view is distinguished with great seriousness from rationalism. A good deal of the power of the main-line view was in reality reason as the capacity to transcend our actual situation. But Niebuhr puts more emphasis on decision. In his view man sees an ideal in the abstract. He can see this with "a perfection" that is lost as soon as he must make decisions among the ambiguities of existence, not least of which is the ambiguity of his own sinfulness.

In one period, Niebuhr stressed the morality of the individual as over against the immorality of society. He has outgrown this position, for the most part, but he still analyzes the operation of the image of God in man as the contrast between the original righteousness of man before he acts (the act of creative self-transcendence, what he calls "perfection before the act"), and the "fallen" state of man within the ambiguities of our sinful world.

There is, however, no such perfection. Actual man cannot even see perfection. Man's vision is tainted by his sinfulness as a total being. Yet there undeniably is in this position, too, a truth in the fact of man's creative self-transcendence.

Again we ask, what does this position do to our view of God? Is God then supremely Creator? Is God first of all Creativity? The Christian answer is positive: God creates because he loves; he does not love because he creates. Therefore, however important the truth involved in the defining of the image of God in man as creative self-transcendence, it cannot constitute the main make-up of the image.

Another important position in today's thought is that of Emil Brunner, who defines the image of God in man

68

as his *answerability to God*. While man, according to
Brunner, no longer possesses original righteousness, he
cannot escape the fact that he is responsible to God for
his life. No matter where man may be or what he may do,
he is in fact so related to God that he cannot escape feeling guilty before God, either in his conscious mind or in
the torments and imaginations of the unconscious.

We ask a similar question of this position: What conception of God does this point of view entail? Is God
mainly Judge? The Christian knows better. God judges,
but he is far more Savior and Father. He judges in order
to save. The Bible even says that God sent his Son not to
judge *but* to save.

In fairness to Brunner it must be said that the original
image that man possessed before the "fall" was not answerability; only the form of the original image now remains as man's answerability to God. We know of no
such historic "fall," however, and with this admission
Brunner and the others agree. Therefore it is better to
make the image central to man's *essential* relation to
God. Its working can be obscured, thwarted by sin, but
its nature is part of God's goodness in creation that must
not be denied by "the fall."

The truth of Brunner's position is powerful. It is connected with God's whole use of law, of guilt, and of grace,
but Brunner's interpretation does not arrive at the determinative nature of the image of God in man.

Others like Karl Barth and Anders Nygren have maintained that the image has been totally destroyed. There is no part of it left in man. The fall was entire, involving the whole man. There is nothing of God in man. Such denial is the most radical in Christian history.

With Karl Barth the emphasis is on the complete sovereignty of God. Man is, even by nature, in no position to help the least bit toward his own salvation. All is by grace and faith. In Nygren there is extreme sensitivity to what he takes to be the disastrous heresy of mysticism, namely that there is a bit of God in every man that makes him restless apart from his right relation to God.

Both Barth and Nygren are afraid of mixing the categories of God and man. Both are also afraid of thinking of God in terms of substance, as some "stuff" that can be in man, or some structure that can organize man. Barth now is willing to speak of the image of God in man as God's call to man. I think Nygren would not object to such a statement of the case. As a matter of fact, Barth and Brunner likewise have come closer to each other, as David Cairns points out in The Image of God in Modern Theology.

An outright repudiation of the image of God in man would really amount to a denial that there is a natural relation between God and man. Indeed, both Barth and Nygren are woefully weak on the point of God's presence in creation; they even stammer on his positive use of creation. Their denial that God is "stuff" is, of course, sound, as is their insistence on the sovereignty of God's grace.

If only they could see more fully how this grace works in creation and in man: offering man free acceptance on God's part and letting him use his freedom to find God!

On this important question of the image of God in man, is there a clear word from God? One fact is obvious and beyond all dispute: the God of the Christian revelation is centrally Love, the God of the Cross and the Resurrection. Simply put, the fact is, God is faithful.

God being Love, his image must be man's capacity for love. Man is centrally made for love, for God's love and for man's. The true image includes the truth of all partial images. Love, for instance, has within it the reality of *reason*, fulfilling the insight of the first position we considered. How can love be high and free without the power to know, to reflect, to evaluate, and in the light of this process to choose? Man is not essentially an animal. Even in the respect that he has reason he is unique in every developed sense of the meaning of terms.

Man also has been given *power over nature*, our second position. His is the world to use. God has put all things under his feet. He enjoys *creative transcendence* over time, a fearful position to be in. This is a sacred place in which to be put. God also holds man *accountable*. He is not only under law, but under the Lordship of the inescapable God. And man's chief relation to God is not in terms of *some bit of God in man*, but in terms of God's coming to man, his calling man.

There is truth in all these positions, but they never fall

into essential relationship until man is understood as created for love by the God who is Love. The image of God in man is man's need for love. The image of God in man as centrally man's being made for God's love gives context and total meaning to all other aspects of the image. Hunger is not food, but it does characterize man's relation to nature. Hunger for God is no bit of God in man, but it determines his very being. Man's emptiness is for God's filling.

No individual and no community can be right until they are rightly related to God. No individual and no community can be real until they are made real in relation to God. The reflection of God's love in man's need for love indicates the reality of God as Love. Christ as the revelation of God's love fulfillingly present in man is God's right relation to man and man's right relation to God.

Therefore we can include still one more view as to the image of God in man. Gustaf Wingren in *Skapelsen och Lagen* (*Creation and Law*) says that the New Testament calls Christ himself the image of God. The Letter to the Colossians does that exactly. Christ as the realization of God's presence in man as fulfilling love, giving man "mature manhood," is in fact the revelation of the true image, the filling of the image in a concrete man. The image of God's love is fulfilled only by the actual presence of God's love.

Christ as the image, therefore, is the reconciliation of the image of God with conscience. To this crucial topic for understanding man, namely the infilling of the image of God in conscience, we now turn.

III

The image of God is the means whereby we adjust to God; the conscience, "what we know together," is the way we adjust to men. God is infinite and perfect Love. Man is finite, made for love. The image is absolute; the conscience is relative. Man himself lives in the conflict of the perfect and the sinful, the unconditional and the conditional.

The only right way we can adjust to God is his way! With respect to God, there is no compromising one whit. God's love is totalitarian in its demand on us. It means full acceptance of him and his way, and complete openness to all men and concern for them. It involves self-acceptance as part of the community of God. We accept ourselves, but only as members of the fellowship, totally to be used for God and for the needs of the community.

God and the mature Christian community, on their part, are totally concerned with each self for his maximum good and development in the good. God asks totally of us what is good within his will for all. The image reflects this reality of our basic relation to God and the demands this relation puts on us.

Conscience is a means for our adjustment to man. It is the concrete rightness we feel in the light of our background, total schooling, and experience. We learn that

73

certain things are right from our parents, mostly informally by the way they live and by the way they share their experience in the ordinary course of life. We learn in school that certain things are right. Many other ideas of right and wrong we pick up or have ingrained in us from life's experience in general and from the way our communities think and act.

The conscience, therefore, varies markedly from person to person and from culture to culture. What some do to God's glory would for others be a mockery of him. Conscience is mostly set by the prevailing religion; not by the religion professed, but by the religion lived. Conscience reflects largely the status quo.

Between the perfect image and its demand on man's conscience there is thus not only a wide gap, but a hurtful conflict. Sinning against their conscience, men are hurt. Such sinning against the conscience is what is generally meant by sin.

But by sinning more deeply and constantly against the image, men are even more deeply hurt. As long as they do not know what the image involves, men are no more than uneasy and vaguely anxious because of this inner conflict. While they then have specific guilt feelings with respect to their conscience, they have only unspecific anxiety with regard to their image of God.

Before they know the better law of God's will, men have a far less keen understanding of what is wrong with them and consequently are far less hurt. When they encounter

74

the better law that interprets the image, the nature of sin bursts upon them and their conflict multiplies. Sin now becomes far more terrifying.

With Christ's coming, the image of God in man became filled by being fulfilled. Conscience received its intended content. With Christ's coming, conscience obtained its perfect standard. Christ showed man the perfect will of God by demonstrating the perfect nature of God and the mature nature of man. Christ showed man his right relation to God.

God reduced in Christ the laws of the Old Testament decalogue to two: love to God and love to man, universal and entire. This concentration of the ten into two commands had already been accomplished by Judaism; Jesus himself had been brought up reciting them daily.

But in Jesus these two laws became demonstrated in life as well as explicated in meaning. In Jesus, too, the law of perfect love became, beyond every command, the Gospel of God's grace. The law of love became fulfilled in the life of Love.

From now on, men must not strive to fulfill this law as law, but, rather, to accept God's life freely as a gift. This new gift of life turns the conscience from an enemy, representing a law impossible to keep, to the correcting friend who enables man to become fulfilled within a new relation to God that itself is the very power for the life of love.

Thus in Christ the full nature of the image is made

clear, conscience is fulfilled, and man is given the power to live the law, no longer as law, but as the life of love. Thus right is real and uncompromisingly maintained even while it is left behind as no longer an enemy or a primary relation to God and man. The amazing freedom of life fulfilled by love takes its place.

But actual man lives in conflict between law and love, between conscience and image. Few find the reality and the power of the Gospel of Christ in this life. Most people get clogged in the attempt to satisfy their conscience by right conduct, and find no rest. Acquiescence in the status quo is almost always the essence of sin. It is choosing conscience rather than image.

Conformity to sinful society is nonconformity to God. And in the light of the full standard of Christ our communities are deeply sinful. Original sin consists in the partaking of this societal heritage that shields our misgivings almost as they arise. We protect ourselves by devious and ingenious rationalizations in the guise of the wisdom of the ages. We try to quiet the protest of the arguments of our socially oriented conscience.

For this reason Kierkegaard is right in saying that man's characteristic relation to God is sin. We repress in our subconscious our unwon battles on the conscious side. But such repression does not deliver us from conflict, for God never loses and never lets go. Therefore, our unwon battles continue at a level below our consciousness. Deep down we hate God who threatens our compromises.

Thus we live by fear of God on the conscious level and in anxiety toward God on the subconscious level. Our relation to God becomes characterized by guilt. Such guilt results in physical illness and mental malady. One woman who could not be cured by doctors was cured quickly after she came to know that her suffering was caused by basic dishonesty in regard to her income tax!

But above all we feel wrong toward God. Because this is the case, either we try to throw ourselves into some religious faith and activity that will persuade us that we are pleasing God, or we grow to resent what we call religion, even to hate the highest form of it. Or else the depth spirit in us, the demonic self we are, robs us of our convictions or produces in us spiritual restlessness or its opposite, spiritlessness. We forfeit the free and fulfilled life for which we are made.

We are made for God, for his love and for man's. When Love's community is real, life becomes satisfying in new dimensions. We become free to live. We become free for creative community. We become free to be ourselves, as persons and as community.

But nothing can bring about this freedom in the full sense, except our becoming right with God. Our fears and anxieties must lose their importance by being focused in our main relation: our fear and anxiety before God.

Only forgiveness by God can make man free. Only forgiveness can fulfill man. Only forgiveness can put man in the relation to God and man where he can find increas-

77

ingly his true nature and grow in it. Therefore, no study of man can be more than a description of man's plight and possibility until it include the prescription by God for man. We now turn to this prescription under the heading of sin and salvation.

IV | Grace Abounding

Sin holds the spotlight among contemporary theologians. We have a new understanding of its depth and stubbornness. Though we are not sure about many essentials, we are sure about the reality and power of sin. We even run the risk of turning sin into a popular topic. To put heavy stress on sin pays off in popularity in some theological circles.

We can be thankful for the rediscovery of the cost and magnitude of sin for it cuts deep wounds into humanity; it even curses nature. If we care for men we must wrestle with the problem of sin. If we ever enter at all into God's nature and purpose we must do battle with sin. Thus every adequate theology must deal with the deadly power and awful reality of sin.

But we must not put a false and one-sided stress on sin. We can talk about sin in grave tones, without ever really coming to grips with it. We can discuss sin without either repudiating it or fighting its power. We can even become theologically "right" by stressing sin without ever taking up the cross to follow the Christ. By so doing we encourage men to emphasize man's sin rather than God's grace; we prompt them to let sin usurp the place of God in human consciousness; we lead them to become more sure of sin than of the Gospel. When sin assumes such proportion in theology, theology itself becomes sin.

I

We cannot indicate the main dimensions of sin without looking at the meaning of sin, salvation, and sanctification. Each dimension exhibits sin in a new light. As always, our examination of these Christian doctrines must be in the light of God in Christ as universal, holy Love. Only the Person of Christ, as we have already seen, exposes sin in all its ugliness and darkness.

We begin with a look at the difference between *sins* and *sin*. In the Prayer of General Confession we acknowledge the many sins we from time to time have committed. We find it easy to confess such sins, if their confession keeps us unaware of our sin. Sometimes deep contrition accompanies the confession of sinful acts not so much out of sorrow for the sins we know we have committed as for the fear we may discover that we are basically sinful. We do not like to think of ourselves as basically evil. So we shudder when we discover the power of sin in us.

Such repentance over a gross or overt act of sin is possible alike for Christians and non-Christians. Why? Because sin is a most pervasive reality; and, too, because our response to it is exceedingly subtle, perhaps even largely subconscious.

Sin is what we are; sins are what we do. Sin is the response of the entire self to God in faithlessness or rebellion; sins are our deliberate acts of faithlessness and rebellion. Because we are sinful we act in sinful ways; we sin and commit sins.

Some distinguish between "material" and "formal" sin. They define the former as doing wrong. Man can do wrong without intending evil. He can be both faithful and loyal, yet do wrong out of ignorance; he can break God's law, fall short of God's command, or miss God's mark. Such unintentional instances of doing wrong illustrate the meaning of material sin. But they are not occasions of sin in the formal sense. This distinction readily lends itself to a sub-Christian and unworthy interpretation. God holds us responsible only for what we know or for what we would know if we cared.

So we return to sin as the source of man's trouble. Sins,

though real and serious, are only ugly flowers on the vine of sin. Sin is always intended by the self. Sin is a chosen state. Sin is what we are and do because of what we choose to be and do.

But our choice of sin is seldom conscious and clear. Sin is a work of darkness; it thrives in the shadows rather than in the light. Seldom does sin involve a well-thought-out course of action in defiance of God. Seldom do we consciously tread the path of faithlessness.

Usually the choice of sin takes place below the level of consciousness. Down in the deep recesses of the subconscious, with consummate craft and in self-deceit, we distort our actual situations and true choices into a caricature. We analyze our situation in the light of self-interest, subtly ballooning the points in our favor and quickly belittling the unfavorable aspects of our situation. We let our eyes dwell on what we think we like, until reason touches up the situation to the point where we become convinced we are doing only what is good and wise.

We sin most deeply by refusing to see ourselves as sinners. We sell ourselves on ourselves, not by clear and conscious deception, but by clever and subtle misrepresentation. Self-interest transplants us in a false world, then prompts our minds to work overtime in search of the defense of that world. Thus reason becomes a tool of self-justification, if not of self-glorification.

We exercise reason in the hope of proving ourselves right and others wrong. Seeing a false world in our conscious minds, we act in accordance with our warped reason. Without conscious intention, and therefore without any feeling of guilt, we do many things others deem wrong; in fact, we, too, would think them wrong if our vision were sound. We even pin the label of evil on such actions when performed by others, unless we pause long enough to remember that we are condemning ourselves by this judgment of them. Whenever the true world manages to pierce this picture we experience conscious guilt.

Nevertheless powerful allies work mightily to keep this conspiracy in guilt under cover. Occasionally we even use repentance to distort and falsify our basic situation. Sometimes we "repent" of our *sins* to protect our *sin!*

So the self-critical are far nearer the Kingdom of God than the self-righteous; so long as men do not feel the pain of sin, they deny God and deceive themselves. But they do not go scot free. Their self-deception exacts a high toll in the deeper self. It begets a guilt-feeling in the subconscious. This in turn aggravates moral decay. And, worse still, moral decay spreads its poisonous contagion.

Why is sin so hard to detect in ourselves? Because it is the very set not only of the self but also of society. Not that this "set" eliminates responsibility, for sin involves choice at every level. Although we cannot choose sin *for* others, we can choose sin *with* others. Our capacity to do this explains our birth into a sinful order. From the very beginning men have joined hands with their neighbors in the hope of making their hiding place secure from God.

Clever and ingenious are man's devices to conceal his depth-hiding from God. Individuals and communities sinning together over long generations have built formidable barriers against the light of God.

Some seek escape in atheistic theory; more seek it in religious practices and doctrines. Because God stands at the center of the human situation, both the self and society feel driven to distort his nature and will. Sinful selves find mutual support and comfort in their construction of some idealistic religion as a refuge from God. Religion in the history of mankind has most often been a product of human fear, and religious practices have usually been a mixture of good and bad. Though the self can scarcely fool itself into looking on the bad as good, or society deceive itself into mistaking darkness for light, both self and society can dim the rays of light in a smoky half-darkness.

Thanks to this mixture, church people can unashamedly defend segregation as an expression of God's will, justify war as divine service, defend ruthless competition in business as a part of the natural order, and reflect hostile and uncharitable attitudes generally; they can bless personal and social evil in the name of religion.

Only rarely does the self have to invent such protection against the light or build such strong support of sin from a fresh start. Usually he has only to acquiesce in the social order. As a matter of fact, he finds it hard to do otherwise. Afraid of public opposition, he takes refuge from persecution in the crowd. He dares not break "faith" with fellow refugees from the light.

The prophets and saints are the greatest enemies of "normal" social order and practices. Jesus *had* to be crucified. They are deemed most guilty of social misconduct who expose man's religious subterfuges and lay bare the sin of churches. Alfred North Whitehead, accordingly, maintains that it is merciful to stone the prophets. Like the ancient High Priest, many can see nothing especially wrong with the practice of letting one person die for the people.

This body of sin, molded through the ages by the set of society against God, suggests the permanent meaning of original sin. In this sense man is generically sinful. We are born into a sinning order.

Theologians illustrate this fact by their tendency to acquiesce in views of God that are unworthy of him. By so doing, they allow views inconsistent with God's universal holy Love in Christ to rob the Gospel of its full powers of judgment and salvation. Worse yet, they permit themselves to be led astray in their search for the full illumination and judgment of sin. They look for this illumination and judgment in religion or "Christianity," but not in Christ as God's universal holy Love come to earth. They fail to see that the judgment is the Light: the Light of Love who came into the world!

85

II

If sin is so deep and serious, if repentance of sin as well as of sins requires such a wrench in the self and such a break with society, then how can the Gospel be good news? Is it not the part of wisdom and kindness alike not to expose people against their will to the full light of God's holy, universal love in Christ? By no means, for all men must pass through suffering on the way to salvation. Indeed, to be unsaved is to suffer. Men who do not know God as Father and who run from him down the dark alley of their subterranean life cannot help suffering.

They suffer from their fear of self, from their fear of others, and from their fear of God. Most of such suffering takes place below the level of conscious awareness. It is not only people who lack inward peace and the sense of ultimate reality who experience such suffering. So also do they who straddle the fence between God and ordinary behavior; these latter suffer from an inability to feel at home among either world-lovers or God-lovers.

They also suffer, of course, who take up the Cross and follow the Christ. But they suffer redemptively. They suffer for others, even for those who inflict their suffering. Unlike other sufferers, they experience the joy of the Gospel even in their pain and agony.

To hope for a life without suffering is futile. No one will ever be saved until his measure of suffering is fulfilled. God has ordained suffering for our good. Only by suffering can we learn to know how false the way of the fearful, self-centered self is, in the first place, and want to find another way, that of the self fulfilled in God. Even then suffering comes, but love's suffering, which, deepest down, satisfies the self and draws us nearer to God. We all must come to God by the way of suffering. The old Gospel song says truly: "The way of the Cross leads home."

By using suffering for God's glory and for his purpose, and not just enduring it as helpless victims, we can triumph inwardly through suffering; in us, as in Jesus Christ, the victim can emerge the victor.

While men may be regarded as "full of sin" in the sense of being permeated through and through with its contagion, they never become so sinful that they can do no good. God lives and works in all men. In fact, most individuals, apart from undue pressure, are a fairly decent lot; they ask only to live and let live. The theologian who paints men as "a mass of corruption" not only distorts the facts; he betrays both God and man.

The wrench in the sinner does not constitute a hopeless chasm; nor his break with society, absolute separation. After all, all men seek right adjustment, which is what salvation is. Very few sinful men ever fall so low that they can no longer applaud the saints. Sinful man, after all, is a sinner seeking salvation. The sinner remains divided in his own response to the Revealer of salvation. But the Gospel hits too hard and hurts too much to let him remain neutral forever.

Why, then, do we call salvation life's truest good? Why is salvation "Gospel"? Because salvation means getting right with God, and such a state alone can give man full satisfaction. To be saved means to be right with God, to be in line with his will. Salvation is life's goal because man is God's creature. Salvation is man's main need because God is life's final goal. So we cannot long continue at odds with God until we begin to be at odds with self. We cannot long enjoy our denial of the very satisfaction for which we are made.

But how do we get right with God? The answer is simple: God has already paved the way for us. God himself came in Jesus Christ as holy universal Love to fulfill the life of past human history in the life of one historical person; his coming paved the way for the fulfillment of the life of every man.

Salvation has two requirements. The first is to be right with God who came in Jesus Christ as suffering and victorious Love; the second, to be right with men.

What does this first aspect of salvation involve? What does it mean to be right with God? The answer is: to accept the only security on which we can fully and firmly rely. Any person who is right with God, by being aligned to his will, knows life's truest security. God alone never fails. He alone can be trusted implicitly. He alone can lend certainty to our life in a world riddled with uncertainty. He alone can lend permanence to our fleeting existence in time. God alone can give reality to the dream of that part of life we have already lived. He alone can brace us for the walk down the problematic tomorrow. He alone can steady us for the jump off the brim over which we cannot look back.

Certainly the hard facts of human existence justify our search for security. Often the healthy and strong die first, perhaps through accident. Disaster lurks behind every corner. Meaninglessness threatens us on every side. Friends may desert us. Possessions may forsake us. Even when we have them, we fear their possible loss or theft. Nothing seems certain in life except death, and people fear what may happen to them after death, despite the advertising slogan of a cemetery in California: "Permanent protection for your precious departed."

Man can find permanent protection only by losing himself in God. He can find safety only in salvation. He can count on the future only if he counts on God. Man can find eternal security only as he seeks security in God. He cannot be saved except by the grace of God. The saved man knows this. So he endeavors to commit his life without reserve or condition into the hands of God—come what may! So he turns toward the path of faith and freedom in fellowship with the Father.

Salvation, in addition to security in God, brings deliverance *from* something. When God gives us a new Spirit

89

in Jesus Christ, he also saves us from the power and pain of self-centeredness, from the fear-ridden, "natural" self. Indeed the presence or absence of salvation can be determined only by the presence or absence of the fruit of the Spirit. The fruit of the Spirit may be thought of as the characteristics of those saved from self: love, joy, peace, and all the other Christian virtues.

The self is a hard taskmaster. No one can be harder on a person than his own self. Self can punish and keep punishing. Self can drive with feverish ambition, keeping him ever restless. Self can plague with blinding fear, denying true peace. The self can dodge discipline and spoil life with fickleness. The self can coddle desire and go to pieces. The self can grieve over self from morning to night. The self can go on, day after day, with no energy and no zest. The self can spurn every attempt to set himself free for faith. The self can go on sinning and still rue his role as slave rather than master.

But when, saved by grace and faith, man finds a new self, the old and all-spoiling self has to release its tyrannical hold on his life. Then he discovers how free and secure the self can be if only he remain within the will of God.

Salvation, insofar as it is effective, also saves us from too heavy dependence on others. We find in God-directedness both a live alternative to and a sure cure for constant fretting over what other people think of us. We neither become overly depressed by their expressions of disapproval nor elated by their words of praise.

Many people suffer from clumsiness in personal relations. They cannot get along with others. They are either
falsely aggressive or unnecessarily defensive. They either
hurt and blaze forth or hurt and smolder.

Only when we know God as our refuge and strength
can we live with others as genuine persons. Only when we
have God as our Father and Judge can we live with others
and with our own strong convictions without constant
tension. Only when we are forgiven by God can we accept
ourselves to the point where we feel no desire to blame
others.

Forgiveness by God and by ourselves releases us from
the tensions which keep us from being generous in our
judgment of others. We no longer feel we have to be
either sentimental about others' faults or shocked by
them. Instead in proportion to salvation's being real in
us, we view others realistically—not blind to their faults,
to be sure—but within the hope and purpose of God.

Once we personally experience God's love in Christ,
once we know the Spirit whose we are, we can also be
saved from our bad habits. Trivial as this aspect of salvation may appear, it is crucial. Innumerable people long
for escape from some habit they loathe but cannot conquer. Many drunkards hate drinking, but cannot leave off.
Many sex deviates deplore lust, but cannot resist its drive.
Whatever the habit may be among the legion that
threaten us, when it rules, we lead an unhappy and en-
slaved life. God can release us from the tyrannical power
of these insidious destroyers of self-respect and freedom.

God likewise sets us free from the bondage of the past. Multitudes find in their own past something they can neither forget nor forgive. Some go to psychiatrists in search of relief. Some try so to change their way of life as to forget their oppressive past. In both instances at least temporarily, the irretrievable past puts under bondage the inescapable present.

Multitudes contain in their lives a whole reservoir of past shame that has never been forgiven or swept out of the subconscious. They feel guilty but cannot tell why. They blame themselves but can find no rational basis for so doing. They cringe within but cannot articulate the reason for their fear.

When a guilt-sufferer genuinely accepts God in Christ, he begins to undergo a radical transformation. With a new Spirit comes a reorientation of life, a sweeping clean of the past and a full facing of the present. The light of salvation starts chasing the clouds from his future. He henceforth sees hope not as cowardly escape but as solid reality.

Salvation also includes deliverance from the wrath to come. Often men live as if they could get away with living for themselves in this life. And, sometimes, they do—in this life! But in the world to come they must face God and face up to what they have done. God's forgiveness of our guilt does not exempt us from the obligation either of paying for our wrong deeds or of working to set things right. We do not get away with anything before God; we only think we do.

In spite of our persistence as sinners, we can have our reward in this life; we can defy God in this life; we can have fun and folly in this life, but, as sure as God is holy and just, in the life to come each of us shall pay every debt not made good in this life.

Salvation is no bargain-counter product. We have to pay for it in full. Though God pays for the guilt of personal relations and freely offers us full restoration to fellowship, we still have to pay for the consequences of our deeds in works of faith and love within the grace of God. Sin is more serious than any human being can fully understand.

Yet we are saved not only from but for something. We are saved for a new self. The more fully saved we are, the more we are in tune with God. The perverted self becomes more and more the fulfilled self. Only experience can teach us what it means to be rid of the fears, drives, and desires that once mastered our lives. Only freedom from their power can teach us the joy that comes when they no longer dominate our lives and spoil them.

We are similarly saved for a new society. A whole new range of experience begins to open up. Lonesome man finds the companionship for which he was made. Instead of fighting others or fearing them, he lives with them humbly, as friends. The experience of salvation enables us to care what others do or think, because we are concerned with them, while not dependent upon their judgment.

Salvation opens the door to the fellowship of the true

93

church, the new society. Even in the home the church begins to become a reality in family life; we become joined in love and faith to those with whom we are bound by blood and birth. Once aware that life apart from the companionship of Christ can never be full and rich, we work to turn the church into a family fellowship of vital prayer and mutual concern. In short, as salvation becomes real we glimpse that community whose character reflects the meaning and nature of salvation.

Above all, the saved are saved for heaven. Already in this life they set foot on the threshold of a new home. In worship and prayer they begin to pull away from ordinary life and reach over into God's side of reality. In companionship with God they see with new eyes and feel with new hearts.

As in prayer and experience they even now soar beyond this earth and life and they commence knowing life on a higher level. They start finding a new focus of fulfillment in God. They know heaven as more than a place of imagination. Indeed they often approach its gates. They even carry something of its far-off glory back home with them. Inevitably they spill some of it into the humdrum of ordinary life.

But heaven remains primarily a place awaiting the saved. They know where they are going at the end of this life. They are going where God is. They are going to be with Christ. They are going home to the larger family.

They are going through resurrection to the place of many mansions.

He who has lost his heart to heaven knows in this life "the power of an endless life." Death is no longer merely an enemy to be feared. The days of unrelieved doubt are over. He in whom salvation is active knows his Father and his home and he waits, while working, to be called home.

Many who do not know salvation regard such talk as nonsense or, at best, questionable speculation; however, many a secular writer seems almost possessed with man's longing for immortality as a basic drive. This deep-set want is due to a need rooted in reality. Thus though men may mock, they cry for what they mock.

For the saved, however, though life never loses either its challenge or its beauty, it always remains touched with homesickness. The saved are pilgrims who can never find full rest and peace on earth, for their hearts are in heaven. Although they may know ever so much heaven here and now, they never fail to remember that heaven, even more, is the home that awaits them.

III

We are saved from sin for God. We are saved from self for community. We are saved from the faults of earth for the fullness of heaven. But such salvation does not come all at once. The *decision* to let oneself be saved may come all at once. At some particular time each person must cross the line from death into life, from self as central to God as central—at least in conscious intention—but it takes time to make the full turn away from self to God. Indeed, God has given us eternity for this purpose. We still can and should, of course, make a significant start on earth.

As illustrated in the life of the Master, when God becomes central to human life how much of heaven's goal can be realized on earth! The indwelling presence of God as holy Spirit at work in life is called sanctification. To sanctify means "to make holy." God saves us by making us holy.

"To be separate" is the biblical meaning of "holy." Normally, holiness in the Christian's vocabulary has a more restricted connotation; "to be holy" means "to be separated from evil." So sanctification means separation from sin and from the ways of the world. One of the most crucial misunderstandings of the Christian faith frequently is rooted in the misinterpretation of sanctification for thought and life. For this reason we must look closely at the questions: What does it mean to be made holy? What does sanctification involve?

The very mention of sanctification repels many people. They take it to mean a kind of unctuous pietism. If pressed, they will even say they had rather remain unsanctified than to become unnatural.

Admittedly they have a point. Often "holy" people do seem queer. And, worse still, some of the "sanctified" are hard to live with! Such people have turned sanctification into a bad word not only for the population in general but also for many Christians. Many devoted Christians still equate sanctification with a stuffy and inhibiting legalism—a matter of avoiding this or eschewing that, whether drinking or card-playing, wearing make-up or going to the movies.

But true sanctification means something quite different. It denotes the process, sudden or gradual, whereby the person who has been saved in intention becomes saved in fact. It describes the action of God in which he fulfills this intention by education, by intensification of intention, and by teaching us how to enjoy the truly good life. Sanctification is the process of becoming genuine. It is an exchange of the false self for the true self, of the unreal personality for the real person. Sanctification indicates the process whereby we are made holy, within the purpose of God for our life.

A non-Christian or sub-Christian understanding of sanctification defines it as physical separation from people who do not live holy lives. Some even treat the absence of a certain "orthodox" profession as a lack of holiness and a ground for excommunication. This erroneous interpretation, though reflected in the New Testament in some instances, stems from the belief that God himself shuns evil people and expects the "saints" to follow his example.

But the life of Jesus causes embarrassment for this view. Indeed, this attitude bespeaks the kind of "Pharisaism" (as the word is ungraciously used by us Christians) Jesus came to destroy. When God walked in human flesh, he walked into unclean Samaria to talk with a "bad" woman, he associated with publicans and sinners and met the accusation of being a winebibber and a friend of the untouchables.

So does he even yet! God loves the sinner completely and comes to him freely—even *into* him, to dwell with him, that God might cast out sin and cancel guilt from within. He still offends our natural goodness and self-righteousness.

Not only does he do it by calling "sinners" to repentance. He does it still more emphatically by identifying the worst sinners as those who trust in their own goodness and hold themselves aloof from the sinners and the despised. Then, as if to rub salt into sore wounds, he says these self-righteous "saints" are the very people the true "saints" should be helping with their company and encouragement.

Christian holiness has as its goals the elimination of sin and the transformation of the sinner into a saint. Particularly does it aim at the transformation of the most sinful —the religiously self-righteous.

Christian holiness means to be like God. It means to partake of his nature and attitude. To be sure, the sanctified in his effort to be one with the sinner does not try to please him by sinning with him. To be holy means to be separate, in thought, imagination, word, and action, from sin and even from needless appearance of sin. The truly sanctified finds no pleasure in evil and no satisfaction in sinful company. He is with sinners because he loves them. He associates with them as a fellow human being touched with divine love for people as people, particularly for those in need, even more for those in moral and spiritual need, and most especially for the religiously self-righteous.

The sanctified separates himself from evil in his inner attitude. The really sinful things, as Jesus taught, are neither what goes into a man nor what he touches. Sinful things, rather, are what go out from his inner self, the lusts that conceive and occasion sinful acts.

Thus a saint seeks out sinners not to judge them but to enlighten and help them, and not too self-consciously, at that. He joins them as a human being who likes and accepts his fellow human beings. By his presence he offers them the only Presence that can truly change them, fulfill them, and thus set them free. Neither threats nor rewards can do that. Only love can rightly fill the self, free it from its false desires and give it peace.

Young women of a new religious order in France choose to live close to brothels and among atheistic labor groups, not to preach, but to be friends, to be of help in need, and to show the lone and lost the heart of God in the midst of human hell. Such living is an example of Christian sanctification.

To be sanctified means, then, to grow in grace. Grace can be had only by being shared. To be holy, we remember, is to be separate from sin. To separate from sin, however, is possible only as, with God's aid, we live more and more for others. Sanctification is from sin but not for selfish reasons. To be made holy is to be removed from sin but not externally.

To be sanctified means being separate *from* because we are lovingly *for*. It is to be separate from sin because we are for God and for others. Just as God, who is ever and by nature sinless and cannot sin, comes to the sinful world because he loves it, so the saint goes into the world because the holiness of God has made him real and overflows his humanity into human fellowship.

Sanctification is, then, *for* the world. Jesus presents the best example of sanctification. He kept himself pure "for their sake." His own conquest of temptation was intimately connected with and, indeed, the very expression of, his holy love, his living for others. Jesus learned obedience through his sufferings for others. He identified his life and passion with the welfare of his people. Thus he became in truth the Messiah.

The Son of God sanctified his ordinary manhood into the Son of Man. In just such a way must we become holy by letting the Son of God rule us until we attain "mature manhood" and come, as the Bible says, "to the measure of the stature of the fullness of Christ." Jesus was in his deepest intention the Universal Man. The Universal Man is whoever under God most fully identifies himself with all men.

Being bid to walk even as Jesus walked, we might start by trying to make all people happy, by so living as to let all men know what it means to be free souls. The more we try to make men happy, as Robert Louis Stevenson pointed out, the more we come to realize that no one can be happy by living for himself. Happiness presupposes goodness while guilt brings sorrow. Therefore we must aim at making men good as well as happy. Goodness presupposes good intentions, a possession always of happy people. But good intentions are not enough. People with the best intentions can be most destructive of other people's happiness.

Goodness requires, besides, the knowledge and the observance of law. Law is a matter of right relations. Right relations are from God for human good. Therefore true happiness does not destroy the law, i.e., right relations. In order to be happy, consequently, we ourselves must fulfill God's intention that we be our true and real selves. We must also help other people to be their best selves. That cannot be done by by-passing the law.

How does holiness work as law? Law is necessary to

101

show right relations, to teach right relations, to correct wrong relations, and to keep guiding into ever more nearly right relations.

Law, however, is only a help; it is no substitute for love. It is only a crutch that does not take the place of walking. Only love can rightly make use of law in any full sense, for the purpose of all law is finally for love. Therefore love alone, as the Bible says, can fulfill the law.

There is no genuine conflict between law and love for those who see the true nature of love as holy and the law as an instrument for facilitating love. Holiness observes law. But the laws of right relations are the fruit of the long outworking of justice. They can be finally attained and fulfilled only by love. True love, therefore, is never slack or sentimental. It is, rather, holy, austere, concerned for others in their total relationship to one other, to themselves, to God, and to the natural order in which they live.

Whenever holiness becomes separated from goodness, or law from love, God is violated. All law is for love; all holiness, for happiness. Consequently both the safest and the most creative response toward sanctification is to live to make all people happy. We fulfill the law of love only as we become inclusively concerned for other people and work in concrete situations to make them happy as whole personalities and communities.

"Happiness" has become a threadbare and shopworn word, tinged with the superficialities of the ordinary and even with escapism. For this reason we must see happiness in the context of holiness and the law. But even when we have done so, no one has the right to happiness except within the trust of God whose suffering and sovereign Love will in the end gather up all human sorrow into a full and inclusive salvation. This godly happiness we may now embrace. Apart from it we shall have little positive satisfaction to offer a doubt-drenched and sorrow-laden world.

Working with a concerned happiness our minds begin to become free to pursue ways and means of helping people. Only thus do we increasingly realize that happiness comes most truly and most fully only within the inclusive, holy love of God. To be holy in relation to happiness is to live humbly and obediently the implications and involvements of a nonsentimental realistic love.

So fulfilling the law within the love that frees the self, we "grow in grace." The saints who have accepted salvation as the act and promise of God experience its fulfillment in themselves.

"Entire sanctification," a term much bandied about in evangelical circles and life's hardest and rarest attainment, is the complete surrender to the will of God and the consistent living of it until, within the grace of God, saints find that temptations lose their power. Even though the "totally sanctified" can still feel temptation and their spirits can still be disturbed by evil imagination; even though they can still be troubled in disposition and less than perfect in decision and act; nevertheless their total self rests in God and finds no happiness apart from his presence.

103

Once for all God has secured the saints' will against basic disobedience because he has won their hearts for himself by their actual experience of the kind of life he offers. Such steadfastness within the love of God and such experience of its fruit are what total sanctification means. It is far more a hope than an attainment; for most people it is unreal and frustrating; for all, its deepest experience lies beyond this earthly life.

"Eternal security," the claim "once saved, always saved," does not involve the loss of ability to sin. The insight that this claim sets forth is, rather, the towline to the shore of heaven that will not give way. But we, of course, can let go of the towline! Eternal security is the confidence that, no matter how much the waves of earthly temptation toss our bark, we shall reach the harbor.

The biblical and historical doctrines we have just discussed have meaning within genuineness of Christian experience. They should neither be denied nor claimed as attained by ourselves. Beyond whatever experience is granted us, they should be the goal of our lives and our far-flung hopes in God's promises.

The Christian doctrine of man is a most serious topic. It precludes every effort to hide our illness or to claim what is unreal for the cure. Sin is real and long lasting. The power of sin, even in the life of the saints, is a terrifying force. Genuine faith never speaks of easy or fast victories over it.

104

Nevertheless, once the hearts of believers have been won by the love of God and their eyes opened by faith, they cannot deny in their own experience the reliability of the grace of God. To that grace they witness: to the greatness and goodness of God.

V | "And the Life Everlasting"

Thousands upon thousands, Sunday after Sunday, end their confession of the Christian faith with these words: "and the life everlasting." How many believe them? For those who do, what do these words mean? Even among theologians no topic is touchier. Many of them would rather not discuss it. They often use, sometimes heatedly, phrases and symbols, words like "resurrection" and "life eternal," but all too often they have changed the meaning so that these symbolic phrases do not stand for life after death. For such confessors, the biblical question still remains: "If a man die shall he live again?" Or perhaps the question does not remain because it has long ago been silently answered in the negative.

On a large university campus the faculty member who represented the university on the Religion in Life Committee came to me for a private talk.

"I have no Christian faith," he said, "but I want others to believe. Am I being dishonest? I believe that there is no God who controls history and that when I die, I'll be cold and hard like a chunk of cement. And that's the end of it. More than that: I know practically every active layman among our churches, and at least seventy-five per cent of them believe exactly as I do. Do you think I should tell the students my stand or should I go on pretending to believe? I have a daughter and I want her to believe. I think faith is wonderful for those who can have it, but I myself can't make myself believe. All these fanciful claims of religion don't spell anything for me."

I looked at him and loved him. What had I to say?

On another occasion a distinguished theologian, an honest and humble spirit, had invited me to dinner. A few of us finally warmed up in conversation concerning life's basic meaning and hopes. The great man's face was sensitive with the world's hurts. Before us sat a giant intellect and a saint's heart, visibly shaken by my suggestion that the Christian faith could not be genuine apart from faith in life after death.

"For me," I had said, "your thinking is profound and illuminates all my experience. You are one of the two men who have helped and stimulated me the most. If only you could believe in a personal God of providence who initiates action for the world's good and who answers prayer; and if only you could believe in life after death!"

Pulling back a bit with pain, the theologian spoke to this effect:

"Lately I have been far from happy about my position that individual life ends at death. My thinking offers no explanation and hope, for example, for idiots. As a matter of fact, I have been considering that even reincarnation offers more of a solution. I may come out for it in my lectures within the next four or five weeks. The Christian position where people are changed all at once at death does not seem to me to take the meaning of this life seriously enough. Why should we have all the trouble of striving in this life and what does it amount to in the end if we are all magically changed? Augustine left the idiots in limbo. The Roman Catholics at least have purgatory after death. That is some better. They take the moral problem more seriously."

Such in general ran his line of thought. A profoundly learned and thoughtful man whose very face showed the deep sensitivity of his nature, thus pondered the three main positions that seem open to us on the question of everlasting life.

Many of Christianity's leading theologians in America have wrestled silently and come to no confident conclusion, or have been forced in honesty, not to deny life after death, but to admit frankly that they cannot be convinced of it. What are these three positions and what attitude should we take toward them?

The first is that eternity is a quality of life; it is *participation* without the right of duration, in the case of man, in the life everlasting; the second is that life is a continual stream of choices and consequences, of living and dying, of repeated *reincarnations* in this world; and the third is that God reawakens us to life *after death* in *another* realm beyond this earthly existence.

Our attitude on all these questions should be one of humble faith and openness. Each of the above positions will be developed only in kernel. Some would say dogmatically that only the last of these is Christian; a very few would call the second Christian, although historically it definitely is not; many others would allow the first as well. In our day, however, the nature of the Christian faith itself is being reinterpreted. Perhaps any view that honestly interprets life in the light of what it sees in Jesus as the Christ has the right to claim his name. Some believe that the very survival of Christianity depends upon such a bold facing of modern man's knowledge. Every man's report should be as humble, honest, and open as possible in this realm. In such a spirit I advance the following suggestions.

The first view of life eternal is that it is a matter of man's *participation* in God's life. It emphasizes quality rather than duration. It is a kind of life rather than length of life. Man as such is not eternal. He is a creature. He lives and dies. But man is not therefore merely an animal. On the contrary, he is a child of God capable of eternal life, of sharing God's own presence and power.

For some this is the only honest answer to man's deepest dread: that life is meaningless. To be sure, we shall all die and be no more. But meantime we are more than we know. At least we do not thus postpone our problems for some fancied existence. We know and take seriously the fact of death. This kind of eternal life is also something we can experience and be sure of here on earth.

For some this means participation in life eternal amidst the busy demands of ordinary life. Life is hard and we are frustrated. It is next to impossible to be the kind of person we want to be—husband, wife, son, daughter, or friend. We fail and feel guilty. We work, and sometimes we succeed even to the point of enjoying the success; but at other times we are disappointed with the results or ache over our own lack of satisfaction in achievement.

Sometimes we feel like the thrifty New England housewife who kept using the apples that were spoiling in the barrel so that most of the apples she used were the spoiled ones while the good ones were always there for the eating! We worry over the one or two things that bother us and fail to be grateful for the many things that are right. We are anxious over possible threats to our planning or living while we never rejoice over the many securities and satisfactions life brings. And what is worse, we cannot by willing change this basic life attitude.

ternal life without beginning or end.
ing reborn. Its character is responsible
ation, from many angles, is the most
tion of life and the one viewpoint that
onds to our actual world while still hav-
ndard of right, wrong, and salvation.
dpoint there is no problem as to the ori-
e is no origin. Each life is eternal by na-
here can therefore be no question as to
There is no end.

life is a matter of free choices continually.
me weighted with the consequences of our
ut, ever and ever, there is a chance to better
though the cards of life are dealt to us ac-
r past, we are always free to play creatively

ation, what we do is put into a reservoir of
ever we receive in life, of good or bad, is due
in the reservoir. We do not, to be sure, get
t once. An evil deed may create consequences
nneled back at a much later time. But we are
o. We get what we deserve. Some interpreters
ation emphasize deeds as acts, others as knowl-
still others as love, but from whatever aspect of
ct, the result is stored in the reservoir. Life ex-

Therefore the offer of forgiveness for those who hold this position is good news. The Gospel of grace means for them that we can be accepted beyond our desert. We are glad for even partial participation in a strength not our own that quiets our anxieties and takes the edge off our fears. We are grateful for the faith that life is not meaningless. In this view while God may not be personal, there is peace to be had. We shall all die, they say, but while we live we can find the resources to be better persons, better family members, better members of the church and the community. If religion gives us no more than this, we can honestly and humbly be thankful for eternal life, for our being touched and moved by our participation in it.

Others who hold this position have more hope, even though they, too, believe that death ends all for each and all of us. They believe that we can become new beings by the power of the Gospel. They believe that by the participation in God's life the basic quality of life itself can be changed. For some of them this experience is a matter of being found at least from time to time within a "Gestalt of grace," a pattern of Gospel power. In either case we do not have and cannot command this power of eternal life. It is a free gift of God. Or in other terms, it is the possibility for us within the hidden resources of reality in its dimension of depth.

For still others of this group who hold that eternal life is an aspect of our experience in this life, everlasting life offers the possibility of being caught up into the ecstasy that can never be contained within time and space and that can never be explained from within our finite and evil existence. It is mystic union with eternity itself. It is sharing beyond explanation in joy at the depth. It is participation in the freedom from self and society, and from the whole world of things, that only those can know who have ever broken through the spiritual time and sound barrier of existence.

All these interpretations offer eternal life by participation. They hold that eternity is timeless, that eternity transcends completely and indescribably the failings and finiteness of time. Reality beyond the limitations of space-time existence has somehow come into people's lives to help them, whether by touching their lives by a new quality of beauty and strength, by offering, that is, a new level of being, or by releasing them into the mystic ecstasy of immediate participation, beyond all knowledge, in eternal life itself.

While life lasts, they say, there is beauty in the wave, even in the breaking of it. At last, however, every troubled sea finds rest. The divided life is freed from the fever of existence. It sinks back into the ocean of being, after having been used on the surface, to rest in the depths of calm. The weary returns home. The tired finds rest. The separated bit of being finds its harmony within the whole to which it now fully belongs. There is peace.

For most people even this view of life eternal may seem unreal. They know only the humdrum of existence with

hibits, therefore, perfect justice within an order of responsible freedom.

Rebirth may be into the order of human beings once again; or according to the classical form of the doctrine, transmigration into the animal realm; or into a higher order of heavens; and at the highest, the delivered self can escape from the round of rebirth to rest within the reality of eternity. This reality has been interpreted as consisting of being, plus intelligence, plus bliss. Such resting is identification with reality. It is being accepted by, and accepting, the center of what is truly real and right, which alone can fully satisfy what is real and right in man.

Such identification is finding the bliss of being in intelligent fulfillment. It is escape from the severed and fragmentary life. It is love's union beyond our divided understanding of it. It is freedom with no overagainstness. It is perfect peace through full finding. Beyond the mere vision of God, it is full participation within the bliss of his perfect being, beyond the lacks and faults of human emotion. This identification is the negation of all that we know, the very finding of the perfect attainment we hoped for in our knowledge.

Here is fruition without frustration. Yet the spirit is free, and responsible choice remains. Those who wish can keep striving, losing or gaining partial satisfactions; those who will can find eternal life itself and enter into it.

No wonder our theologian friend was attracted. Who

115

can see and not admire such freedom and justice, with such a wide spread of possibility? No credulity is needed to believe in irrational beginnings or in miraculous endings. The problem of evil is met fully without hopelessness.

Interest in this doctrine is rising sharply. All over the United States and Canada, I have come across people who believe in reincarnation while professing Christ. A Presbyterian minister, for instance, told me that in a ministers' discussion group to which he belonged, most of them had confessed, once they had "let their hair down," that they had abandoned the Christian point of view of eternal life in favor of the doctrine of reincarnation. Recently several leading writers, religious and secular, have openly or subtly taken leads along this line.

With classical Christianity at the crossroads, decisions have to be made honestly and creatively. For most educated people, the world view of the Christian faith as a whole in its supernatural dimensions is a shell. Emptiness is bound to suck in some faith. What shall it be? The traditional views of immediate translation into heaven or hell are hollow. Emptiness cannot be filled by emptiness! Perhaps taking the Christian center and rethinking in its light the doctrine of reincarnation may be a creative step. Certainly this second view, of reincarnation, is far more reasonable, considering all problems of beginnings and becomings, than the first view's claim that there is no rhyme or reason to our origins and ends before and beyond this life.

I personally have been long and heavily tempted to make a try at such a synthesis. Now with the world becoming one, if it remains, and with our leading Western universities importing religious teachers from the East to teach students the religions that brought forward views like reincarnation, not to mention the success of missionaries in our midst from non-Christian religions, we Christians had better think long and deep concerning these religions, not only to be honest with ourselves, but to do justice to the central realities of our faith.

Reincarnation is certainly an improvement on the emptiness of naturalism. No wonder our great-minded and great-hearted theologian pondered the possibility of reincarnation as a step beyond his own position, which is basically in our first category as described above. I even suggested to him that evening that with his creative capacity he might develop a view going beyond both reincarnation and traditional Christianity to some form of fulfillment implicit in the Christian faith, but not yet brought to light. The classical Christian center seems to me to involve, in any case, a far more just and dynamic view of eternal life than has so far been expressed in traditional formulations, a view which accepts and incorporates whatever is true in the first two.

III

The Christian view of life after death is not easy to describe. The authority for it is Christ as the context of

God's love. Our standard of truth is: "God is faithful." That affirmation on the subject of life everlasting implies everything basically Christian. In humility and honesty we must leave the far future in God's hands. As Roger Shinn puts the case: It is not so much what we believe as Whom we believe. All that is needed is to draw the implications of the main confession.

With the first point of view in this chapter I agree that life everlasting is basically a *participation* in the life of God. It is first of all a quality of life. We are not interested in mere continuation of life. That could be both bad and miserable. It could be a decidedly selfish wish, based both on the fear of death and on a drive to be at the center of things. It could also amount to a postponing of life's present problems for the sake of some fancied solution by or after death. The New Testament talks of a new life, a new being, not a mere continuation of life. For this reason many biblically minded thinkers dislike the term "immortality" and use the term "resurrection" instead.

Nor should life be thought of as eternal in its own right. That would mean that man himself had become self-sustaining forever. That would imply that man can become independent of God. To speak in such fashion is indeed to make man God. It is to be Platonic and not Christian. The Christian knows that man is mortal by nature. The breath God gave him in creation is the breath of earthly, not of eternal life. Man lives and dies as a human being. His life beyond this life, whatever it is, is surely a life of relation to God. It is a life of participation in God's immortality. It is a new being, a new quality of life. With this main assertion I reaffirm my agreement.

Nevertheless, must we substitute quality for quantity? Why not have both? The better life is, the more it deserves to continue. If the basic meaning and reality of our lives are partaking of God's love, that quality ought to insure the quantity. If everlasting life is life beyond the evils of temporal change and failings, why should not everlasting life *last*? The posing of quality as an alternative to quantity not only prejudices the question, but makes the answer necessarily deficient.

The longing for such a life is no more selfish if it is desired for a lifetime, or for eternity, than for an hour. For that matter, life everlasting in Christian terms is the death of selfishness. Such is its quality. No one can enter eternal life in reality unless he is willing to give up his own centrality in order to find a true center in God and in a community of love. Such a losing of self into life everlasting is the basic threat to selfishness. How, then, can the hope of such life after death be selfish?

To face God and eternal life aright, each person must face reality. Flight from God is the flight of fear. Acceptance of God is the acceptance of the love that involves the acceptance of self and others. It is the acceptance of life. How, then, can a genuine faith in life everlasting involve the postponing of problems in this life for the sake of some mysterious solution in the next?

We can, consequently, accept the positive truth of this first position without falling prey to its negative conclusion. We accept participation and permanence, quality and quantity, a new life now and in the world to come.

The second position presented reincarnation as eternal life without beginning and without end, the life of continuously responsible freedom on man's part and of continuously perfect justice on the side of reality. This view, we saw, makes a strong attempt to be honest and realistic in its dealing with the mysterious question of life after death. Reincarnation offers life after death for each and for all. We have stressed this position in the belief that Oriental religions will be heard from with great vigor in coming generations. Many of the emphases of reincarnation are of utmost importance for Christian thinkers who have done little, for instance, with the question of the meaning of animal life and pain.

The most appealing part of reincarnation is its reasonableness and its morality. If all we knew of life were that it had always been here and had always been a mixture of good and evil, reincarnation would be even more tempting than it now is. As it is, we know that our main evidence is of a lightning quick history which has burst out of the unknown. In the light of Christ, our most adequate context for understanding the meaning of our total experience, we see that our world has not always been here, but has come into being as a special creation with a special goal. There are still problems aplenty and no one can be

glib about ultimate matters. Our little world history, however, points toward God's deeper meaning for us, not only
in the future of our world within this cosmic process, but
in the future of all life beyond death.

The governing thought in reincarnation I can accept
insofar as it stresses both our responsible freedom and perfect justice in the universe. To this justice, however, the
Christian faith adds God's perfect love beyond our own
deserving and capacity. God is seen in Christ as the sovereign Love who controls all the conditions of this life and
beyond.

We can also maintain and develop reincarnation's inclusion of the animal world as an enriching aspect of the
Christian faith. Christians must be increasingly sensitive
to God's purpose for the whole of creation. Even animal
suffering has its place there. The fulfillment of animal life
in some way is surely in accordance with God's most inclusive plan. I have tried to indicate several ways of such
fulfillment in *Evil and the Christian Faith*. The God of
perfect love is even more concerned with animal life than
any ultimate reign of justice could be!

For a Father's love, however, each and every individual
is everlastingly important. The Christian faith because it
believes in a personal God of love believes also in the
perpetuation of human personality. God whose love is
everlasting loves every individual forever.

Life everlasting denies the perpetuation of what is falsely
individual. The selfish and the finite who take themselves

121

too seriously cannot participate in God's perfect love, while the truly personal life of love lives forever in it. The Christian faith teaches the perpetuation not only of the personal, but of the person. Such perpetuation is not only by participation in the divine life but by the eternal partaking personally of it.

Would a God of love create us to find no fulfillment beyond this life? Is the wish for fulfillment selfish? If we have to choose between believing in a selfish man and a selfish God, it is far better to keep faith in the ever-faithful God of creative concern. Thinking to be noble in not desiring life after death, we become most ignoble in our accusation of God as the creator of such a world as this with nothing more to follow! The Christian views of God and of life after death are inseparable. Apart from life's continuation there is neither conquest of evil nor fulfillment of life. God is not the God of frustration but of the fullness of love.

Eternal life involves, naturally, the divine fruition of community. Man is not a person apart from others. He lives in, through, for, and by community. Individual life as such is a myth. True individuality is always reality of self-being as a social self. The Christian faith promises, by its very bedrock authority of God in Christ, that Love cannot lose his own.

How, when, and where we shall live after death we cannot tell, but we know that we shall be as Christ is. For us to try to predict the details of personal and community fulfillment is far harder than for a cocoon to envisage the life of a butterfly. No earthly eye has seen, no earthly ear has heard, and no earthly mind has conceived what heaven will be like. All we know is that the God we meet in Christ will exceed immeasurably every expectation and all imagining.

We have no right to believe, of course, that a magical change will take place at death. The meaning of this life has to be taken with all seriousness. Morality would be violated if God were to translate all immediately into the eternal perfections. This much we can surely learn with profit from the doctrine of reincarnation. The Christian view must be fully as moral, fully as patient, and fully as dynamic as any and as all alternate positions.

A weary life desires escape from all life's problems. There is much appeal in the Buddhist doctrine of nirvana, which literally means "being blown out" of existence. Fear is fond of such an escape. Death as cessation is dear to a large side of our experience. We cannot build on our desires, however, one way or another, but only on God. When we build on God we shall find his mercy underlying the next life still offering us the challenge of growth and the chance for new grace.

Life everlasting can be had only by freely accepting God's life of love. Love alone is eternal; love alone is free. Perfect love casts out fear. God has given us freedom of

123

choice in order that through it we might find freedom of life. Freedom of life comes only as, through freedom of choice, we learn that God's will for us is best.

God made us for fulfillment through freedom. In making us for himself, he created us for unconditional and universal love. We are free only as we find this kind of love from, for, in, and through God. The anxiety of the loveless is a chain of fear.

Our earthly experience and whatever similar experiences may be in store for us beyond death exist for the sake of our free choosing of God as we learn from the consequences of our action that God and his way alone are worth having. God never shoves heaven at us; like the father of the Prodigal Son he leaves us to come to ourselves as we discover the results of our lives. When we are ready, however, he is already there to offer the freedom of love and the reality of eternal life.

The final outcome is in God's hands. We can trust him for the best result possible. He will find, but never force. He will free, but never force. He will fulfill, but never force. God is Love and he is faithful. Does not such faith give light on the way and strength to walk it?

The Christian who believes, in line with all classical Christianity, that Christ truly rose from the dead knows—whatever elements of truth the doctrine of reincarnation may have on the lower levels of life— that for man the final truth is personal resurrection. The disciples encountered the same person they had known before he died. To be sure, the resurrection of Jesus is a mystery both for history and for thought. So is man's living again. But in both instances we are dealing with the mystery of the faithfulness of God.

When God is unreal and unknown, life after death becomes either a threat or an escape. When he is known as real, living, and Lord, our faces turn toward death with the quiet assurance of those who put their lives into fulfilling hands. Life everlasting, in the Christian sense of fulfillment, has the deepest meaning of all for those who within a life of love have already begun to glimpse the faithfulness of God. For them argument has less and less relevance, for they rest on the reality of God.

"And this is eternal life, that they know thee, the only real God, and him whom thou hast sent, even Jesus Christ."

Ferré, Nels Fredrick Solomon, 1908–
　　Know your faith. ₍1st ed.₎　New York, Harper ₍1959₎
　　124 p.　21 cm.

　　1. Christianity—Essence, genius, nature.　ɪ. Title.

BR121.2.F4　　　　　　　　　230　　　　　　　　59–7149 ‡
Library of Congress

Date Due

DENIS DE ROUGEMONT

Denis de Rougemont was born in Neu-châtel, Switzerland, in 1906, and was educated in Switzerland and Austria, but has made his home principally in France. He is the president of the Congress for Cultural Freedom, was the founder of the European Cultural Center in Geneva, translated some of the volumes of Barth's **Dogmatik** into French, and was associated with Emmanuel Mounier in the founding of the French international personalist review, **Esprit.**

The author of more than twenty books in the fields of literature, religion, philosophy, and politics, De Rougemont's work has been translated into twelve languages. He is best known in the United States for **The Devil's Share** and **Love in the Western World.**

The Christian
Opportunity

The Christian Opportunity

DENIS DE ROUGEMONT

Translated by
Donald Lehmkuhl

Holt, Rinehart and Winston

New York · Chicago · San Francisco

Copyright 1944, 1947, 1954, © 1963 by Denis de Rougemont
All rights reserved, including the right to reproduce
this book or portions thereof in any form.
Published simultaneously in Canada by Holt, Rinehart
and Winston of Canada, Limited.

Library of Congress Catalog Card Number: 63–11869

First Edition

Designer: Ernst Reichl
81813–0113
Printed in the United States of America

Acknowledgments

Grateful acknowledgment is made to the following publishers who have so generously granted permission to reprint from their publications:

Christendom (a quarterly which continues to be published as *The Ecumenical Review*), for "A Common Language" (Spring, 1941); and "Ecumenicity and Federalism" (Summer, 1947), which appears in this volume under the title, "The Ecumenical Movement and Federalism."

Harper & Row, Publishers, Incorporated, for "The Crisis of the Modern Couple," from *The Family: Its Function and Destiny*, edited by Ruth Nanda Anshen. Copyright 1949 by Harper & Row, Publishers, Incorporated. Copyright © 1959 by Ruth Nanda Anshen. A new translation of this essay appears for the first time in this volume under the title, "Crisis in Modern Marriage."

Harper & Row, Publishers, Incorporated, for "The Mission of the Artist," from *Spiritual Problems in Contemporary Literature*, edited by Stanley Romaine Hopper, copyright © 1957 by Harper & Row, Publishers, Incorporated.

Réalités, American Edition, for "The End of Pessimism" (August, 1957, No. 81).

The Student World, for "The Cultural Responsibility of the Church" (Vol. XXXVII, 1944, No. 2).

The Third Hour, for "The Christian Opportunity" (1947, Issue III); and "False News: 'God is Dead' " (1954, Issue VI).

Prefatory
Note

The essays that constitute this volume are not by a theologian, nor by an apologist for any denomination, but by a free writer, that is, one who represents only himself, and addresses not a confessional or partisan public, to confirm his prejudices, but a public consisting of all those, Christian or not, for whom religion is a reality or at least a permanent problem.

Personalist in philosophy, federalist in politics, ecumenical in religion, and long concerned with the myths that are the creators of all poetry and with the archetypes of love as it is expressed in the Western world, I see that in all these realms I have constantly sought a certain fundamental coherence whose principle I should like to indicate here. Whether in metaphysics or practical morality, political action or poetry, if I become concerned with the ultimate direction of what I see, write, or do, it is always to certain choices of a specifically religious nature that my thought is attracted.

The religious phenomenon, in the very broad sense I assign to it, includes certain subversive experiments of *avant-garde* poetry, as much as the ordering effort of traditional dogmatics and the speculations of modern knowledge, whether scientific or esoteric. I imagine that such a nonconformist curiosity in this realm may explain my fruitful friendships, whether successive or simultaneous, with men whom, in so many respects, everything seemed to set in unremitting opposition to each other: from Karl Barth to André Breton or Teilhard de Chardin; from the strictest theologians of Europe and the United States to the writers furthest from all dogma, although regarding themselves as Christian; finally, from Western thinkers most conscious of their own values, to certain spiritual leaders of Islam and India. Lacking the power to establish an actual dialogue between these extreme figures who touch me so nearly but remain convinced that they have nothing to say to each other, I have composed my personal dialogue. In the course of the incidental orientations which the chapters of this book represent, I believe I have always taken into account the diversity of the inner interlocutors who have sustained my quest for a vital unity.

Yet I observe that in our time the religious phenomenon in the broadest sense is considered suspect not only by rationalists and atheists, but by a whole theological school that dominates Protestantism today and happens to be the very one from which I have learned most. I must acknowledge this paradox, for it is at the heart of my book.

Whatever may be solid in the theological framework of my essays I owe without a doubt to Karl Barth.

Yet man does not live by discipline but by assimilated truth. To avoid and denounce systematic error is vital for the teacher, but to accept the risks of error or heresy is no less vital for the spiritual seeker, who must invent his *person* and discover his vocation.*

Here I do not speak against an admirable master, but think of his disciples (of whom I was one when I wrote several chapters of this book), those who adopt his intensely exclusive style and parody his all-or-nothing approach, his indefatigably hammered-out "all this, yet nothing but this," his dramatic manner of

* This concept is explored in Chapters 10 and 12.—ED.

ceaselessly *excluding* whatever risks distract the mind's attention, the soul's expectation, from the point where it is crucial for the Doctor of the Faith to circumscribe and impose once and for all: Grace is here and not elsewhere; all the rest is unbelief or even rebellion. . . . This Lutheran-Calvinist pathos constitutes the strength but also the weakness of a school which has been able to revive a strictly Protestant thought and has made it into an interlocutor finally—or once again—valid, on the threshold of the great ecumenical dialogue.

There is no Church without orthodoxy, which is *rectified* knowledge (*recta cognitio Dei,* in Calvin's words) as it must be preached by "ministers of the Word" and communicated by those who serve the sacraments. But in the life of the spirit, which is not collective, Spirit alone can show the way to the appropriation of truth. Yet Spirit reveals that there are as many ways as persons created by it.

Sometimes I tell myself that these ways are all "heretical" in the eyes of the Church's coherent doctrine, but redeemed by their convergence beyond the various *anathema sit.*

I tell myself, too, that the discoveries of science are not made by those who apply the rules, but by the man who dares imagine, starting from a tiny defect in the rule (neglected by the professors), something which calls into question the great premises that are undisputed on the scale of everyday realities. Similarly a man can discover in the orthodoxy that educates him the tiny defect, just as great or as small as himself, through which he can slip toward the truth that awaits him, and which was reserved for himself alone.

I do not believe in man in general, the German *Mensch,* the Latin *homo,* in whom classical Europe has believed, and who was invariable, eternal, so that one could speculate on his unalterably true or false relations with an unchanging God.

There are men, men who evolve. There have been, there will

be, men for whom all the categories of thought in which Barthian dialectic functions—or Thomist reason, or pragmatism, or existentialism—do not yet, or will no longer, exist. There have been and there will be men ignorant of the "daily bread," the wine, the grain, and the sowing of which the gospel parables speak; ignorant of relations of consanguinity or of egalitarian justice, of the patriarchal organization of society—from which the trinitarian system is inseparable—ignorant of the conception of the "person" assumed by Greek tradition and Roman vocabulary, even of the conception of Unity or of plurality within Unity. In the nearly million years (it appears) that he has lived and died and thought a little, man has changed so much—and his fundamental conceptions with him—that we cannot assert without a narrow pride that in the course of centuries, of the thousands or millions of years to come, he will not change much more radically still, as only the intuitions of a few adventurous, rather despised minds among us have dared assert. Barth has convinced us that Christian dogmatics must not be linked to a philosophy that is by definition transitory and less than the truth. But it is inevitable that its theology is indissolubly linked to a history of Western thought, to a brief slice of history (whether three thousand or eight thousand years makes no difference), to a province, a mere canton of man's evolution in space and time.

Not that I derive from this argument a refusal to conclude *hic et nunc* on the relations between man today and Spirit, or speculations on a future still nonexistent for us and which would be absurd *today*. The fact that all our languages are transitory, that they develop and will one day pass away, cannot justify our errors of syntax or vocabulary. And the fact that our present modes of thought remain linked to the old Greek logic, for instance, cannot excuse our sophisms or our blunders.

But it would be an error henceforth to link the divine absolute to *our* most "faithful" formulations and thereby to exclude in advance all that can live outside them in God.

This corrective proposed, I must add that whatever the development of my thought during the last twenty-five years—for certain of the essays included date from 1937—I have not felt the need to modify or retract anything of importance in these early texts. It is not on this or that specific point that I have altered; rather, the perspectives in which my early conclusions can be set today seem to me more open.

DENIS DE ROUGEMONT

Ferney-Voltaire (Ain)
January, 1963

Contents

ONE

The Christian
Opportunity
in a Secularized
World

1 False News:
"God Is Dead"

"The death of God" has been, since the end of World War II, an obsession of a significant sector of contemporary literature. Originally propounded by Nietzsche, it was taken up again about 1944 by a group of writers who had gained a sudden and fortuitous popularity; repeated daily by their disciples, it is treated as self-evident by those who seem to live on rumor alone. The self-righteous are angry when they hear it uttered, as if they were really obliged to come to terms with a weighty proposition; such an attitude is incomprehensible for genuine Christians, who certainly ought to know that the existence of God is not affected by a local argument conducted in time and space. This irrational behavior is no less apparent in the divided camp of the agnostics. We are already beginning to hear about mystics and saints without God. Malraux wonders whether God's death does not also imply the death of man—a stimulating idea but rather difficult to understand. Using God's death as an excuse, young writers indulge themselves in the masochistic pleasures of describing an "absurd" world.

However, as far as I can see, this theme, although everywhere mentioned, has up to now never really been discussed. The effects of Nietzsche's desperate defiance and Sartre's methodical af-

3

firmation on modern psychology, society, and culture have been only vaguely analyzed. Have we ever asked any of those who say that God is dead just what they mean by such an assertion? What God is dead? The God they imagine, or the God to whom so many people pray? A convenient caricature, or the First Person of the Trinity? The God about whom philosophers speculate, or the God whom prophets announce? A psychological attitude, or an ontological reality? Or is God only a password in the new conformism? To insist upon a little honest clarity would be a way of pointing out to these modern writers a few of the inextricable difficulties into which their assertions plunge not only their own but all Western thought.

Let us be careful not to do these writers an injustice by suggesting that all they mean to say is, "As far as I'm concerned, God no longer exists"—for there would be nothing new in that. If this was all they were saying, they would simply be relapsing into the metaphysical spleen of romanticism, or even back into the rationalistic platitudes of Western atheism, which they flatly reject. On the contrary, they insist upon the novelty of their message, taking advantage of the dramatic style that typifies the aftermath of the war, and on its objectivity. They claim they are announcing *news*, the bad news of God's recent demise. They behave as if they were writing a gospel (good news) in reverse. We must, therefore, first examine the sources of their information, and then its credibility.

I shall not discuss the inventer of the phrase "God is dead." After all, Nietzsche is sufficiently well known.[1] Moreover, he partially disowned his pronouncement when one day he wrote, "The refutation of God: only the moral God has been refuted." But the case is quite different with Jean-Paul Sartre, to whom general ignorance ascribes the authorship of the rumor under consideration. Sartre's major argument, of course, is not con-

---

[1] See the brief and admirable work of Karl Jaspers, *Nietzsche and Christianity* (Chicago: Gateway Editions, 1961).

cerned with the essence of God or the Devil, but with their existence, which, according to him, would seem to *diminish or suppress man's responsibility.*

If this is Sartre's position, we must necessarily conclude that for Sartre the supreme moral value is responsibility, and that this moral value is more important than anything else, for in its name the question of real existence can be decided. God and the Devil *must not* exist, for then man's responsibility would suffer. And so we are presented with a kind of fanatical morality, a morality ready to negate any reality that gets in the way of its overpowering passion for responsibility.[2]

"Perhaps the truth is sad," Renan said.[3] He was far from being happy about this conclusion, but he never decided to deny that truth exists. Perhaps truth is not existentialist. Perhaps God forcibly limits man's responsibility, though it remains no less real. Apparently it is enough for Sartre to decree that God does not exist, and right away he is dead.

Where does this passion for responsibility come from? From a wish to affirm man and his power, Sartre would reply. Malraux and Jaspers give a similar interpretation to Nietzsche's cry: a proclamation of man's accession. But this reveals a strange ambiguity. As a matter of fact, Sartre does not use the word "responsible" in its original and literal meaning of "capable of responding" (for one's acts and thoughts before God or man), but in the sense of "capable of deciding" (what one is and will be). Therefore, "responsible," for Sartre, does not imply that man is charged with a mission, but rather that he is an adventurer who assumes risks and perils with sovereign independence. Man is responsible, not as a human creature, but as a

---

[2] For God in himself, even if one believes that *he is not,* remains a reality in any event for the overwhelming majority of human beings.

[3] I believe no one has ever noticed the similarity between this phrase and Rimbaud's observation, in *A Season in Hell:* "truth which surrounds us with its weeping angels."

demiurge; not man as man, but man as God. This last meaning is the most important. One has the feeling that Sartre betrays a refusal of reality as "given": first his own ("I will make myself according to my own idea"), and then the reality of others ("Hell *is* the others"). Nevertheless, he notes the limitations of intellectual arrogance, the delirious borderline of an overcompensating individualism, which cannot help denying itself if it wishes to rejoin morality. Thus Sartre will deny himself for the sake of some collectivist dictatorship, for it is only there that he believes he has refound the "involvement" which his doctrine favors but otherwise makes impossible and unpracticed. (It is well known that, prior to the Hungarian revolution, Sartre made common cause with the Communists, even though they had attacked him personally, and—more to the point—had criticized him as a petit-bourgeois individualist.)

This rapid survey of sources brings us back to a fairly simple position. Sartre's announcement that God is dead tells us only that man ought to refuse the kind of God that Sartre imagines: an inconvenience for man. However, this does not really prove that God no longer exists, or that he no longer helps man or judges him. As a matter of fact, from a numerical point of view, never in history have there been so many who actively assert their belief in God as there are today.

Let us now assess the credibility of the news that God is dead. It is obvious that the mere fact that most men reject it provides no basis for evaluation.

Apart from the realm of polemics—whether Nietzschean or anticlerical—taken literally and logically, the sentence "God is dead" is utter nonsense. For either "God" means nothing—in which case there is nothing to die; or "God" means Life, Eternity, the Whole, Being per se, the Unknowable—and in that case to speak of God's death is nothing more than a lot of noise. If the Eternal God had lived and then died, he would not have been the

Eternal God. We would be saying, in effect, that he died because he was never alive—which is absurd. And if God the Unknowable were dead, that would be the same as saying we know everything—which is also absurd.

If the Revealed God were dead (after having lived as a Person), an unprecedented cosmic event would have occurred in time and space (but where and when?). But it would have been an "event affecting being itself," as Jaspers says. How can we believe that Nietzsche alone has heard of this event, or that Sartre has been especially informed of it? If the scriptural revelation of the Living God is considered problematical, what are we to say of the upside-down revelation these two men offer us? We are trapped in the absurd.

Their news simply has no credibility.

The fact remains that the God of Christianity, of Judaism, of Islam, the God who is interested in every man (even, as the Bible says, in the welfare of a sparrow) and in the intimate details of his life, the God to whom so many millions of human beings, suffering or meditating, geniuses or humble men looking for a way out, have prayed and will go on praying for help in their trials, both great and small—the personal God, in a word, omniscient and omnipresent, is unbelievable to many contemporary minds. For them he is absurd—as absurd as all the absurdities I have just enumerated. But this is not surprising. It is even quite easy to explain.

A personal God is unbelievable and absurd in a statistical conception of the universe, in terms of the imaginative framework in which the cosmos is viewed today. It is merely a question of scale. The transitory vermin that man represents on earth is no more than an atom in the solar system, which is itself an atom in a galaxy, which is, in turn, an atom in a time-space continuum in a universe indefinitely expanding (talk about counting the hairs on a man's head!).

On the other hand, the personal God becomes not only believable but indispensable for the *meaning* of every individual life the moment we turn our eyes to man, to the individual man, to "me." A good, close view, straight into the secret heart, shows this to be true. "God is known in the heart," Pascal says. The same applies to the study and discovery of fundamental energy in the nucleus of the atom, the heart of physical reality.

If our scientists had restricted themselves to examining our cities, our landscapes, our heavens, our automobiles, our economics, our politics, or the fate of the masses, nuclear energy would never have been visible or understandable; it would still be unimaginable to this day. Similarly, it is ridiculous to "search for God in nature," or in history, or in political, economic, or social preoccupations, because he is perceptible only to the heart, that is, to the most intimate part of every real and distinct person.

It is normal, then, that the personal God should remain absurd, except in an encounter that can take place only in intimacy; just as the transmutation of energy is achieved only in the smallest particles, and love, only in the heart.

2 Secularism

The word "secularism" has become current in Anglo-Saxon and German Christian circles. For the French it evokes recollections of the Revolution, when the wealth amassed by the monastic orders was confiscated by the state.

In my usage, secularism is both an action and an attitude.

As an action, it is the confiscation of the spiritual riches of Christianity by men or groups of men who no longer believe in Christianity.

As an attitude, it is exemplified by many among us who do not believe in a transcendent reality. It is atheism brought into the real world, organized, lived, and daily practiced, but progressively stripped of its controversial elements, at least so far as they are conscious. This "death of God" as a psychological, not ontological, phenomenon poses some very specific questions for Christians. How shall one confront this century that wants to be limited strictly to itself, no longer believing in a "world without end"? What new forms must evangelism assume to become suitable for our era? How must one address all those people who have decided that the word "God" is meaningless? And all those who are convinced that the words "church," "salvation," "vocation," "faith," "obedience," and "worship" are a pack of lies, illusions, inanities, and flights from reality? Face to face with a century virtually atheistic in its customs, theoretically atheistic

9

in its doctrines, what must we be, what must we do, if we are Christians?

In this simplified form, the question seems crushing, beyond the strength or knowledge of any living human being. Nevertheless, every one of us who believes is constrained to do something about it. The situation in which a Christian finds himself today is utterly *insane*—that is, if he feels obligated to live and think according to his faith in a world where that faith is denied, more or less serenely ignored, or, even worse, where Christianity is accepted and ridiculed under the forms of its traditional deviations, its caricatures: in short, in a world where it does not exist. Indeed, some people accept Christianity as a guarantee of middle-class order, while others ridicule it as if it were simply a system of morality and a more or less hypocritical evasion.

It is in this almost impossible and untenable situation, however, that the Christian must speak. And so I hope the following reflections will not give the impression of a man merely developing his ideas, but rather of one offering a hopeful prayer asking that good use be made of the sickness of our age, whose victims we all are.

A Century Limited to Itself

Let us begin by describing this sickness. Most contemporary descriptions of our period made by Christian analysts begin with the banal notion that the twentieth century is more out of joint and less Christian than other periods—the Middle Ages, for example. Consequently, such descriptions more accurately betray their authors' fears and resentments than they portray the century as it actually is. I shall try to avoid this approach as much as possible.

In the twentieth century, the secularization of existence assumes two aspects that must not be confused: the loss of the meaning of the holy, and the loss of the meaning of transcendence. We are witnessing the final phases of a long deterioration, or even destruction, of the dimensions of holiness in public and private life. This general *profanation* is the result of numerous concomitant causes—popular rationalism, urbanization, mechanization, and increasing democratization. Falling under the influence of these diverse elements, twentieth-century mankind tends to eliminate the forms and rituals which our ancestors considered sacred. The heads of democratic states are no longer ritualistically isolated personages, clothed and consecrated as kings once were. War is no longer a game obedient to prescribed laws, a solemn drama reminiscent of God's ordeals and judgments. Mechanized farming loses its magical and symbolical characteristics, which used to play such an enormous role in the religious myths of antiquity. (In this regard, it will be noted that almost all the parables and metaphors found in the gospel are drawn from farming—the sower, the grain of wheat that must die, the vine and the vine shoots, the sterile fig tree, and so on.) This symbolic language, pregnant with the rudiments of natural religion, loses much of its efficacy and persuasive power in an era of supermarkets, airplanes, transistor radios, and subways. Catholics, whose religion is still sacramental, have recently been especially concerned with this. French priests and monks, for instance, have been wondering whether the gap between the pastoral framework of the gospel and the daily life of the factory worker might not be one of the reasons for the more general gap between the Church and the urban masses. But what conclusions are they to draw—that urban life and machines must be condemned, that rural life alone is suitable to the divine order of creation? Or, on the contrary, that the language of the gospel must be modernized?

We shall return later to dilemmas very similar to this; consequently I will not attempt to define a position in this particular case. I will say, however, that despite legitimate worries—and there are some—I am inclined to think that the first form of secularism, elimination of ritual sacredness from existence, may be a blessing as well as an obstacle to faith. It can do harm if it deprives man of a sense of mystery, of a sense of natural correspondences, of a sense of reverence. But it may also be a blessing in so far as it eliminates the confusion between natural religion and faith by removing the former. Indeed, from the point of view of pure faith, progress can be shown by the fact that men today are less tempted to confuse Christianity with any ancestral religion—whether patriarchal, rustic, or monarchical. Furthermore, the sacred, or the sacramental, belongs to the reign of nature, of social physics, or immanence, and for this reason it did not fail to awaken distrust in the apostles and the first Christians. It tends to be spontaneously modified every time a new community or society is established. Thus Christian society in the Middle Ages reconstituted a sacramental conception of life, and thus it is that modern revolutions have been led, as if by a sociological law, to re-create pseudo-religious ceremonies and symbols for the masses. There is no more reason to congratulate ourselves on these revivals than to lament the decline of older forms of the sacred. As far as faith is concerned, these phenomena will always remain ambivalent.

The case is completely different with the other form of secularism, the one I have called the loss of the sense of *transcendence*. Our analysis of this point must be particularly careful.

As a mass, twentieth-century humanity believes only in the present century, in the here and now, and nothing beyond it. Consequently, the dimensions of the beyond are reduced—that is, of eternity, transcendence, and of God in his creative and authoritative totality. The gospel speaks of "the heavenly kingdom." Man has become man's only goal, life the only goal of life, and time the only goal of time.

Every aspect of human life, without exception, is touched by this mode of secularism. I shall offer three illustrations of it:

one in philosophy, one in politics, and the last in the very religion of our churches.

Philosophy

Following Nietzsche's example, as we saw earlier, twentieth-century philosophy proclaims that "God is dead." For some recent French philosophers and writers this theme may be even more central than they are willing to admit. In this they are distinguished from their Anglo-Saxon contemporaries, who do not even experience the need to indicate that God is dead; they behave as if the question were of no consequence to them, as if the time for serious and honest thought had begun with Marx and was continued only by Freud, neopositivist logic, and sociology.

In France the whole corpus of new philosophical and literary thinking—arrived at in cafés—establishes the "death of God" as indisputable dogma and goes on to say that what matters now is existentialism or surrealism, sociology or Nietzsche. The most coherent of the current "schools" founded on this dogma is that of the Parisian existentialists. "Existentialism," the leader of this group has written, "is nothing more than an attempt to draw every possible conclusion out of a coherent atheistic position."

It is a curious thing, but I know of no other system of philosophical thought closer to Christianity than existentialism in its description of the human condition. Man, it says, is *responsible* for what he is. Man chooses in *anguish,* because his ethical choices *involve* all humanity. If God does not exist, man is entirely *forsaken,* abandoned to the utter hazard of his own choice. In the long run, man is not what he imagines himself, not what he feels about himself, but *what he has done.*

All this seems exceptionally close to the Christian conception of man "thrust" into the world of sin—a sin that existed before he arrived, but for which he is nevertheless responsible in every single one of his acts. One day I said to Sartre, "In short, your philosophy may be summed up in these words of Pascal: 'the misery of man without God.' " And he replied, "Yes, but with just this difference: there is no God."

There is no better way to describe the secularist situation, considered, of course, without illusion and without bad faith. And I think we should be happy that an existentialist movement is taking place among us and that it frankly poses honest and real questions. We ought to be delighted that the belief—or rather, the fundamental disbelief—of the century has been expressed so coherently. Great progress has been made, if, indeed, real progress lies in the clarification of genuine human dilemmas and in the realistic and efficacious delineation of the decisions man must make and the risks he must run.

I shall not discuss atheistic existentialism as such; I am using it only as an example to describe more clearly the secularization of modern thought and to pinpoint where the denial of transcendence by modern thought *changes everything* in man's attitude toward life. Existentialism is a privileged case in this regard. Indeed, it uses Christian terminology as its source—and that permits an exact comparison, term for term, with the Christian position. But, at the same time, because it does not believe in God or his transcendence, existentialism distorts the Christian meaning of its key words, emptying them of significance through using them over and over again; or, in the proper meaning of the term, *secularizing* them.

Take the word *anguish*, which is borrowed by the existentialists from Kierkegaard. In their eyes, this word defines the condition of the man who chooses in total freedom, but who, by his choice, implicates in it the whole of mankind. This is a thoroughly agonizing choice, for man is responsible for his decision, but nevertheless can decide only by virtue of an arbitrary movement whose results, good or bad, will become apparent only in the course of time.

Externally speaking, Christian anguish resembles that of the atheist. In point of fact, the Christian, too, must choose; he also must involve himself, through choice, in the total fate of mankind; he also must know himself to be responsible and must find support in a reality that is "undemonstrable" to others— that is, in his faith.

The difference between Christian and atheist lies in the fact that if the Christian, in consequence of sin, chooses badly, he knows that his action does not affect the *truth,* which remains intact and supreme in God. A bad choice made by an atheist, on the other hand, makes everything false, leaving no place to turn. "We are alone and without excuses," one existentialist remarks. The Christian also knows that he is without excuses, but not that he is without pardon. His anguish is meaningful: it is directed like an appeal toward God and toward God's order. It does not rest upon nothingness, but upon *pardon.* It is thoroughly leavened with hope and confidence. That is why it is completely different from the anguish of the atheist, which is "pure" anguish, too pure and irresolute to be true. In fact, it is so pure that it is reduced to a kind of simple uncertainty which is ultimately abandoned because, "after all, one must live." It is also true that atheistic responsibility is less real than Christian responsibility. For the Christian must truly answer *to* God and answer *for* his acts before God. But to whom is the atheist responsible? To whom must he render account? To the future, which alone will decide, the existentialists say. Therefore to History, to an abstraction. And it is exactly the same for the atheist's *involvement,* for his *freedom,* and for his *abandonment.* All these words lose their reality the minute one asserts that God does not exist here and now. In that case, involvement is no longer an act, but simple assertion of an existing condition to which one submits, and which leads to nothing definite. Freedom, too, is no more than a gamble in the void. And abandonment is dissolved into a kind of vague, worried indifference in which everything is permitted and there are no sanctions, but orders are still given.

Thus the description of atheist man drawn for us by secularist philosophy is both exact and meaningless. It is a portrait in
which every detail is correct, but whose over-all impression is
one of falseness or nonexistence. One recognizes the nose, the
eyes, the mouth, the proportions of the body, but not the man,
the personality, the one who is called into question and from
whom answers are demanded.

In the same way, it would be possible to criticize a large number of Christian notions that have been secularized by modern
thought. I shall mention only two of them.

Scientific determinism with its system of rigid laws—a concept which still exists in the minds of the half-educated, if not
of the experts—is a secularization of the idea of the divine order
of creation. Similarly, the Fate that we invoke is but a secularization of Providence. In both cases, the process consists in replacing the action of the divine Person with an impersonal system, against which there is no appeal.

Finally, the modern idea of revolution, of immediate and
salutary change on the collective level, is a secularization of the
Christian notion of individual conversion. It is unimaginable
apart from ideas formed by Christian thought, or developed in
ideologies which have issued from a Christianized world.

Politics

If we pass on to politics, we shall see the concrete results of
man without God.

Totalitarian political regimes are the direct and fatal consequence of man deprived of transcendence. Marxists, like the
Fascists, completely reject transcendence and have inevitably
arrived at the logical consequences of such rejection. Everything
that matters, they say, takes place in the here and now. Since
they must succeed at any price and at once, the most brutal tactics are justified. Putting aside all illusions, we can agree with

to piety, and results in the creation of illusion in the minds of the faithful.

And another example. Churchmen who are called upon to participate in public demonstrations, political congresses, banquets, memorials for the war dead, and so on generally try to sound like everybody else, to make themselves "acceptable," to show off, but always to end their speeches with some kind of reference to the "Almighty," which fools nobody. This is called, rather smugly, "lending a religious tone" to such gatherings. As far as I am concerned, these men are *collaborationists*. For, after flattering the century with their attitudes and the very style of their thought, when they add their "religious tone" it can only be a false note, for which they are readily pardoned because of their profession. In this way they further the belief that God is not the Unique Reality, but only a necessary complement, or traditional ornament, of our civilization. To my mind, the "religious tone" is the most insupportable dissonance that has ever assaulted the ear of man, Christian or pagan.

The Dilemma

Here, then, is the dilemma that confronts us in the twentieth century.

On the one hand, this century has become conscious of itself. It has dared to draw with rigor the consequences of its atheism in both philosophy and politics.

On the other hand, the churches, in confronting the century, are both absurd and feeble. Absurd because everything in which they believe is regarded by the triumphant systems of this century as an illusion or as held in bad faith. Feeble because the churches act as if transcendence were not the sole reason for their existence; as if they did not truly believe in it, as if they hoped to make themselves acceptable for other reasons—

moral, political, or even religious, in the natural meaning of the
term; in the sense that "people ought to have religion."

However, I do not think we should be discouraged in this
situation. For if the churches become true churches once more,
they have nothing to fear from secularism, even triumphant secularism. It depends completely upon us, therefore, whether the
churches are to become authentic again. And the perfectly un-
mistakable and clear challenge offered us by the doctrines of the
century affords an unhoped-for opportunity, perhaps the greatest in all history, to reply unequivocally.

Christian Responses to Secularism

When a question is both serious and total, as it is with secularism, we cannot reply to it by arguments, but only with our
whole being, with our manner of being, with the strength of being
that is revealed behind, and indeed beyond, every argument.

But Christianity's very being is a tension between the transcendent and the immanent. This means that we are not to offer a pure, verbal, isolated transcendence in opposition to the
century, but, instead, a transcendence which is involved in immanence, which makes the immanent truly serious, more serious than it believes itself to be. And more modest, too.

Someone may ask: Must we, too, become secularized in order
to act against this atheist century? Must we adapt ourselves, or
should we, rather, stand as partisans of the sacred and the transcendent? To this I reply: We must do both at once, depending
on the situation, and generally just the reverse of what we are
doing today.

Facing this century, immersed in this century of atheism, we
must set up churches where we worship in transcendence, and
where we confront the problems of our time, too, but in the name
of what transcends them. At present we are very far from that.
There is a miserable mixture of secularism and pietism in our

churches, the one almost always manifesting itself exactly where the other is needed.

Earlier in this essay I have said that most sermons today—and not only in the United States—are filled with the commonplaces of middle-class morality. Their morality is secular, but on the chance of an association of ideas, they are couched in pious tones and ornamented with biblical trappings. This is precisely what we do not need, precisely the opposite of what we should look for from preaching. Our sermons must consist of nonsecular reflection, conscious of the presence of the transcendent, but expressed in the most natural language of our time. I repeat: a person newly accepted in our churches finds secular thinking presented in pretentious terms. And this combination is doubly ineffectual: first, because our contemporaries detest any language that erects a barrier of fifty years between them and their preacher; and second, because once the barrier is surmounted, one sees that it was hardly worth coming to church for such platitudes. Perhaps you think I am being a little harsh, but our contemporaries who are unbelievers are apt to be even harsher if they happen to attend one of our religious services.

I wish all sermons would begin, "In the name of the Father, and of the Son, and of the Holy Spirit." Let these words be taken with such seriousness by the preacher that everything not said in the name of the Trinity is eliminated from his preaching! And I wish, too, that the truths preachers declare to us were presented solemnly or joyously, soberly or passionately, but never with that false sadness, that proper pseudo-religious accent that fools nobody and is enough to make even genuine truth look ridiculous.

As for our places of worship, it seems to me that they have been secularized where they should not have been, and are often inaccessible when they should be permanently open to the public. I wish our Protestant churches would stop being completely secular in their decor, architecture, and ornamentation. They should *not* be simple meeting rooms, virtually impossible of access and almost always closed; rather, I wish they would once again become consecrated sanctuaries that anyone may enter at any hour of the day.

I have talked about the churches first, and that is natural. For "the judgment will begin," as St. Peter wrote, "in the house of God." Besides, if we want to do something about this century, we must first exist, and a Christian truly exists, as such, only in the Church.

Now, if we leave the sanctuary where we have joined together to worship the transcendent, we find ourselves in the streets, in the middle of a century which denies a God who is both judge and saviour. We find ourselves in a century that challenges our belief and expects a serious reply to this challenge. Just how are we going to show this century that we believe in Eternity?

I have come to think that the testimony of a Christian outside of church—that is, when it is no longer a question of worshiping God but instructing and convincing men about him—may assume two forms, one positive, the other indirect.

I see the positive form of testimony less and less in the "revival meeting," in the emotional appeal to crowds, in all the procedures common to political propaganda since the advent of radio and mass communication. I do not think we can compete with the times on that level. I think, rather, that we must simply declare what we believe, speaking soberly, not agreeing to a discussion of the existence or nonexistence of the object and subject of our faith. The proof that I believe in the existence of God is that I do not feel the need to resort to propaganda in his favor. One does not propagandize to prove the existence of the Alps. They exist, and it is sufficient to say so to those who do not know it. It is unnecessary to "sell" the truth of the Spirit, which does not belong to us and is not a virtue to lecture about, or an opinion to inculcate, or a doctrine of some party to propagate. Let our age pursue its propagandistic methods, which are unsuitable for absolute certainties. And if we are asked what we believe, let us simply recite the Credo.

Now for the indirect form of testimony. This consists, I believe, in placing in question the pseudo-certainties of the century.

For wherever transcendence is denied, as in totalitarian states, no doubt is permitted about immanent realities. But as soon as such states are absolute, they become idols and, often, bloodthirsty gods. The absence of doubt on the question of immanent realities encourages the construction of a new world of "necessities" around us, which in turn tends to exclude even the possibility of doubt. Therefore, if we believe in the transcendent, we shall doubt some of the necessities our present age venerates under the name of "law," and which it, itself, manufactures in order to avoid acknowledging its responsibilities.

The Christian, let us not forget, believes in the transcendent; *consequently*, he doubts the false absolutes fabricated by the century. He is the man who doubts in the name of his faith.

Earlier, I described some of the atheist's political and philosophical false absolutes. I had hoped to show that these doctrines and practices, entirely and consciously secular, afford a rare opportunity for us to come face to face with the genuine dilemmas, the genuine questions, of our time: the *whole* of man and his destiny.

In conclusion, I should like to give an illustration that seems extremely important to me.

It is not accidental or coincidental that simultaneously with the appearance of the first truly authentic totalitarian movements (children of our century), we have also achieved the power to destroy the world. I am speaking, of course, of the hydrogen bomb.

Hardly had man asserted the autonomy of the earth and the "death of God," than he found the means to destroy the whole earth and bring about the death of man. Hardly had he said, "I believe only in this world," than he saw himself confronted with the end of this world. The limit of man's liberty had been reached: the freedom to bring about instantaneous self-destruction.

So, today, an unanticipated dilemma is posed: that of a beyond transcending our madness, or a vast collective leap into nothingness. We have entered an era of enormous risks, of decisions that affect the whole world.

We have the opportunity for greatness in our time, and we must meet its challenge with a free and confident heart. Free because we are not, like the unbelievers, devoted utterly to the present form of the world, but rather to its transformation. And confident because we know that whatever happens in this world, even if it must one day collapse, the drama of time has *already* been played. Truth is *already* victorious beyond time, through him who could say on the cross: *All is accomplished*.

3 The Christian Opportunity

For centuries, since the Renaissance, Christianity has been forced into a defensive position.

The ecclesiastical hierarchies first protected their temporal powers at a point when they were being justifiably contested by the state, and then had to protect their spiritual powers, which certain states had unjustifiably assumed.

The doctors of the Church had to protect themselves against the successive attacks of that skepticism, first of Cartesian science, historicism, and philology, and then of the sociological and philosophical systems which started to multiply at the beginning of the nineteenth century, and which could not be translated into the traditional theological categories.

As for believers, they had to defend themselves against the daily and ever intensified threat of ways of thinking and living that conformed less and less to spiritual laws. Without knowing it, without daring to admit it, Christians in Europe, as elsewhere, became a slightly persecuted minority. This subtle persecution of pinpricks, half-smiles, and intellectual ironies based on "science's latest progress"—the very tolerance shown toward the "survival of religions"—did as much harm to the churches as the Roman persecutions did them good in the beginning.

There was to be seen everywhere in the eighteenth and more
especially in the nineteenth century the exhaustion of the fuller
expressions of Christianity. There was a falling back under the
pressure of unbelief, and, to save the rest, those positions which
were too directly menaced by skepticism were abandoned. For
example, the mystical movement disappeared from the heart of
Roman Catholicism, while the transcendental theocentricism of
the Reformers gave place, among Protestants, to an amoralism
centered on man.

In order to save their bodies, the churches very quietly re-
nounced, if not their very soul, at least this flaming vehemence
which was always a sign and a symbol of spirit.

One of Rome's faithful sons, the great Paul Claudel, could at
the end of this period write that, to the question—"If the salt has
lost its savor, wherewith shall it be seasoned?"—modern Catholics were generally answering, "with sugar," a remark which is
unfortunately valid for many other churches and summarizes a
whole era.

I think that with World War II, this era came to an end, and
I base this assumption on a few facts.

It is a fact that totalitarianism broke the false peace that
seemed to exist between secular society and the churches. It has
suddenly become evident that Christians are a minority, and totalitarianism fought them openly in the name of non-Christian principles (such as nationalism), which Christians previously had
thought they could tolerate. Nazism was finally crushed at great
cost and after a great struggle, but its brutal promotion and its
downfall have been, for all churches, a test of strength, a challenge, a purification, an occasion for awakening.

It is a fact that the non-Christian, or anti-Christian, secularist
cultures which pretended to take the place of religions and lead
the modern world to a godless paradise have shown their real in-
capacity, in the face of attack by barbaric dictatorship, to give
life purpose, an ideal, and a morality more effectively than
Christianity.

It is also a fact that the latest developments of science imply less and less of a fundamental challenge to the truth and validity of Christian dogmas. In the last century the very opposite was true. The time of scientific arguments against Genesis, or the creation of the world by God, and the existence of the soul, now seems to belong to a bygone era.

Finally, it is a fact that for the last two or three decades the three great branches of Christianity have again found courage to reaffirm their sometimes extreme positions, with a refreshing independence of outside criticism. There has emerged a revived Thomism and serious biblical scholarship among Catholics, the re-establishment of Protestant dogmatics due to the initiative of Karl Barth, and the birth of a strong and purified Orthodox Church in the East. If we say that the period of defensive struggle has now ended for them, this is only a way of challenging the Christian churches, for today there remain to them only two alternatives: either to go back to sleep or to assume the offensive.

After two world wars, what do people find before them? Yesterday's conquerors and conquered both look in vain for a new Utopia. Some feel frustrated by the collapse of rationalist passions, which have become exhausted by the catastrophes they helped unleash, and which the simple search for material comfort can hardly replace. Others believe that by rearranging a few objects—wealth, for example—life itself can be arranged. Still others, making a theory of their weakness, formulate doctrines of "the absurd" in a philosophical jargon which at least makes them harmless. Faced with this abdication of thought and morality, the state feels compelled to extend its powers with such general laws that each man's personal vocation is necessarily undermined.

In other words, the churches no longer find hostile doctrines in the world, but a doctrinal void that has no precedent. This vacuum calls, in a dramatic way, for something substantial, for offensive action, for initiative.

Today the churches and their preachers have less reason than

ever to concern themselves with refuting the arguments of those
who do not believe in God; they must simply give testimony
of their beliefs with naïve aggressiveness, in order to help men
who are drowning.

As a layman belonging to the Church, and seeing its opportunity for action in the outside world and hearing the call of
misery in our time, I would hope for the following:

1. That the Church should stand for the kind of livable human
relationships it represented in the dark centuries before the
Middle Ages, its masterpiece. We have to re-establish the meaning of the living community, which has almost been killed by the
gigantism of our administrative machine, by the reign of money,
by industrial nomadism, and by mass deportations. All these factors tend to leave everything to the state and its rules, which
often may be useful but are never rules of life. I look forward to
a Christian sociology for the twentieth century.

2. That the Church might present an ideal of livable cultural
relationships, daring again to support and give leadership to an
intellectual vanguard instead of keeping its backward and suspicious position and becoming identified with the academic, both
in sacred art and contemporary culture. Its present stance only
leaves culture in a state of disorientation. Instead of indulging
themselves in virtuous indignation, our theologians should adopt
a policy of constructive intervention toward new schools of
thought, which are unprovided with principles of integration,
common measure, or spiritual ambition.

All the culture of the West—music, painting, philosophy, literature—came from the churches and the monasteries; but, unfortunately it has gone out of them! It is time that we organize
a search party, find it and bring it back again.

3. That the Church should stop protecting the sad and inef-
fective bourgeois morality which too many Christians today mistake for virtue; it should restore among its believers the meaning of personal vocation, which is the foundation for specifically
Christian morality.

"Be good!" the preachers have told us for the last two centuries. "Be mad!" said St. Paul to the Corinthians. "Dare to be improbable!" said Kierkegaard.* The latter are the voices which the most genuinely searching minds outside the churches seem especially eager to hear today. They can be caught by "the madness of the cross," not by middle-class wisdom. They are looking for something that drives ahead without shrinking from the risks of life.

4. That in the political domain the Church make absolutely clear that the message of its Founder is above all nationalism and state absolutisms. If it should ever happen that a really international spirit is established on our planet, it would only be in the name of something transcending our national, political, and racial boundaries. This is why the ecumenical movement assumes a capital importance in our century, even in political terms; it can offer the best model for a world union which respects national diversities. It can, it *must* do this; if it fails, I see nothing ahead of us but tyrants and their wars, in turn creating even greater tyranny.

Let me add one thing more. This program which, to my eyes, summarizes the greatest opportunity that Christianity has in the twentieth century, would remain a Utopia if Christians depended on the churches to bring it to fulfillment. The churches, as organized bodies, can only support and give a framework for Christian action, which will be implemented, as it always has been, by individual persons and small groups; by a few "fools for God" like St. Francis of Assisi; by unassuming people gathered in a room; by mystics whose appearance will suggest nothing extraordinary; by men who will be told that they exaggerate, that they are dreamers and lack common sense.

* Kierkegaard refers here to the incomparable, the unique man, who has received a precise vocation from God. He adds, "Every vocation is without precedent and therefore, to the one who receives it—for example, Abraham—seems completely improbable."

TWO
Christianity and
Culture

4 The Cultural Responsibility of the Church

There are striking similarities between the principles of the Atlantic Charter, drawn up during World War II by Roosevelt and Churchill, the United Nations Declaration of Human Rights, and the statements formulated by the great ecumenical conferences. But it is none the less remarkable that none of the latter documents makes any allusion to the building of a new cultural order. The continued neglect of this question by the churches has been a major factor in the general confusion of the postwar period.

It must be remembered that the youth of nearly all countries have been subjected to years of military training and almost constant indoctrination by the military mind. The general lowering of educational standards should not, therefore, be surprising; the standards of classical culture are abandoned, not only in countries torn to pieces by the war, but equally or even more so in countries like the United States.

In modern warfare, everything contributes to a lowering of the intellectual level. Ideas become propaganda; the great need is to simplify all problems; and judgment is made in terms of utilitarian exigencies rather than the demands of truth. It is hard to resist the pressure to put all the evil on one side and all the good on the other; we tend to be suspicious of those who maintain an attitude of exacting criticism or a normal sense of justice.

Besides, war has always had the effect of making the cultural standards of the prewar period outmoded, even in victorious nations. Today's youth can hardly be expected to respect a culture that produced Buchenwald and can find no better use for its technical genius than the development of the hydrogen bomb; in such an atmosphere we should be able to understand the strong demand for new leaders, new values, and a new ideal. There is a powerful current of desire to start anew and not fall back into the traditional errors or return to the disciplines of the bourgeois era.

This demand, since it springs from material and spiritual chaos, may include the transfer of the violence of war to the realm of the spirit; along with a taste for adventure we have seen a tendency to intellectual oversimplification. Today's youth cannot be expected to be free of the eternal illusions of mankind, and we should not be misled by their pretending to be extremely matter-of-fact and cynical. They are hungry for answers to their questions, for guidance, for catholic ideals (in the etymological sense of the word catholic), and "total" solutions in the cultural realm. For the bourgeois period has been an era of division, of the absence of relationships and a common measure between ideal and practice, between the diverse disciplines of the spirit, between diverse human and social activities.

The Task of the Churches

If the Christian churches cannot provide this firm and truly catholic direction, embracing all the aspects of life, the abyss will widen between the religious world and culture. The latter will set itself against Christianity, and probably with the following orientations: science (scientism), pagan eudaemonism, the cult of those values which are said to "belong to life," the creation of new religions and virulent nationalisms.

But if a church is to be in a position to intervene in the cultural process, it must be based on a firm doctrine, on a theology which is at the same time rigorous and vital within the church. A church whose theology is vague has nothing more to say in the domain of culture.

Such a church can still give counsel in the political field. It can, for example, approve a document like the Declaration of Human Rights, which does not emanate from a theology or even directly from Christianity. It can rally to a political attitude inspired by pure humanism. But the realm of culture is a wholly different matter. Here a church cannot adopt ideologies made by others. It cannot speak effectively except in the name of its own theology and by relating what it says in the most direct way to it.

Thus it is that the Roman Catholic Church led the philosophical movement of the Middle Ages. Thus the Reformation of Luther and of Calvin fought successfully against the Renaissance and inspired a vast cultural movement. Later, when the Roman and Reformed theologies became atrophied, they no longer dared nor yet were able to intervene as inspiring influences in the cultural controversy. The abyss began to open between the Church and culture. A Christian of the nineteenth or twentieth centuries, for example, could believe the official doctrines of his denomination and at the same time admire Wagner, or Whitman, or Renoir, without even asking himself if this was at all compatible with his creed. For theology had in fact ceased to be living, precise, and exacting—and therefore inspiring.

Thomism inspired Dante; Calvinism inspired Rembrandt; Lutheranism inspired Bach; Puritanism inspired Milton. But the liberal Protestantism of the nineteenth and twentieth centuries has inspired not one artist, musician, poet, or creative philosopher. Because it made no clear, strong demands, it did not offer the creative instinct a framework and fixed boundaries to be at once a stimulus and a guide.

First, then, if the Church has nothing to give to or demand of culture, the latter will thereby find itself impoverished and disoriented; it will be cut off from its roots. For all Western culture was born of Christian theology and liturgy, whether in conformity with the Christian code or in revolt against it. (The great modern philosophies, those of Descartes and Hegel, were born of controversy which was clearly theological in its origins.)

And in the second place, if culture loses contact with the Church, with its doctrine and its worship, then the Church loses its most effective means of acting on the age, of transforming its beliefs into creative action. Creativity in general eludes it. All that is created is then created outside the Church or in opposition to it, and becomes difficult to integrate into a Christian conception of the world. This is particularly striking in the Protestant countries, where a concern to relate any work of culture to a genuine theology has almost entirely disappeared—for lack of a firm theology. The Roman Church has kept a stronger hold on intellectual creativity because it is zealous to preserve the rights and duties of theological criticism in all fields, and not only in a negative and restrictive manner.

What, then, can the churches do to contribute toward the creation of a cultural order in the chaos of tomorrow? I propose a simple reply. The churches will be able to act and inspire if they are based on a firm and complete doctrine. They will be effective to the degree to which they intervene in the name of their theology. They will be effective if they make demands instead of losing interest or following belatedly the trend of the day.

Vocation: The Fundamental Principle

In order to pass from the theology of a church to social, cultural, political, or economic applications, it would seem to be a good idea to define certain principles or intermediary stages between theology and ethics.

The intermediate category that appears the most fruitful in the cultural and social realm is that of *vocation* (in the Calvinist and

Lutheran sense of the term, which is wider than that of Rome).
The gospel teaches us that *every* man is capable of receiving a vocation, a special call, which distinguishes him from his kind and
endows him with an inalienable dignity to the degree to which
he obeys the call. This is the fundamental principle of any social
order that can be called Christian. One can also accept the idea of
general or collective vocation, applied to a nation or even to a
generation. Every being, whether individual or collective, for
whom the Church can pray, is capable of receiving a vocation.

Now the great social and cultural maladies of the modern age
all have this one common characteristic: that they deny personal
vocation (whether nationalist, racial, or class collectivism;
whether biological, moral, or bourgeois materialism; individualism is likewise a morbid deviation from the sense of vocation, for
it denies social and community implications). The chief criticism
of this is the following: an ideology which denies personal vocation, or a social regime which deprives man of the freedom to
obey his vocation, is incompatible with Christianity.

All the totalitarian ideologies, for example, deny by definition
the fact of personal vocation. They replace it with an *ersatz:* the
function of the citizen within the state or the party, as decreed
by the state or the party. They deny diversities, or qualify them
as morbid, reactionary, individualistic, antisocial. They are,
therefore, incompatible with the Christian order, which presupposes union in diversity.

All the *unitarian* doctrines seeking to establish a mechanical
and rigid homogeneity, whether imposed from above (state,
tyrant), or from below (egalitarianism to the uttermost), deny
personal vocation or the vocation of a group, and consider it
dangerous or scandalous. These doctrines are thus incompatible
with the Christian order, which implies union and not uniformity,
and respects diversity of endowment, diversity of members in the
same body, many mansions in the kingdom of God.

A social order cannot be termed Christian unless it is founded on respect for vocation, and unless it assures to every man (and to each group or collective entity) the liberty of realizing that divine, unique, and inalienable vocation.

A Christian social order will thus be ecumenical rather than unitarian. It will be federal rather than centralized (in the cultural, religious, and social realms). It will put the rights and duties of the individual (that is, the individual burdened with a vocation), before the rights and duties of the state (the organism whose task is to secure in a material sense the freedom of the individual).

The Social Consequences of Vocation

1. A Christian doctrine centered on the idea of the vocation of individuals will always put the emphasis on duty rather than on rights. Let us take the example of an army. Military regulations do not define the rights of a captain, but only his duties and functions. It goes without saying that army organization is such that a captain will always have the means of exercising his duties: that is his freedom; he has no other. Now the *Ecclesia militans* resembles an army far more than it resembles an abstract constitution defining the rights of the individual independently of the duties of his office.

2. A Christian doctrine which takes seriously the fact of the divine vocation of a man or of a collective body, will condemn any system which mechanically impedes the realization of that vocation. It will therefore condemn, in the name of theology, the great bureaucratic machines in which individuals are treated abstractly in terms of the requirements of the machine and not according to their real vocations. It will condemn the system of private capital to the degree to which it sets in motion the means of material power by the chances of stock market operations, for instance, and not according to the rights derived from the exercise of a vocation. It will condemn every economic system which

makes man the plaything of the interests of the state, of a trust, of material production, of individual or collective will to power.

3. The churches will fight on behalf of everything that assures to an individual or a collective body the legal liberty and the material means to accomplish his vocation. They will do it in the name of their doctrine, and with great precision. They will not do it in the name of conceptions that are purely humanistic or religiously neutral, such as progress, social justice (of the "left"), the social order (of the "right"), national interest, or economic prosperity.

The duty of the churches is to rethink all these categories, and to criticize them in a specifically Christian setting. For example, there must be a redefinition of freedom in terms of the functioning of a Christian doctrine of vocation. (Freedom from want does not mean prosperity as an end, but the accordance of the material possibility to everyone to realize his vocation, and so on.)

Thus, and thus alone, will the churches regain an effective authority. They will cease to identify themselves, in the eyes of the man on the street, with this or that social class, with the established order, or with the reform of the moment. They will cease to be dragged in the wake of movements initiated by others, with motives and to ends that are not necessarily Christian.

The Cultural Consequences

From the point of view of an ethic founded on vocation, two dangers threaten modern culture: (a) a false universalism, the product of an education which has no color—confessional, philosophical, or regional—and no definite ties with a real community; and (b) nationalism, or spiritual autarchy.

The vocation of a man or of a group is that which both distinguishes and integrates that man or that group. These two factors should be reconciled and vigilantly safeguarded: the universal factor and the one that sets him apart.

It is greatly to be desired, for instance, that institutions of education (colleges or universities) be founded on a confessional (i.e., denominational) basis plainly stated, side by side with lay, neutral, or non-Christian institutions, and that all instruction, in every field, be dominated by the doctrine of the Church in question, as is the case in Roman Catholic institutions and the Calvinist University in Holland. This would result in the creation of centers of culture which are clearly diversified, but which favor intellectual striving and a greater integration of culture and theology.

But at the same time, in order to safeguard the universalist factor, it is necessary that in denominational schools reasonably thorough instruction should be given about the other denominations: the ecumenical department. For we come to know ourselves only by learning about others, just as we come to know others better by understanding ourselves.

The general attitude, then, would be to deepen and integrate to the highest degree each cultural vocation of the group, whether religious or national, and all with a view to the union (federal or ecumenical) of these vocations in a far more comprehensive whole—the body and its members; never to seek union through the neutralizing of differences and peculiarities, but, on the contrary, to seek to compose them.

The second problem to envisage is that of closer collaboration between intellectuals and the Church. In the present state of affairs this organic collaboration is lacking. Only the ecumenical movement has given to a certain number of scholars, historians, and writers the opportunity of working for the churches as a whole. But most Protestant denominations lack the means of bringing into organic contact the creators of culture and the Church as such—the Church as a body of doctrine and as a community. In this field everything remains to be created. And something must be created if we wish to avoid the development of tomorrow's culture along lines that diverge more and more from a Christian conception of the world.

5 A Common
Language

Europe held many surprises for me when, after an absence of
several years, I returned there in 1946. A great intellectual alert-
ness, often allied to a kind of cynicism which was easy enough
to explain; a profound need of realism but too little knowledge
of world conditions to sustain it; renewed interest in metaphysics; and finally a general politicalization of ideas—that was
the picture of intellectual circles there as it appeared to me.
Quite naturally, the counterpart of most of these traits could be
observed in religious thought. But what surprised me was to
find in the latter a lively consciousness of the need for true community and for new communal structures. I saw among the intellectuals—obsessed as they were by politics—neither invention
nor systematic research in regard to new political forms: they
held either to the old regime of parties or to a totalitarian solution
of the Marxian type.

Community consciousness had been reawakened in the
churches of Europe by the Resistance as well as by economic
misery; hence it was missionary as well as charitable, offensive
as well as defensive. From the missionary point of view, it was,
and is still, manifested on the one hand by an urge for social
action which would lead the Church to enter the sphere of political economy by suggesting to it institutions more consistent

with the Christian idea of man, and on the other hand, by a desire for action within the Church itself, to the end that it might
be led to offer in its worship service a structure more efficacious
for spiritual life, a more organic discipline for the faithful. It is
this second trend that I want to examine. Among Protestants as
well as Catholics it has taken the form of a liturgical revival.

But before going further, I want to underscore the fact that
the impetus toward social action and the liturgical revival, far
from excluding one another in principle or revealing two tendencies in conflict within the Church—as often happened in the
nineteenth century—sprang from one and the same spiritual
attitude. In fact, if on the one hand the "social" Christians seek
to Christianize society outside the churches, if on the other hand
the "liturgists" seek to make devotion within the Church more
communal, it is because both are intent on conforming to the
doctrine of the Incarnation, in the light of which their efforts appear equally necessary and thus complementary. Here we have
a parallel to the way in which the two commissions of the World
Council of Churches. "Life and Work" and "Faith and Order,"
are drawing closer together.

Signs of a Liturgical Revival

Let us first of all cite a few facts.

A well-defined movement has emerged among the Catholics of
France to have the Mass said in French and to popularize trans-
lations into the vernacular. At the same time influential bishops
have been recommending to the faithful the reading of the Bible.
Seminary courses and recent theological writing indicate a
serious effort to purify the doctrine of the sacraments of Aristotelian concepts and magical overtones which had made it so
difficult to reconcile with the Protestant or Orthodox concepts
of the gospel. The intended objective, however, is not to draw
nearer to other confessions, but to render the Roman liturgy more

appealing and efficacious. In Paris, the Holy Orthodox liturgy is said in French in two churches, and an Eastern Rite community of Benedictines was formed during the war with a liturgy likewise translated into French. On their part, several Lutheran churches are in process of a pronounced return to their original liturgy, after having suffered for two centuries an impoverishment comparable to that of the Calvinist churches. But it is precisely among the latter that we can best observe the phenomenon of liturgical restoration, since it had to start from so near the zero point.

In Calvinist circles in France and Switzerland, among many of the younger pastors and among students of theology and influential laymen, the legitimacy of liturgy in itself is no longer argued. Rather, various proposals for a revised order of service are being considered by church committees, and certain specific problems—such as the place in the service to be assigned to the Decalogue—have been discussed. (According to Calvin and his Strasbourg liturgy, the Decalogue should be recited *after* the promises of grace.) One notices that young Barthians, in spite of the distrust which Karl Barth continues to voice in regard to liturgy ("It's theatrical," he once said), are not the least active in this sphere. In the French section of Switzerland the movement called "Church and Liturgy," freely inspired by Anglicanism, has already won several parishes. Several religious "communities" of men or women have sprung up in the country. I know of three in Switzerland and one in Burgundy near the ancient Abbey of Cluny. There the liturgical life holds a place which is constantly growing.

These are scattered symptoms and may not yet be discernible except in limited circles. How much importance should one attribute to them? Are we in the presence of the beginning of a genuine liturgical renaissance or only of sporadic revivals, accidental and with little promise of continuance? Is there behind these preoccupations and these beginnings a common necessity that ties them together? No one can answer as to the future. But as I try to place within our epoch the several signs I have just mentioned, they seem to me a direct answer to the profound need of this day.

Community and Language

The whole world feels it, many have voiced it: our century no longer has genuine *loci communes*. As we have seen in earlier pages, it has lost that common spiritual measure which conferred upon the medieval and classical civilizations their grandeur and their sense of unity. We live, for example, in a great confusion of contradictory ethics: the fact is that in a single day we have to make decisions now in the name of conscience, now in the name of some science or other, or again according to the national interest, or the prejudices of a class, or a romantic ideal, or a fashion, a psychoanalytical theory, a system of hygiene, a party, and so on. The result is that the *loci communes*, the common and accepted expressions—today we speak of them as standards of values—cease to be truly common and have themselves become indeterminate. The words *liberty, authority, spirit, justice, democracy, truth* take on as many different meanings (and often incompatible ones) as there are standards of value in our heads. It has come to this, that if war breaks out in the near future, we can be sure that all the countries will wage it in the name of liberty, of justice, and of democracy, for these terms designate such contradictory realities that there will remain no other possibility either of exchange or arbitration save that of the nuclear bomb. At Babel, men divided because they began to speak different languages. Our situation is worse: we all pronounce the same words but at the same time give them different meanings. It is speech itself, the sign and gauge of the human community, that is stricken to the heart and on the verge of losing its primordial functions of definition, regulation, and communication.

The totalitarian regimes thoroughly understood that the problems of communication and of language are closely united. To the anarchy of vocabulary, hence of moral and political judgment, they opposed regulations that were schematic and sweeping, but temporarily effective. It was the party that dictated the actual meaning of words, thus re-creating an appearance of order. It was the party that both supplied and imposed new symbols, that is to say, the plastic language of gestures, of insignia, of uniforms. This sociological need for ritual appears thus far to have escaped the attention of the democracies. It is here that the liturgical renaissance is integrated with the forces of our era; in fact, it represents the only serious attempt among us to surmount the verbal anarchy which I have just defined as being at the same time the sign and cause of the community disintegration from which we are suffering.

Liturgy and Semantics

According to its etymology, liturgy signifies a "public work." By definition it is therefore a communal reality. Futhermore, it is a reality creative of the true community, and that for two principal reasons. First, the liturgy is *performed* by the people, it calls out their participation, their avowed loyalty, both inwardly and outwardly, and thus demonstrates its existence and furnishes the pure prototype of a public *order* freely accepted. The situation of the man who is receiving the sacrament should be considered the true foundation of all Christian sociology. Second, liturgy is a language of co-ordinated sentences and gestures; it thus guarantees and defines the common meaning of the words and their actual authority.

It is on the second point that I should like to insist. It might be said that theology and philosophy play more exactly than liturgy the role of defining activities in regard to the vocabulary. But it must be noted that terms such as *grace* or *liberty* are defined by theologians and philosophers in an analytical manner; they make (and this is to a certain extent methodically inevitable) abstractions of their living context. It seems to me that the liturgy, on the contrary, defines these same terms by synthesis, within the body itself of the community, by the entire context of the service and in immediate liaison with physical gestures and attitudes; hence, by inclusion, through an enrichment of the sense of their value and efficacy. Simplifying for the sake of symmetry, one might say that theology provokes reflection in regard to certain terms, while liturgy makes of them reflexes of the entire being.

Let us take another comparison: one feels all the difference there is between the word *attention* analyzed by a psychologist and the word "Atten-*shun!*" pronounced by a drill sergeant; or again in the exhortation "Let us attend!" pronounced by an Orthodox priest in the divine liturgy. Similarly with the verb *to believe* in our conversation and the verb *I believe* at the beginning of the Credo. And in the same way one may well reflect on the fact that the words *peace* or *liberty,* to which all our parties, doctrines, and revolutionary sects give their own one-sided definitions (winding up by making them contradictory), recover only in the liturgy their full weight, their complete meaning, immediate and concrete. ("The *peace* of God which passes all understanding"; "go in *peace*"; "*deliver* us from evil"—*deliverance* always linked to *pardon,* to glorification, and so forth.)

In the last analysis, the full meaning of words which have elsewhere become so hard to define authoritatively—grace, liberation, spirit, peace, justice, truth, society, good, and evil—was given to our Western civilization by the Bible. And liturgy makes these words live in their biblical context, thus unceasingly restoring them to their spiritual etymology. For liturgy is composed chiefly of quotations from the Psalms, the Gospels, and the Epistles. In turn, many apostolic salutations and doxologies which our liturgies draw from the Epistles were themselves taken by the authors of the Epistles from the first liturgies of the Church. That, at least, is the thesis advanced by Professor Cullmann of Basel.

Of course, what is true of single words is also true of a large number of compound expressions, proverbs, and popular sayings stemming from the Bible, transmitted by the liturgies, and forming an important part of our literature. Remove the Bible and suppress the national liturgies, and you will render incomprehensible not only the literature of the Middle Ages, but innumerable allusions, turns of phraseology, quotations not indicated by quotation marks, poetic devices, semantic qualifications, processes of reasoning, exclamations, and so on in works as diverse as Goethe's *Faust, The Flowers of Evil* by Baudelaire, Nietzsche's *Zarathustra*, the *Four Quartets* of Eliot, and the novels of Gide. A fat book might be written on this question: To what degree is the slight common meaning which our vocabularies still preserve due to biblical and liturgical recollections?

Liturgy and the Ecumenical Movement

One might argue at length, I admit, from a strictly sociological and cultural point of view, the practical importance in the world of today of a vast liturgical restoration, where the churches are much in the minority. But what appears to me beyond doubt is the need for such a restoration for the *rapprochement* of the different communions.

Before and after the war I took part in numerous meetings of European intellectuals organized for the purpose of confronting the theological or political positions of the great Christian communions and of finding an area of agreement. But from these discussions each man went out with an increased feeling of the inherent correctness of his own system, which seemed to me to be contrary to the goal envisaged. And in fact, in this plan, union would not operate save in the form of a not very desirable compromise, or by the abdication of one of the doctrines represented

—something very unlikely. Things are altogether different when a Christian assists or takes part in the liturgy of another communion. For a discussion, however fraternal, brings into play, exercises, and stimulates the faculties of distinction and exclusion; while in the other case, before the living reality of a different religious experience, it is the spirit of comprehension and of participation that comes to the front. It may happen that the reaction is negative and that the visitor feels repelled, estranged, by what goes on before and around him. But the feeling of respect which pervades the ceremony, the fact that all are turned toward the cross on the altar, the expectation of the successive acts, all this holds the attention in a current of participation, retards judgment, and predisposes to a sort of receptivity which the intellect too easily prohibits. The man who discusses is reduced to the minor but immediate necessity of being right; he sends back the ball, he does not want to be hit; whereas he who assists at a worship service is plunged into an existential situation where he does not feel himself questioned save in a more fundamental manner. Even if he is in an inward state of refusal, the fact that the expression of this refusal is suspended permits an act of comprehension more profound and concrete. That is why the Orthodox and certain Anglicans are not wrong when they reply to those who question them concerning the doctrine of their church: Read our liturgies, or better yet, take part in our services.

But this brings us to a more specific point. The Anglican who takes part in the Lutheran service or the Lutheran who takes part in the Roman Mass, discovers that the liturgical structure and most of the words pronounced are well known to him. And because he is familiar with the language it is easier for him to distinguish what is really specific in the spirit and style of the church he is visiting. Conversely, the believer from a non-liturgical church, attending an Orthodox, Roman Catholic, Anglican, or Lutheran ceremony, will be tempted to attach excessive importance to the vestments, the music, the setting; that is, the decoration. If he stops there, it is he who at that moment is the victim of the "materialism," the "sensualism," and the "theatrical" forms with which he reproaches the ritualists. The setting conceals from him the real drama whose spirit alone is important to those engaged in it. He will be tempted to reject all hope of fraternal association with a church which he will have judged only by appearances—of which he has, moreover, exaggerated the importance. The obstacle to union, or at least to comprehension, will in this case come from the absence of a common language, precisely that language which liturgy offers to the other churches.

We now see the real and not accidental bond that unites ecumenical striving and the liturgical revival, especially among Protestants of the Calvinist tradition. The one brings the other along, summons it, and assists it. The French and Swiss pastors of whom I spoke earlier feel very strongly that in re-establishing a liturgical framework in their services they rediscover the great commonplaces of primitive Christianity and at the same time, without ceding anything of doctrine, arrange new ways of approach, ways more truly right and practical, toward the four other communions. One of these pastors, Max Thurian, has recently republished important fragments of the liturgy of Calvin under the title *Joy of Heaven on Earth*. It is noteworthy that the Decalogue is put into French verse and that it is to be chanted, just like most of the prayers, the Credo, and the doxologies. May one hope that, on the other hand, while insisting that the Mass be said in the living language (as it originally was), the young Catholic priests will think also about facilitating reciprocal understanding and reducing certain external and nonessential obstacles which have created so much misunderstanding, so many avoidable arguments? When the Calvinists have a complete liturgy and the Catholic Mass is said in French, I do not say that unity will be achieved, but I do say that the people of the churches will see better that it is not the use of candles or a few embroidered vestments that is the cause of separation; they will see better the slight difference there is between the words pronounced in the various churches; and finally, they will be enabled in a measure to evaluate much more justly what unites us and what is still irreducible. Doubtless this will be only a first step toward the desired federation. And while it is certain that it will not be enough, the necessity for it seems to me to be no less clear.

For a Modern Worship Service

I do not want to conclude these remarks leaving the reader with the impression that I am making myself the advocate of a "return"—to whatever it may be. To establish the fact that liturgy answers to a common need and challenge of our time and would enable us to re-establish (between Christians to begin with) a common language—that is not to appeal to the past, but rather to an act of creation. The error of many Protestants, once the generation of Luther and Calvin had passed away (and above all during the Puritan period), was precisely to imagine that by suppressing the liturgy they had rediscovered the "purity and simplicity of the primitive worship service." But the primitive Church was liturgical; today we realize that. All our attempted returns to the past are liable to errors of this kind; that is, the "returns" are imaginary. Therefore, it is not because the primitive Christians had a liturgy that we should have one, but by virtue of modern need and with a view to the future. And we do not respond to that need by restoring archaic rituals which, though often very beautiful, probably did not die out without a reason. Let us not forget that Gothic was modern in the Middle Ages! We need a modern worship service, a living one—and after so many "venerable" texts, a youthful liturgy.

Yet the fact is that liturgical evolution seems to have been arrested for centuries. After the Council of Trent the Catholic Mass was, for practical purposes, suddenly fixed in a single form and never varied again. The great vitality, the diversity, the profusion of rites that characterized the Middle Ages were for a time prolonged in the churches that issued from the Reformation; then they became congealed there also, and have changed little save in the direction of continued impoverishment.

But it is perhaps the very excess of this impoverishment, paralleling the dissolution of the genuine community, that is giving birth to the revival which I pointed out at the beginning. And perhaps those churches that are most impoverished, most denuded, will point the way to a new liturgical *life*. Two reasons, principally, lead me to believe this. These churches, from the very fact of the meagerness of their ritual, are more free than others to *innovate*, that is, to reply to the vital question of today in a manner both direct and new. Moreover, it happens that these very churches have just undergone an impressive theological reorientation without parallel in the other communions. I am thinking of Karl Barth and Emil Brunner, of their very numerous disciples, and in general of the astonishing theological vitality one has seen in France, Switzerland, and Holland in recent years. The Reformation churches seem to me in a good position to avoid the double danger of timid traditionalism and irresponsible fantasy in innovation.

The true problem of the century is that of the community. It is bound up with the problem of a common language. Liturgy can contribute toward re-creating and authenticating this language, but only under two equally determinative conditions: it must remain biblical at its source, and it must find a contemporaneous form. It is only in a creative effort, surpassing both our riches and our poverties through a general forward movement, that our present divisions will be able to transform themselves into converging diversities.

6 The Vocation and Destiny of Israel

"A prophet," Karl Barth wrote, "is a man without biography." *"Er steht und fällt mit seiner Mission."* In other words, he exists only within his mission. Or, literally translated, these words say: "He rises and falls with his mission." We know nothing else about his life, and we need know nothing else in order to recognize the full scope of his message, since it is God's message. Jeremiah might have been only a stammering shepherd if the Eternal had not spoken through him. It is really noteworthy that the only biographic detail which the Bible gives about him is his difficulty in expressing himself. Not only was he not historically destined to become a great prophet—psychologists can wear themselves out on this point—but he even had an obstacle to overcome, in human eyes the most decisive obstacle for a man called to the ministry of the Word.

What is true of the prophet is also true of his people—above all a prophetic people. What is *biographically* true of a man whom the Eternal chose is no less true of the *secular history* of the Jews, themselves bearers of a mission for which nothing seemed to prepare them. Without intending a paradox, it might be said that Israel would have had no history without the promise God made to Abraham. This tribe "rises and falls" with the mission it incarnates: "preparing the ways of the Lord," hoping for and preaching the Messiah, actively waiting for the invisible—for even more, the never-seen, which no other people on the face of the earth was ever able to imagine, and which does not correspond to any historically determined need.

History (as described by Hegel or Taine, or by dialectical materialism) undertakes to reconstitute the immanent evolution of a people, to the degree that one can with probability make generalizations as to its fundamental style and reduce it to statistics. It deals with what may be determined from partially measurable factors (geography, economics, and so on), or expressed in our more or less naïvely positivist language. What can such a science teach us about the *destiny* promised to the tiny nomadic tribes that originally made up the Jewish nation? Analogically speaking, History did not have the slightest reason to suppose that the people of Israel, had they not been "elected," would have turned into a tribe any different from so many of the tribes that to this day inhabit the Near East, all of them so remarkably persistent in maintaining the characteristic traits and pastoral customs of the time of Abraham. We have no secular information that reveals to us why this particular tribe escaped the monotonous and conservative fate that even today weighs on the inhabitants of the desert. It was chosen among thousands, and without reason, or with no other reason than their astonishing inability to conquer and construct . . .

So the annals of Israel are those of an unforeseen and humanly unforeseeable power which was never immanent to the mediocre circumstances of the Hebrews. What we do know of their "history"—and here the word takes on a new meaning—is the consequence of God's acts, whose instruments they were. But unruly instruments! What belongs to them, what is really theirs in these annals is their truculence in the face of their destiny, their constant revolts, mistakes, and outbursts of disbelief. And all their glory belongs to God, to the calling that spared them a shabby destiny, despite themselves.

Faith and Idolatry

Reflection on the age-old struggles related in the Old Testament insistently and grandly leads us to the fundamental opposition of a calling and a destiny. And the Jewish nation is impossible to understand apart from this opposition.

A nomadic destiny, a messianic calling. A visible, insignificant destiny; an invisible and triumphant calling, such as that which the prophets preached to the people and which alone lifted them up, brought them together, and gave meaning to their lives. These people wandered without end in the desert; their movements were aimless until God elected them. Henceforth their way was fixed, but it was no longer their "own"; it came from God, went forth toward God, and it was God's law that pointed it out. It is for this reason that their *telos*, their final end, is transcendent and mysterious, like God; essentially unique, like God; and, like God, the object of faith alone. It is a matter of faith, not of sight. We are dealing with absolutely new categories, which will play a determining role in the ethic of the West, however masked in the present world by the pagan names of idealism and realism.

But the conflict between faith and sight is, in the long run, only another aspect of the conflict between calling and destiny. It helps us understand the spirit of revolt that endlessly tormented the twelve tribes. To mortal eyes, an invisible goal is a threat and an affliction at least as much as a promise. It is a threat to "immediate interests" that seem neglected in favor of a completely uncertain future; it is an affliction that drives men to look for something visible and tangible as a protection. Thus the Hebrews rebel, escape into the worship of false gods, who are reassuring because made by "the hand of man." But prophets return uninterruptedly, denouncing the idols and the traitors who worship them:

> My people inquire of a thing of wood,
>   and their staff gives them oracles.
> For a spirit of harlotry has led them astray,
>   and they have left their God to play the harlot.
>
> Hosea 4:12

This "spirit of harlotry," this idolatry that is reborn as soon as Israel ceases to believe in what its eyes cannot see but which constitutes all its greatness, is really the rebellion of profane destiny against a liberating vocation. And just as this rebellion, this destiny, and this need to see, are concretely symbolized in the statues of foreign idols—for they imitated their neighbors when they doubted their calling—so their calling and its implied faith are also uniquely and unequivocally symbolized in the ark of the covenant in the midst of the people. The ark is also called the ark of testimony because it testifies to God's will, the conditions of his alliance with Israel.

The Rule

The tables of the Law are kept within the ark. The Law is the sacred rule: it reminds the people of both their beginning and their end, in so far as they are a new people, elected by God and set apart from others.[1] It is to the tables of the Law that every

[1] Jewish "racism" must be seen as justified in the beginning only by the spiritual calling of the people. It is not at all biological. It becomes so only in so far as the signs of vocation are considered as worth-while realities in themselves. Undoubtedly this inevitable error began to take place from the beginning, to the degree that relations between the elect and the Gentiles were codified. We know perfectly well how far this was carried out. In *Against Apion*, Josephus says that a register of priestly women (i.e., descended from the families of priests) was kept by those who offered sacrifice. "And they did not marry those who had been captives, for fear that they had had contact with foreigners. Can there be anything more precise for exempting some races from contact with others, since our sacrificers could prove their descent from father to son for two thousand years by authentic documents? If someone failed to observe this law, he was removed from the altar, and was no longer allowed to perform any of his priestly functions" (Bk. I, 7).

gesture and thought is referred. Nothing may be neutral or left
to chance; everything is measured and judged in the light of
the entire nation's predestined end: God Eternal and his service.

The ark of the covenant seems to us like an almost ideal example of measure in the Greek sense of the term, the canon and
rule of a civilization. It is the initial principle, the final standard,
and—concurrently—the living source of every national act, material as well as political and spiritual.[2]

The history of civilization offers us certain other examples of
a commonly accepted "measure" that are equally grand and
rigorous: ancient India, Periclean Greece, imperial Rome, the
medieval papacy, the Aztec and Egyptian empires, China during
the great dynasties. But the measure of the Hebraic tribes is
distinguished above all the others in that it is a vocation that
came from a personal, single, eternal, transcendent God. It is
not the normal product of a historical evolution, fecundated and
crystallized by the intervention of a great leader. Consequently,
it is more "total" than any humanly conceivable measure, since
it does not originate in circumstances or persons necessarily imperfect or partial. It permits no contingencies, no possibilities
of escape or neglect; there is no refuge "far from the face of
the Eternal."

Because it is *God*'s Law, and because God is the Eternal, the
Law is the ultimate consciousness of the Hebrew people. And
because it is God's *Law*, defining truth, in itself it carries the
permanent principle of every action and of every thought. A true
measure, then, and perfectly common. During war, the ark was
carried in front of the armies as a symbol of the people's unity.

[2] I have gone into more ample detail on the capital importance of a common
rule for every culture in *Penser avec les Mains*. There is an abridged version of
the present study in that book. From the perspective of the history of the Jewish people, that summary suffers from (among other things) a serious gap, for
it appears to end with Israel's final abandonment of its destiny after the birth of
Christ. Here I am happy to be able to delineate developments not mentioned in
my book.

But its use was forbidden during civil war, for it is an indivisible standard.

God is in heaven, his Law is on earth, and priests exist to watch over the covenant. And if these "clerics" commit treason, giving in to their well-known and immemorial weakness, if they forget that God is a jealous God, the prophets rise up against them and denounce their idolatry.[3] Please note that in this instance the idea of idolatry represents more than the worship of images from which it draws its name. It includes everything that is only sight and not faith, everything that refuses obedience, and any conception of another god. An idol is anything that turns one away from his vocation. An idol is any act or thought, however beautiful, which cannot be consecrated to the priestly ministry of the chosen people, anything not ordained to that end which the prophets are constantly announcing.

But the worst idolatry is making an object of worship of the common rule itself—that is, the Law divorced from the end for which it exists. This is the idolatry of making man submit to the "letter" of divine legislation, converting it into *man's* own creation, forgetting its Author. It is then that the letter kills man instead of helping him by incarnating the spirit. This is the ultimate temptation to which the Pharisees were to succumb, those learned rigorists and doctors of the Law whom the people honored very much as later they were to honor princes of the Church, bishops, and cardinals. In the name of the Law they condemned the very one who had given it; fidelity to the letter of the Law

---

[3] The compilation of the Mosaic books of the Bible is attributed by Wellhausen and his school to the disciples of the great prophets. By this theory it was prophecy, the most finalistic element of Israel's religion, that gave legal expression to the common rule of the people: the Ten Commandments. Thus the end creates its own means.

Today this hypothesis is out of fashion. We have returned to the ancient idea of a single leader, Moses, who gave the rudiments of the Law to the Jewish people after the flight from Egypt. The prophets, then, not only recalled the people to their true God—as against the priests of false gods—but denounced the excesses of legalism.

made them incapable of recognizing Jesus Christ, the one for
whose coming the letter had prepared, and who alone gave it
meaning.

While reading Josephus, the greatest secular historian of the
Jews, I came across a passage that seems to confirm this interpretation of the Law, the common rule of the Hebrew people.
"Our lawgiver, Moses," he wrote in *Against Apion*, "has been the
only man whose words and actions have been consistent."[4] For
he not only formulated just laws, complete and detailed, but he
made sure that everyone learned about them.

This knowledge produces an admirable consistency among
us, because nothing is capable of bringing such consistency
to birth and keeping it alive as having the same feelings about
God's greatness and being raised in the same manner of life,
and observing the same customs. For you never hear God di-
versely discussed among us, as among other people, neither
by the common people who say casually whatever comes into
their heads, nor by the philosophers. . . . We believe that God
sees everything that takes place in the world. Our wives and
our servants share our belief: from their mouths can be learned
the rules for the conduct of our lives and that all our actions
must be directed toward pleasing God.

A Poor but Faithful Culture

A twentieth-century man can experience nothing but fright at
the spectacle of a social order so fanatically linked to, and suspended from, the Invisible. Modern man resents it as an affront
to the creative liberty he thinks necessary to his pride. What lost
wealth, he imagines, how many inventions neglected and scorned!

4 Bk. II.

We love life and progress, increase and diversity, and every rule appears to us as if it were made to be broken.

Yes, wealth is our latest god—it is the secret of expansion, but also of the ultimate anarchy, of modern culture. We have a culture becoming more and more fragmented, cut off from its common roots, arriving at a point where communication is no longer possible. The various elements are no longer able to activate any other; each is imprisoned in its own specialization, forging a special language in contempt of any common meaning, and summoning up finally the age-old curse of the Tower of Babel, the ultimate dispersion of mankind.

The dilemma every civilization must face, and especially urgent in our own, is clearly defined by a comparison of what may be called our anarchical wealth, almost pointless in its excess, with the meaningful poverty and grandeur that the Law of Israel imposed. What is lost and what is gained by sacrificing to a rule is most perfectly illustrated by the Jewish example.

Just what becomes of culture in a world where nothing is tolerated except "the one thing necessary"? The man who has a vocation is not good for anything else. "Israel carried the future of the world in her bosom. As soon as she was tempted to forget herself in the vulgar ways of other peoples, a sort of somber genius showed her the underside of everything, and—in bitter ironic tones—proclaimed that justice in the ancient manner must never be sacrificed."[5] Thus every secular attempt to alter the culture was viewed as a revolt of pride against God. The culture of Israel is poor for the same reason that it is pure. Its poverty is the condition of its grandeur. What is great is that which fulfills the measure, not what exceeds it; fidelity, not wealth; not means in themselves, but means measured by the end. That is why the very poverty of Israel guaranteed the cultural fidelity of the Hebrew people. It is a form of asceticism, destroying in the

[5] Ernest Renan, *Histoire du peuple d'Israël* (Paris: Calmann-Levy, 1889), Vol. II, Bk. IV, 265 f.

bud everything that would satisfy too soon or too humanly the vast hope for a Messiah.

No abstractions, for immediate obedience, both "in spirit and in truth," is the worship to be given to the living God. To abstract is, first of all, to remove one's self from the immediate; in a certain sense it is also to doubt. For the Hebrew, then, to be limited to the concrete is to remain faithful to the Law. From the very beginning, even his language is dedicated to this higher calling. Bare of abstract terms, useless for any metaphysics,[6] the Hebrew language compels its religious writers to invent metaphors which cloak the highest ideas in ordinary clothes—indeed, almost in work clothes. This philosophical "poverty"—but do people need philosophers when they have prophets?—is consequently the negative aspect of an unequaled poetic splendor. (Western Christian poetry is great in proportion to its use of biblical or Greek sources; sublime, to the degree that the synthesis of the two traditions is dominated by the biblical element.) Among all the songs ever written, only the great prophetic passages have captured the true meaning of the Greek word "poetry"—to make, to act.

No figurative or imaginative arts: they are forbidden in the second and third commandments. "Thou shalt make no graven image, neither of things high in heaven nor low on earth, nor in the waters lower than earth." Every form of plastic art is condemned. "Thou shalt have no other gods before me": This condemns mythology and that kind of imaginary story by which the Aryans came to be satisfied with illusions.

No purely technical sciences: the wisdom of Solomon is not a knowledge of causes but of natural signs; it does not wish to manipulate things, but to discern the divine intentions in them, in

[6] "The Hebrew's difficulty in explaining the simplest philosophical notions, in the Book of Job, in Ecclesiastes, is surprising. In Semitic languages, physical imagery is really earth-bound, obscuring abstract deduction . . ." (*ibid.*, Vol. I, Bk. I, 49). But where Renan sees obscurity, I see the proof of a living actuality, of the efficacy of the learned language, identical with that spoken by shepherds.

order to make of them a spiritual burnt offering to their creator.

Finally, Renan notes: "The prophetic spirit, and the institutions that are born from it, virtually forbid commercial and industrial development."

What is left, then, of what we call culture? Philosophy, fine arts, storytelling, science, industry—everything is sacrificed to a single necessity: the fulfillment of a spiritual calling. The means for the fulfillment of this vocation are the most elementary devices of communication: writing, speech, and action; tradition, prophecy, and war.

But this extreme poverty, this residue of fanatical exclusions, really safeguards and guarantees the possession of what the Western world itself defines as the supreme good: harmony amid dynamism, the over-all meaning of life.

If we acknowledge that the aim of every culture is the concentration of natural and social power in the hands of the man who is responsible, whose mind is fixed upon an end to which he dedicates his works, we see that the poverty-stricken culture of the ancient Hebrew was the best suited to the supreme goals of the spirit—however, this was not so much because of its poverty as because of the absoluteness of its rule and the promise that it contained.

Let us return to Josephus for a moment:

As for the reproach they make against us, saying it is an enormous defect not to be bent on inventing new things, either in art or language, whereas other peoples are praised for their continual changes, we say exactly the contrary. It is through virtue and prudence that we remain constant in observing the laws and customs of our ancestors; because it proves that our rules for living were perfectly established. Clearly, it is only those laws and customs that have not this advantage that must be changed, when experience demonstrates the need to cor-

rect their defects. Thus, as we do not doubt that God gave us
these laws through Moses, could we without impiety fail to
observe them very religiously? And what conduct may be more
just, more excellent, more holy than that declared by the
Ruler of the universe . . . ? And so what form of government may be more perfect than ours, and what greater honor
may be rendered to God, since we are always ready to offer
the worship that we owe Him, since our priests constantly see
that nothing irregular is done, and since everything is no better ordered on days of solemn festival than on any other day
among us?

The Fall of Israel

Everything depended upon the Law, which itself depended
upon the promise of the Messiah made by God in the earliest
times.[7] But finally this promise was incarnated. And the Jews
misunderstood it, using the pretext of the Law, the "shadow of
things to come" (Heb. 10:1), in order to expel Christ, who was
the "spirit" and final reality of the Law.

From that moment the Law was "accomplished," as Christ
said, and in a twofold manner: it had arrived at its goal—the
Messiah was come—and it had lost its meaning by condemning
the very thing it announced. Christ brings a new rule with him,
founding a new Israel. What is more, he is himself this new
law, this covenant, and those who still worship the ancient law,
now declared old, become the idolaters.

[7] Abraham and the prophets had already seen the "day of the Lord." St. Paul
and the author of the Epistle to the Hebrews (11) forcefully insist on the unity
of revelation. It is a great commonplace of Reform theology to see in the Old
Testament the history of Christ before he comes; to see in the prophets the
apostles before Christ, and in the apostles the prophets after Christ. So the
Bible means nothing but the Incarnation, which is its very center, beyond itself.
"*Tolle Christum e scripturis, quid amplius invenies in illis?*" (Luther: *De Servo
Arbitro*.)

That is why the Jewish people, who did not believe in their victory and rejected the new law, are today a people without any rule and measure, without boundaries and without a home. Without hope, they create Utopias. Without obedience, they imagine fatal laws. Without the Messiah, they prepare for messiahs who will never come.

Israel's Heritage

A quotation from Christopher Dawson is helpful at this point:

Although Christianity by its very nature broke with the exclusive nationalism of Judaism and assumed a universal mission, it also claimed the succession of Israel and based its appeal not on the common principles of Hellenistic thought, but on the purely Hebraic tradition represented by the Law and the Prophets. The primitive Church regarded itself as the second Israel, the heir of the kingdom which was promised to the People of God; and consequently it preserved the ideal of spiritual segregation and the spirit of irreconcilable opposition to the Gentile world that had inspired the whole Jewish tradition. It was this sense of historic continuity and social solidarity which distinguished the Christian Church from the mystery religions and the other oriental cults of the period, and made it from the first the only real rival and alternative to the official religious unity of the Empire.[8]

These lines of Dawson, I think, succinctly define the double heritage that the Church and Europe have received from the hands of Israel. First there is the divine heritage of "collective election," for Abraham's posterity after Christ is the entire mass of believers, Gentiles or converted Jews, who compose the Church. There is also the human heritage of the idea of an all-encompassing rule which was to ensure the grandeur of the Church, but

[8] Christopher Dawson, *The Making of Europe* (New York: Meridian Books, Inc., 1956), p. 43.

whose deviations and perversions have been ravaging Europe since the seventeenth century and today even threaten to destroy it.[9]

This is not the proper time to retrace the surviving elements of the fall of Israel in our culture and civilization, although these elements are at least as fundamental to the Western world as Greek reason and Roman order. My intention is simply and swiftly to show what the heritage of Israel means to the Protestant faith.

We know perfectly well the role played in the Reformation by the return to the Old Testament and to prophetic traditions. But do we know just how significant this is in our evangelical churches today? From the earliest days of Sunday school, every young Protestant is nourished by the very sources of pre-Christian Judaism, which become his fables and mythology. Goliath, Joseph sold by his brothers, Jonah and the whale, Balaam's ass, David and Jonathan, Absalom caught by the hair, the young Samuel thrice called by God—whether history or legend, these figures are far more familiar than the metamorphoses of pagan gods; so much so that one may say the Old Testament was the true antiquity of Protestant Europe.

But there is something more important than this poetic background and these examples of a morality which is sometimes scandalously anti-middle-class. The theme of vocation and the theme of the chosen people are both profoundly moving for the spiritual feeling of a Protestant.

The simple fact that, from the beginning, Calvinism has been a minority church, exposed to persecution, is really not enough to explain the frequently noted resemblance between the scattered

[9] As soon as the rule stops being transcendent, it becomes human, contingent, and partial. No longer total, yet still wishing to be totalitarian, the result is a police state of a Fascist or Stalinist type. Of course, it would be absurd to hold Israel responsible for what are merely "profanations" of the idea of an all-encompassing rule.

tribes of Israel and the "little flock" that was driven from its country long ago. Nor can it explain the resemblances between the similar forms of social activity and attitude adopted by the two peoples.[10] What is really convincing about this analogy, what imparts to it its only acceptable meaning and reality, is that in both cases, persecution and minority isolation are considered normal. They express the spiritual destiny of those whom God has chosen, collectively as a people or a church, to be his witnesses in an unbelieving and rebellious world. By virtue of this election about which they are so certain, by means of a perilous grace and in genuine faith, Calvinists have considered themselves since the end of the sixteenth century as charged with a mission in a sinful world that God has not abandoned. Just as Mosaic law maintained the Jewish people, despite sin, in a temporarily livable economy suitable to await the coming of the Messiah, so the charismatic ethic of the Calvinists attracts them to the notion of managing the earth's goods. They must assume control of them, utilizing these riches "as if not using them," in the name of the Lord and by his command, who came and will come again. This is unquestionably the real root of the Puritanism that appeared during the eighteenth century. In his celebrated book, *The Protestant Ethic and the Spirit of Capitalism*, Max Weber insists that this was the origin of modern capitalism and of its principal ethical values. But Werner Sombart replies that capitalism is older; indeed, that it is of Judaic origin.[11] This is hardly the place to discuss these two explanations of the origins of capitalism. No one—not even Marx—has been able to define it clearly. But I will repeat that both hypotheses associate the impulse toward capitalism with religious attitudes—attitudes in any

10 For example: the spiritual and material cohesiveness of the various members of these scattered and persecuted nations, a spirit both traditional and vigorously innovating; financial genius, high standards of culture, and the like.

11 Other authors, such as Labriola, ascribe the capitalist phenomenon to the accumulation of wealth in English convents of the Middle Ages and to the banks of northern Italy.

event that emphasize "election." It is curious to note that the parallel may perhaps be best seen in the considerable deviation by which the Jewish spirituality of the Eastern Jews turned into its opposite when it came into contact with Western customs. Of course, those who have stopped believing in the mission of their people and who work in a vacuum, exercising psychological faculties strongly developed in their race by centuries of waiting for the Messiah, are most liable to distort their own true strength. Similarly, the vigorous asceticism and active pessimism of the Puritans, yielding in the New World to the temptations of immediate and accessible success, were partially transformed into a will to abstract power (the founders of the enormous trusts of the last century are a perfect example), as well as into plainly moralizing utilitarianism. Both these deviations show the loss of an understanding of the religious goals of the Puritan ethic. What was originally self-renunciation and obedience to faith they changed into an absurd despotism. *Corruptio optimi pessima . . .*

The Collective Vocation

These few observations—which, moreover, call for every imaginable nuance—lead us to the central problem of Protestant, especially Calvinist, thought: the example of Israel and her fall.

All of Calvin's theological ethic is based on vocation: the calling of the "little flock" or of the church, the calling of every member of the church. But Israel, which was the chosen people, seems to have betrayed her mission; the Diaspora appears to many as her punishment. Would it be possible, then, to lose one's vocation? And what happens to someone who rejects his orders and is blind to his true goal even when it becomes incarnate? Is he lost forever? Is man's refusal capable of modifying an eternal decree, when God predestines every man before the day of his birth?

This is not a gratuitous problem—it reaches the heart of the

Reformation faith. This is really what St. Paul is talking about in Chapter 11 of his Epistle to the Romans. This text unquestionably illuminates the final mystery of Israel as profoundly as possible.

"I say then, that God cast away His people? God forbid. For I also am an Israelite, of the seed of Abraham, of the tribe of Benjamin. God hath not rejected his people which he foreknew," that is, predestined (Rom. 11:1–2). Nevertheless, Israel did not obtain what it sought; the elect obtained it and the rest were "blinded" (Rom. 11:7). Thus it is through the failure of the children of Israel that salvation is come to the Gentiles, in order to "provoke their jealousy" (11:11). By not recognizing their Messiah, the Jews forced the apostles to preach the message to the Gentiles; they lost the national, and exclusive, benefit of revelation. But it is here that St. Paul points out the mysterious reversal of roles in the long run: "Now if the fall of them be the riches of the world, and the diminishing of them the riches of the Gentiles; how much more their fulness!" (11:12.) "For I would not, brethren, that ye should be ignorant of this mystery, lest ye should be wise in your own conceits, that blindness in part is happened to Israel, until the fulness of the Gentiles be come in. And so all Israel shall be saved" (11:25–26). ". . . for the gifts and calling of God *are* without repentance" (11:29).

Hoc est verbum praeclarum! This is a marvelous utterance, Luther exclaimed, referring in his commentary on Romans to the verse just mentioned. Speaking of the same verse, Calvin said, "It is a strong, beautiful sentence." Calling, at least *this* calling,[12] is really irrevocable. It cannot be lost, even if he to whom it has been given opposes it with all his might! Even his rebellion merely serves to abet divine Providence. His rebellion only extends to all humanity the benefit of the promise that he

---

[12] Always careful not to speculate arbitrarily on biblical passages, Calvin notes this reservation: "Isn't it also necessary to understand this of every calling, but particularly of that through which God has adopted the posterity of Abraham: seeing that the remark was distinctly and discreetly made of the afore-mentioned?" (*Commentary on Romans*, 11:29.)

received, while his final destiny remains in the hands of God's most secret counsel. "As for me," Calvin wrote, "I apply this name of Israel to all God's people; in this sense, after the Gentiles are all entered into the Church, then the Jews, retreating from their rebellion, will become obedient to the faith . . . However, the Jews will hold the first rank, since they are the elder children in the House of God" (*Commentary on Romans*, 11:26).

The world's fate, one could even say the date of its ultimate salvation, depends upon the conversion of the Jews. So we observe the profoundest reasons for the ambivalent feelings (as Freud would say) that all Christian history has exhibited toward the people of Israel. Everything depends upon them, and they reject! This partially explains the blind hatred some feel, and makes meaningful the attitude of religious respect that others have for them. Perhaps it is not going too far to ascribe the sudden and periodic pogroms during the Middle Ages to this contradictory passion. But I doubt that this explanation could have any bearing on Hitler's anti-Semitism, which would, in any event, be the most impure example of it. It remains a fact that Christendom not only may never be disinterested in the fate of the Jews, eternally linked to its own by God's decree, but it must judge Israel differently than the world does. It is not in the name of transient interests that we must take a position, but in the name of faith's promise, and in a missionary perspective which reduces the theses of political nationalists to their proper proportions. The drama is much vaster than our arguments can compass, and its outcome depends neither on us alone nor on them alone. "Their fall has made the riches of the world," and those riches are called salvation.

7 Theology and Literature

Christian theology is the mother of Western thought, just as the Church service is the mother of almost all the arts.

1. Music was born in church choirs and convent chapels. Painting and sculpture came to life on altars, in naves, and around sacred architecture. Our earliest poetic rhythms were diffused by Church Latin. What is important is not that all these classical arts emerged from the Church at the decline of the Middle Ages, but that they constantly indicate, in both their spirit and their history, the influence of their origin.

2. Although generally less recognized, the relationship between our disciplines of thought and theology is no less direct nor less fruitful to observe. Ever since the days when philosophy was only the handmaiden of theology, its most violent (and even most successful) efforts for emancipation have merely confirmed a dependence upon theology. This dependence certainly no longer exists by right, but it remains no less so in fact and nature than in origin. The most powerful and living ideas of the twentieth century all began in specifically theological arguments. Marxism is no exception to this rule—as a quick glance at the writings of the young Marx on Hegelian dialectic will show. Today the technical vocabulary has changed, the references to dogma

have disappeared, the logical apparatus belonging to physical
and mathematical sciences tends to replace that of scholasticism
(so the philosophers claim, at least, with a sometimes suspicious
insistence), but the central discussion remains theological,
whether we like it or not. This is true whether, like Bergson, we
admit it at the end of a career; or try to disguise it, like Heideg-
ger; or ignore it, like Dewey.

3. The relations between theology and literature are not as
clear, nor as easily defined and verifiable. It is true that certain
direct and acknowledged influences have been the objects of
famous works: that of St. Thomas on Dante, Calvin on D'Aubigné,
Jansenism on Pascal and Racine, Swedenborg on Balzac, New-
man on Gerard Manley Hopkins. But I do not think that the
whole problem has been adequately explored, either by the doctors of the Church or by literary critics. Nevertheless, how would
it be possible to deny the significance of this question in a day
when literature does as much to mold cultivated minds as radio
and television to form mass opinion, and when Christian teaching
in the city seems reduced to an intermittent whisper? Is the generally mutual ignorance of theologians and writers really of no
importance? Does it not matter to them, and to the élite in
general?

Clearly, theology has no need of literature and can remain disinterested in it without harmful results. In the same way, since
theology's main purpose is to formulate and criticize Christian
dogma within the Church, it is perfectly right in leaving to
others the problem of applying its criteria outside the Church.
It is not quite so obvious however, that literature can with impunity dispense with theology. And it is certain that when literature does ignore theology, the effect is felt within the Church
itself. For the clergy and other influential members of the faithful simply cannot avoid the influence of what they read, and they
experience an ever increasing difficulty in judging literature from
the viewpoint of their faith. The vocabulary of devotion and of
literature, the atmosphere, the problems placed under scrutiny,

the moral values—they have all become too different and are practically without any common standard. Just who is at fault?

4. Of course, I am the first to worry about theologians dabbling in literary criticism. You can see this kind of attempt almost any day in religious magazines—reviews and articles by amateurs trying to talk about books "like anybody else," trying to make you forget they have a "specialty." My idea would be rather to demand that literary critics have at least a minimum of theological knowledge, in which they seem terribly lacking. Again, I am the first to protest against the quoting of fashionable writers—or rather, those who were fashionable fifty years ago— as is done by so many modern preachers who hope to ornament their sermons. The Word of God gospel does not need a helping hand from literature; if anything, it is the other way around. If it happens that a pastor or priest considers it appropriate to speak of a book, I expect him, both as a believer and as a writer, to speak as a theologian, not as a man of culture, a moralist or artist.

These preliminary reservations notwithstanding, I should like to ask something quite definite of the young theologians who will read me. I should like some of them to devote themselves to the examination, criticism, and—should the occasion arise—spiritual guidance of the literary tendencies of the age. But I repeat, they should always do this as theologians, not as amateur *littérateurs* or men of taste. Without prejudging the success or outcome of such an attempt, it would in any event have the advantage of giving the faithful—and their clergy—certain criteria for judgment. They would have a vocabulary to work with, and consequently a distinct orientation of their minds which would gradually enable them to re-establish elements of a common standard between belief and reader within the same individual.

Having said this, I shall now return to my original intention, which was to raise a question and suggest some working hypotheses for studying it.

5. The general ignorance of modern writers of the rudiments

of theology condemns them to rediscover, every twenty years, Americas that have long since been colonized. Someone really ought to write a history of the principal schools of modern writing from a strictly theological point of view. Such a history would show not only what the writers unwittingly owe to the religious climate of their time, but above all how they suffer from their lack of knowledge of even the existence of traditions, whether orthodox or heretical. All they can do is gather, at great cost, bits and pieces of traditions, as can be shown from the encyclopedists to the existentialists, from the German romantics to the symbolists and surrealists. In *After Strange Gods,* a book that is really too short, T. S. Eliot has sketched out a study of heresies in modern literature. For myself, I have tried to show how the troubadours, whose doctrine formed the model for *Tristan and Isolde* and from whom virtually all our modern novels derive, were strongly affected by the Manichaean heresy. Consequently, this heresy has survived to the present day, although so vulgarized and distorted that it is unrecognizable. I use this small example for lack of a better one, as an indication of the kind of thing that should be attempted. As for the *avant-garde* schools of writing today, much might be said about their endemic revival of the best-known deviations of mysticism, gnosticism, Arianism, and romantic liberalism. Who would and could expain all this to the disciples of these movements? You would need a theologian. Moaning to heaven and pointing accusing fingers is to fail in clarity and to forget that, for many of the best among us, today, the *avant-garde* fills the role of a courageous and ardent spirituality.

Why should the theological obscurantism that marks contemporary culture be met by theologians with a consistent refusal to become informed, made up of scorn, indifference, moral indignation, and middle-class timidity? Actually, theological accuracy is the thing required. Because of the demands of our parishes, too often used as a pretext by Protestants, are we going to leave this century's intellectual élite without help? Are we going to turn our backs on intellectuals because they are flashy, scandalous, and badly behaved, confirming them in their conviction that the Church is all right for the lower middle class but not for free and "advanced" minds? Will we let them go on thinking that the Church tolerates nothing but the bad art of a century ago? I should like to make some suggestions for further study to readers who, like myself, believe it necessary to bridge the gap between theology and today's writing. They are only examples and presented in no particular order.

6. At the present time, writers are interested in theological extremism, whereas liberalism tended to flatter their prejudices and consequently was of no real help to them.

Kierkegaard is a good example. He was not a theologian in the strict sense of the word, but his works exhibit a perfectly coherent and uncompromising theological attitude, and had an enormous influence on Ibsen, Unamuno, Rilke, Kafka, and a great number of young poets, novelists, and essayists in Europe, England, and both Americas. It is interesting to note that, though his influence has been obviously effective in a large number of conversions, they have rarely been conversions to any particular church. Is this not a sign of disturbing incompatibility between the élite and church circles?

7. A theology that is orthodox—and I do not mean atrophied —favors, supports, and nourishes works done in the classical manner, whereas liberal theology is linked with romantic movements.

The romantic writer believes dogma to be an impediment to his creative flights, whereas the classical writer finds both support and fertile restraint in it. The romantic, like Kant's dove, imagines he can fly better in the void. The other, more confident of the strength of his wings, seeks out a heavy atmosphere in order to give full vent to his energies. Dante asks Thomas Aquinas for a framework, solid guideposts, effective and valuable constraints for the follies of the imagination. The impetuous

D'Aubigné does the same with Calvin. On the other hand, I suspect the romantics of having gone through the theology of their
time, and in the name of liberty, of looking for intellectual license
or simply a quickly mastered facility.

8. Generally speaking, literature is encouraged less by a partic-
lar dominant theological doctrine than by an atmosphere of theological controversy mixed with political questions.

An example of this is troubadour poetry, born in the second
half of the twelfth century, right in the midst of the conflict between Albigensians and Catholics, the feudalists of the north and
the "Democrats" of the south. Evidence could also be supplied
by Calvinist poetry of the sixteenth century, Elizabethan drama
and poetry, and, in our day, the renaissance of religious poetry
in France during and after the Occupation.

9. A church with a definite liturgical tendency offers the best
ground for harmony or significant conflict between the theologians and writers of any given nation.

I will limit myself to only one example: the Anglican Church,
whose Book of Common Prayer has formed the poetic language
for more than four hundred years, and whose role in the history
of English letters is crucial from John Donne to T. S. Eliot, including Dean Swift, Bishop Berkeley, Coleridge, Lewis Carroll,
and twenty other names of the same order. Of course, this argues
neither for nor against ritual, but indicates a possible path for
fruitful research.

10. Theological literary criticism would show the public the
foolishness of the current notion that the only authors who should
be considered "Christian" or "religious" are those who talk
about God or deal with religious subjects.

Here again, "it is not those who say Lord! Lord! but those who
do my Father's will. . . ." We must take this warning seriously.
Doing God's will by writing is not simply talking of God and his
will, or even talking about them with a simplicity too easily
achieved at the expense of mystery, to which Anglo-Saxons seem

addicted. I am familiar with a large number of religious works whose journalistic style is incompatible with any kind of spiritual reality. Although their authors never stop mentioning that reality, they fail to *express* it. They abandon themselves to obvious propagandistic efforts in favor of "spiritual values." At the same time, however, they betray a lack of Spirit in the very genesis of their work. They forget that the style of writing often communicates on its own account a "message" more genuine and influential than the declared object of the work. Sometimes these two messages conform and reinforce each other. More often, alas, they contradict, and one secretly destroys the other in the reader's mind. What one must remember here is that every literary work, even when its subject is secular, implies a theology —whether the author knows it or not. And that theology is expressed by the very movement of its style more faithfully and convincingly than by its argument. An explanation and clarification of such a theology would render an important service to the writer no less than to the public.

These brief comments will serve their purpose if, by their very inadequacy, they inspire young theologians to push further into an area I merely hoped to point out.

8 The Mission of
the Artist

A few years ago I was asked to speak on "The Mission of Art as a Creative Expression of the Human Spirit." I would not have responded but for the bearing of the subject upon a conference of ecumenical study bringing together some artists and writers and some Protestant, Anglican, and Orthodox theologians.* It seemed to me that this title, since it was proposed specifically by Christians and not by any vague or hazy humanists, merited a serious *mise au point*.

To me, the expression "Mission of Art" rings false. Art, with a capital letter, is one of those official allegories we have inherited from the nineteenth century and from romanticism (with its admiration for Wagner and Baudelaire), and which our forebears condemned and strove to modify. This allegory marks the existence of a sort of "religion of Art," born of the romantic sects and brotherhoods—pre-Raphaelites, symbolists, and so on—and which in our time has lost its sacred vigor, but subsists nevertheless in the form of a very widespread prejudice amongst the Philistines, "the people," in Hollywood, and in inaugural addresses. Art, with a capital letter, is something ideal, something

* International Conference on Christianity and Art, convened at the Ecumenical Institute, Chateau de Bossey, Celigny, Switzerland, May, 1950.

76

distinguished, something vaguely *en rapport* with the Infinite, not useful for anything; it is respectable, interests women more than men, and is the business of certain specialists who, from time to time, are permitted to escape from the too-real cares of daily life, and who elevate souls and soften morals—in short, men who resemble in this misconception that other misconception which most of our contemporaries have made for themselves of the Christian religion. It is not serious if we admit with Talleyrand that "whatever is exaggerated lacks seriousness." No serious artist says that that he is creating "Art" unless it is to defend himself against the tax collector or a suspicious policeman.

On the other hand, the word "art" is a serviceable term which denotes the ensemble of artistic activities and the objects that result from them.

In either case, whether it is a question of romantic exaggeration or of a generic term, it is evident that Art, with or without the capital, cannot have any "mission." Neither a false god nor a word can have a mission. Only a man is capable of receiving one.

Next, I have some doubt about the adjective "creative" as it appears in the proposed title.

The use of the verb "to create," in relation to human activity is, I believe, rather recent. This manner of speaking of the human act by comparing it, or even making it equal, to the divine act, not only raises anew at the very beginning a synergist doctrine that demands examination, but coincides historically with the impoverishment or loss in the modern epoch of the belief in a Creator God. I am not at all sure that man is capable of creating, in the true sense of this term: that is, of producing an absolute mutation, an absolute novelty in the universe. What is currently called today a "creation" is in reality only a slightly different arrangement of elements already known according to laws known or knowable. Therefore, it is a *composition*. Before romanticism we were content to say that a musician composed an opera, that a painter composed a picture. But today we say that he "creates" a symphony, that he "creates" forms. No one can prove that a man creates something, because no one can know the totality of existent things, with their structures and their inner relationships. I shall limit myself, therefore, to the classical term "composition" in speaking of works of art.

So much having been said, let us consider now what is the mission—if there be one—of the men who compose books, pictures, scores, statues, pleasure grounds, poems. And, first of all, what is the nature of their activity and what are its proper ends?

The Nature of the Artistic Activity

All sorts of people make things, objects, and instruments. *Homo faber* designates a great part of humanity: workers, artists, scholars, legislators, and artisans.

Let us ask what difference there is between the man who makes a poem, a musical score, a picture, a façade, and the man who makes a machine, an equation, a law, a shoe, a chemical product, or a photograph.

For about two centuries now, we have been accustomed to answering this question in an apparently simple manner. We think that artists make useless objects (or, as we say in French, *gratuits*), and that others make objects which are necessary in our daily lives, such as automobiles, telephones, computers, farm equipment. We cannot do without a razor, says the modern man, but we can, by dint of sacrifice—and even without much sacrifice—do without a picture or a statue. Art products are a luxury and the other products are necessities. All our education leads us to believe this, and if it is necessary to justify this habitual belief, our professors have recourse to certain interpretations of Kant, according to which an object of art would have its end in itself, and would serve no end, therefore, but that of being contemplated

—which is to say, honored with a glance on the way to the dining room.

These criteria of utility or necessity, on the one hand, and of gratuitousness or uselessness, on the other, are inconsistent and absolutely superficial. They teach us nothing concerning the nature of the work of art. But they do teach us something about the nature and attitude of the society that accepts them: the knowledge that this society has lost the sense of the holy. Many civilizations have existed, and perhaps will exist, for which a stone or a piece of wood, sculptured or painted in a certain manner, has been infinitely more "useful" than an electric razor is for us. These objects have been regarded as eminently useful because they contained a power, an exalting or terrifying quality, a meaning. They were taken seriously by the peoples who believed that the meaning of life, the fear of death, the sense of dread before sacred power, are serious things. Whereas we consider as serious, and therefore useful, whatever permits us, for example, to go more swiftly, though it matters little from what motive or toward what end.

The fact that even in theory we hold a work of art to be destitute of direct utility proves simply that art does not respond to the most potent desire of modern man; that modern man should be able, therefore, to dispense with it; that he has in truth no need of it (as we call useful that which we need); and that he believes he should respect it only by virtue of a kind of prejudice. From which, it may be said in passing, we should be able to deduce the utter vanity of the actual attempts made to vulgarize art in order to give it publicity. Art's necessity is that it must arouse, awaken. To do this, it must put to sleep the various natural necessities that stifle it. Therefore it must change the total attitude, the entire orientation of modern man—before setting out to distribute reproductions of van Gogh!

If, therefore, I set aside the criterion of utility or lack of utility as being too relative, too variable, and too subject to change in meaning according to the religious condition of a society, I find myself once more before the initial question: In what respect does artistic activity distinguish itself from the other activities of man?

I would suggest that the difference is here, that, as distinct from all other products of human action, *the work of art is an object of which the necessary and sufficient* raison d'être *is to* signify, *organically, and by means of its own structure.*

As it consists in a structure of meanings, forms, or ideas, the work of art has for its specific function the bribing of the attention, the magnetizing of feeling, the fascinating of meditation —and at the same time it must orient existence toward something that transcends sense and forms, or the words so assembled. It is a trap, but an oriented trap.

It is true, of course, that an equation is an object which has no function other than that of signifying. Nevertheless, its structure remains entirely analyzable and reducible to its elements, which can be grouped in other ways—as the equal sign shows —without destroying their significance; which is not the case with the work of art.

But if, in searching for the nature of the work of art, I define it as a *calculated trap,* we see that the understanding of its nature is tied up with that of its end: a trap is made in order to capture something. In the work of art, nature and aim, essence and intention, are inseparable. It is a question of a single and identical function, which is to signify something by sensible means.

The Aim of Artistic Activity

It will perhaps be thought that I am not giving proper value to beauty, and that my definitions will run counter to some classical definitions in much the same way as they run counter to our current and commonplace ideas. In fact, there are those who insist that beauty should be the aim of art, and that the proper function of the artist should be that of "creating beauty," as it is said. I confess that I am not at all sure about this. And I will make, on this point, three remarks of very unequal importance.

The first is a simple statement of fact that I throw into the discussion without presuming to judge it. The principal artists of our epoch, such as Picasso or Braque, Joyce or Kafka, Stravinsky, T. S. Eliot, or André Breton, *do not try to make beauty,* and without any doubt would refuse to say that beauty is the aim of their work. For meaning and spirit it matters little whether the work be beautiful or ugly, charming or odious; the aim of the artist is to express or describe realities at any cost, and even at the price of ugliness if necessary. Academic artists alone, the false artists, still try to make beauty or to flatter it.

My second remark is of a much more serious nature. It seems to me that "beauty" *is not a biblical notion or term.* The Scriptures speak to us of truth, justice, freedom, and love, but very little or not at all of beauty. They do not tell us that God is Beauty, but that God is Love. Neither does Christ say that he is the beauty, but that he is the Way, the Truth, and the Life. This way is not beautiful, but rough and painful. This truth is not beautiful, but liberating. This life does not open into beautiful harmonies, but passes by the narrow gate of death.

Is it necessary to think, as one has written, that in the Bible there is a question of a "terrible lacuna"? A gap which the Greek ideal would have filled to overflowing by amalgamating itself into the Christian tradition—a debt discharged through distinguishing itself anew at the time of the Renaissance? Or must we, on the contrary, ask ourselves whether our notion of beauty is not subject to serious revision?

Finally, my third remark, which is entirely independent of the first two, will take the form of a confession. I find myself incapable of making any use of the *concept* of beauty in itself. Obviously it happens that as frequently as anyone else I exclaim,

"How beautiful it is!" before the most varied things, such as a
landscape or a building, a human being or a work of art, an
airplane, a sporting exploit, a fruit, an heroic act, a sentiment . . .
But this enumeration, by virtue of its heteroclitic character,
shows that beauty is not a specific property of the work of art.
We can describe anything as beautiful. It is a subjective qualifica-
tion, a term convenient but vague, an exclamation. If I exclaim
that a work is beautiful, it is easy to see that this "beauty" which
I attribute to it resolves itself upon analysis into very diverse
realities. In saying, "How beautiful it is," I wish to say—I ought
to say—"How well it is made," "How true its proportions are,"
"How much more free or strong one feels for having seen this,"
"How it excites the passions, or is of inexhaustible interest,"
or simply, "How I love it"—because one calls "beautiful" whatever one loves with intensity. Thus, after all, behind the word
"beauty" we find again justice, or truth, or freedom, or love.

To put aside the Greek concept of beauty is not therefore to
deny art. To declare that the Bible scarcely speaks of beauty is
not for a single instant to say that the Bible excludes art; and
similarly, to state that modern artists do not seek beauty primarily and in itself, does not signify that they are bad artists.
Very much to the contrary, all this is tantamount to saying that
art is something other than a search for beauty, and that those
who make a work of art assign to themselves a very different
aim.

I believe that the aim (conscious or not) of all true art is to
make objects of real significance; therefore, it is to signify, to
render the viewer attentive to the meaning of the world and of
life.

This accepted, what the artist succeeds in signifying need
not be understood by him prior to the work itself. There is not,
first of all, a certain meaning, and then afterward a determination
to illustrate it by a work. Rather it is by the work, and in it
alone, that a certain meaning manifests or reveals itself. The

critics or the public, or sometimes the artist himself, will try afterward to "disengage" this significance and isolate it from the work by an effort of translation or abstraction. But in reality the meaning is tied to each detail just as it is tied to the work as a whole—if it is good—and truly exists only within it. If it were possible to express this meaning by some other means, the work would lose its *raison d'être.*

We will qualify, therefore, as "great" that work which commands attention most imperatively and for the longest time; that which carries furthest man's meditation upon his destiny and upon the order of things. And we shall call "lasting" that work which plays its role as a trap most efficaciously for many generations and peoples. The current expressions, "I have been captured by this work," or "It is very gripping," appear to me accurate and revealing, from this point of view.

The Mission of the Artist

If such, then, is the nature and end of the work of art, we may now consider under what conditions an artist is able to fulfill his particular mission.

There are two things that I should like to indicate at the outset and in the simplest manner possible. The artist fulfills his mission:

1. In so far as he is a *good artisan* (craftsman), and,

2. in so far as his works *signify* in an efficacious manner.

This calls, naturally, for some explanation.

The good artisan is one who has a mastery over his means, who plays well the rules of his particular game, who, in short, constructs exactly and craftily his traps for feeling, reflection, and imagination. Let us call all this—that is, the ensemble of the processes of the craft and the rules of composition—*rhetoric;* assuming, that is, that we wish to make a place for the skills. But it is precisely a respect for the skills, a love of their proper uses

and laws, that from the outset distinguishes the true artist
from the amateur—any person who feels himself inspired or
moved and thinks he can replace rhetoric by sincerity. I am not
certain whether it is Laforgue or Valéry who has written: "The
bourgeois are those who believe that there is something in the
world more important than a convention." Or let us cite Baudelaire
once more: "It is clear that the rhetorics and the prosodies are
not arbitrarily contrived tyrannies, but a collection of rules required by the organization of spiritual being itself, and at no
time have the prosodies and rhetorics prevented originality from
putting itself forward distinctly. On the contrary, to understand
how they helped in the hatching of originality would be infinitely more true."

Sincerity has scarcely any significance in art. It certainly has
none when it is a question of the craft of the artist, because this
craft is, by definition, made up of artifices. On this point the
moderns committed a strange error when, after romanticism and
some of its by-products, they believed they must betake themselves, as they say, "to the school of Nature," and so no longer
accept any guide other than sincerity, or even naïveté. I state
it as a fact that a man possessed by the need to express himself,
or to express something by means of a work of art, is absolutely
incapable of expressing sincerely what he wants to express unless he has first of all mastered his rhetoric. When Jean-Paul
Sartre gives his disciples the precept of not "writing"—that is to
say, of explaining oneself, no matter how, without trying to
"write well"—he gives the formula for modern mass production
and deprives his disciples all the more of the means for really
expressing their message. Apropos of this term "message,"
which we especially abuse—and not only in Christian surround-
ings—it is impossible to "deliver a message" (as we continually say) unless we surrender ourselves to the mastery of its
means of expression, to the point of being able to adapt them,

make them serve, orient them, and this even to the least detail, in the direction and according to the *sense* of what we want to communicate. To express a message of truth, but "no matter how," is almost certain to express something altogether different from the message in question; it is to be indifferent to the disorder of language, the absence of inner coherence, and finally, of truth itself. After all, what we first perceive in the work of art are the means—the words, the colors, or the forms, the sounds and their relationships or groupings. And most certainly, even if all the rules of the game are known and applied with care, one can never be sure of winning; in other words, the artist is never *sure* that the public perceives truly what he has wished to say, but at least it is necessary to place the maximum number of chances on his side.

Of course it is possible to object that the public perceives in a work, first of all, not the technical means in themselves but rather the author's style. If I have not mentioned style as the third condition whereby the artist fulfills his mission, it is because in my view style is born of the conflict between the first condition—the craft, the means—and the second—what the artist wishes to signify, the message. If there is no style in a work, it is because there is no drama between the means of expression and what one wishes to express, between technique and significance, between rhetoric and message. And if there is no drama, it is because one of the two terms is strongly deficient or even absent. In the latter case there would then be no *art* properly so called. There is only an almost empty form—and that is academicism; or a formless message—and that is everyday communication, justifiably without art. Or further, if the means are not put in question (or to the question) by a very exacting significance, one will fall into what we call "pure rhetoric," into eloquence and formalism. If, on the other hand, the meaning we wish to express is too intense and imperative for the means at our command, we fall into obscurity or nearly so, or into an inarticulate cry.

Let us come then to the second condition, the significance or message.

On this point I will be brief and limit myself to a few formulas. I think an artist (it being granted that he is a good craftsman) fulfills his mission in proportion as his work elicits in the spectators, readers, or hearers a sense of liberation; manifests what is true, that is to say, makes a truth possible to feel; evokes the order of the world, the laws of man's destiny; constructs or reveals forms in feelings, imagination, ideas; and finally, leads to increased delight.

A single remark upon this point: It is evident that a classic work of art, a work of Bach, for example, is founded on the order in man, evokes the order of the world, and renders its laws comprehensible and even lovable. But some entirely different works, which seem to have no purpose other than that of evoking the present disorder, chaos, and absurdity, the noise and the frenzy of things deprived of meaning and related by a drunkard—I think of certain parts of Joyce's work, or *The Waste Land* of T. S. Eliot, or the stories of Faulkner, the painting of Picasso—these works dialectically, nostalgically, in revolt and defiance, still bear a witness to the lost order of the world, because art, all art worthy of the name, never has had and never can have any other object.

Such being the two conditions which an artist must fulfill to be equal to his mission, it becomes clear that criticism, the evaluation of works of art, ought, on one hand, to bear upon the skill and the means, and on the other, upon the meaning and value of the realities revealed by those means—for which our attention has been "bribed" by those skills. That is to say, criticism ought to be at the same time *technical*, on the one hand, and on the other, metaphysical or ethical—which is to say, in the end, *theological*.

Outline for a Christian Meditation
on the Activity of the Artist

I realize full well that in speaking of a theological criticism of works of art I shall shock not only the great majority of my contemporaries, on the public side, and some artists, but also the theologians. The latter will say that it is not their business, that they must occupy themselves with the dogmas of the Church. With that I agree. Note that I do not say that this theological criticism would necessarily be the business of the theologians. They are often badly prepared by a strongly didactic turn of mind—most of them are saddled with some teaching obligation —and in any particular case it is a question of developing first of all a power of comprehension and of nourishing it with a living experience of art. But perhaps it may be proposed that those who would devote themselves to the criticism of art—and every artist is more or less of this number—might at least make an effort to go beyond the stage of total lack of theological culture in which we see them today.

It is within this perspective that I run the risk of suggesting, neither a scale of judgment, nor a doctrine, nor a canon for the arts, but a theme for meditation which may perhaps be of such a kind as to sustain, and at best motivate, the judgments one brings to bear upon works of art—and this through making us more attentive to the spiritual situation of the artist.

What does the artist really do, after all? In the exaggerated language we have inherited from romanticism, without reflecting at all upon the import of the words, we customarily say in the twentieth century that:

1. The artist *creates;*
2. he *incarnates* in his works certain realities;
3. he is *inspired.*

I say again, these three verbs are used improperly and justly
deserve the greatest severity on the part of the theologians. But
the exorbitant misuse itself suggests a possibility of faithful and
sober usage. The three everyday verbs I have just cited—to create, to incarnate, to inspire—evoke irresistibly the attributes
of the Holy Trinity.

If we are able to say of the artist that he creates, it is not
merely the consequence of a Promethean or Luciferian overesti-
mate of human powers. In composing—with what he has learned
from the world and with what he is internally—a work external
to himself, man imitates symbolically the act of the Creator in
forming the world and forming Adam. And certainly we must
question whether this human work adds anything to the world, in
spite of the fact that it is something which was not here before.
Man is only able to rearrange that which God has created *ex
nihilo*. But in the artist's love for the work which he detaches
from himself—not in the work in itself—there is a parable of the
fatherly action, an attempt to love the creation as the Father
has loved it.

Why has God separated the world from himself? Why and
how does he love it? In what way is this object of his love distinct from him, and what autonomy does it enjoy? These questions and many analogous ones arise and fix themselves in the
mind that pauses before the mystery of the First Person. Thus,
to meditate upon the mystery of the Father would lead at one
and the same time to the best understanding of the act of the
artist, and of its limits or its relativity.

In the second place, we have seen that the artist, in composing
a work of art, tends to signify something which would not be
perceptible otherwise. Let us not say that he incarnates a reality,
for it is not a question of flesh. But he renders this reality intelligible, legible, audible, by physical means. What takes place
then, on the side of the spectator, the reader, the auditor? It happens that the expression veils what is expressed, while manifest-

ing it at the same time to our senses. For what is expressed is not separable from the means of expression, or is so by abuse only. What makes manifest is at the same time that which conceals. The meaning of a picture, for example, is not distinct from the colors, forms, proportions, and style by which, but also in which, it exists. It is possible therefore to see them and not see it. In the eyes of reason the means remain essentially heterogeneous to the reality they express—why those and not some others?—and yet we would know nothing of it without them . . . I do not press the matter. I am obliged here to limit myself to indicating the point of possible departure of a dialectic which would find its model and perhaps its norms in the doctrine of the Second Person of the Trinity, and in a meditation on its mystery.

In the third place, the artist is currently credited with being inspired. The most determined adversaries of romanticism, such as Valéry, have never denied that the primitive impulsion of a work of art might be a "gift of the gods"—a single verse, for example, or the vision of a form, on which the operations of the technique afterward develop themselves. The inspiration, whether it operates at each moment or intervenes only at the start and in a single instant, is an undeniable fact of experience. But whence does it come? What Paul Valéry calls "the gods," without compromising himself, would be for certain other people the Holy Spirit, and for still others a message from the unconscious. Sometimes we imagine that this instantaneous vision has revealed in a lightning flash the existence of a secret way, which it remains only to follow; and sometimes we have the impression that we invent the way while advancing upon it. This problem, let us observe, torments not only the artist but also, and more consciously still, the scholar of today. Do I invent, he says to himself, or is it rather that I discover a reality? Do I project into the cosmos the forms of my spirit, or is it rather that I espouse by the spirit some of the objective forms of the real? And the man who receives a call sometimes subsists in this doubt to the point of anguish. Do I surrender to some obscure determination of my desire, or am I really responding, rather, to a summons received from somewhere else? Where does the voice come from? Who speaks? Myself, or the Other? Such is the predicament the intervention of the Holy Spirit creates in man.

Once again it is my purpose here merely to suggest some possible direction for thought. I limit myself to submitting this notion: that Christian meditation upon the act and work of the artist can deepen, inform, and instruct itself within the framework of meditation upon the doctrine and mystery of the Trinity; and that Christian meditation will find in the vocabulary and dialectical arguments employed for nearly twenty centuries by trinitarian theologians the whole of a theory which introduces us better than any other to the human mysteries of the act of art.

I will add one last suggestion. We know that most heresies have resulted in interpretations which represent either excesses or deficiencies from the standpoint of trinitarian doctrine. May we believe that the deviations or excesses expressed by such-and-such an artistic school reflect these heresies, or does this perhaps happen in the course of development, unknown to those who express them? And would we not have here the principle for a theological critique of the development of the arts? Certainly, if so, we should be able at last to go beyond the stage of arbitrary judgments upon tastes and colors, or upon the import, moral or otherwise, of works of art, judgments based ordinarily on day-before-yesterday's fashion, or upon bourgeois prudence, or upon the envy of those who hold contrary views. It seems to me that some attempts along this line would be worth the labor and the risk—and by laymen first of all.

The Function of Art

By way of conclusion, I shall try to summarize in two sentences the conception of art I hold, upon which the preceding pages are based.

Art is an exercise of the whole being of man, not in order to compete with God, but in order the better to coincide with the order of creation, in order to love it better, and in order to re-establish ourselves in it. Thus art would appear to be like an invocation (more often than not unconscious) to the lost harmony; like a prayer (more often than not confused) corresponding to the second petition of the Lord's Prayer: "Thy kingdom come."

9 Crisis in
Modern Marriage

Since there is no such thing as a family without marriage, at least in the Western meaning of the word, it is clear that all family problems are, in practice, subordinate to those of the married couple. Consequently everything that damages the relations between husband and wife strikes the family at its very root. It is obvious, therefore, that family problems would be radically changed in character in a society which systematically questioned the cause, manner, purpose, and permanence of the joining of a man and woman as a couple in order to have a family. We are not dealing with a mere possibility; society today is very close to bringing it about. The crisis of marriage, which had been latent in the Western world for centuries, is passing through a phase so acute today that a single statistic is sufficient to characterize it: in 1961 there were two divorces for every five marriages in the United States.

For the first time in the Christian era the family is seriously threatened. Up till now it had survived all kinds of political upheavals, social and economic changes. Feudalism, monarchy, class distinctions, capitalism—one by one they have disappeared in various countries without entailing notable alteration in the status of the family. But today an enormously profound revolu-

tion is noiselessly taking place. Its consequences are not easy
to predict. In this study I shall limit myself to a description of
some of its symptoms and to pointing out one of its causes which
seems especially unnoticed.

The Modern Marriage, Founded on Love

If we consider all the various kinds of marriage institutions
found among great civilizations and primitive tribes, we see that
modern Western marriage is distinguished from all the rest by
one outstanding and specific characteristic: it tends more and
more to rest on free choice, purely individual in its motivations.

In every other civilization, and even in ours up to modern
times, the mutual choice of husband and wife depended largely
upon collective influences: religious regulations about exogamy
and endogamy, levirate or sororate law, to mention only the
most familiar; social rank, race, religion; and later, level of education and wealth. The margin for purely individual choice allowed by these rules, taboos, and conventions remained quite
negligible in most cases. Today the situation is reversed. In the
majority of cases the collective influences I have just mentioned
not only play an insignificant role, but are no longer sufficient to
constitute the obstacles or restraints they still were even as late
as the nineteenth century. This evolution seems to parallel the
evolution of sexuality, which with the Christian era became partially detached from the collective unconscious and broke away
from religious rites, tending toward integration with the individual dialectic through a process of interiorization and greater
awareness. (Remember that the expression "sexual problem"
is relatively recent, appearing for the first time about 1830.)

On what will we base individual choice, now that it is "free"—
no longer limited or predetermined by collective rules? Of all the
elements that traditionally contributed to its motivation, only
one remains: love.

Besides, we must really ask what kind of love it is, and whether this sentiment itself has not changed in character or even nature now that it is isolated from the priestly, religious, or rigidly conventional atmosphere of the societies in which it first developed.

Romance

The kind of love on which most marriages in the Western world are based is a generally slight fever which is considered infinitely thrilling to contract. The Anglo-Saxons call it "romance," a word that reveals its origin in the Romance country of southern France, a point we will have reason to mention again.

In a conversation with the editor of an American magazine for which I was writing an article about the extraordinary emphasis laid on "love interest" in movies, novels, and advertising, the editor suddenly said to me, "But my dear fellow, if one doesn't marry for love, just what the devil does one marry for?" This spontaneous outburst, sincere and direct in its naïveté, sums up current thinking succinctly. Modern man, especially in America, can conceive of absolutely no other reason to marry except romance. It just never enters his head that one can, or must, marry for dozens of different reasons, romance perhaps being the least important. In his eyes, every consideration of social standards or education, every notion of compatibility of character, background, age, material wealth, future prospects, family circumstances, career, religious persuasion, ideas of upbringing, intellectual or spiritual communion, has become secondary. The important thing is romance. If they love each other, he thinks (with this type of love), let them get married! For romance has every right, and it behaves as if it had every power. Under the influence of its excitement, rational motives count for little or nothing. The time is over, it is believed, for marriages of reason, convention, or convenience. We are free, and that means we shall marry the man or woman we love—for that reason alone, come what may. The only significant thing is to be sure of the authenticity of feeling. If it is genuine, it will overcome everything. Even more, people can live on love; their emotion will become more exalted by resisting conventions—which, by definition, are stupid or tyrannical—and this gives it the promise of permanence, if one is necessary.

But here is exactly where the weakness of this point of view becomes apparent. Even if we admit, along with all the novels, popular songs, movies, magazines, publicity agents, and women's clubs, that romance can and must vanquish all obstacles, we are compelled to recognize, nevertheless, that there is one thing against which it is powerless and which in turn may overpower it: permanence. But permanence is the meaning, the very *raison d'être* of marriage, from the social and family viewpoint.

One must therefore state that, in the present state of Western customs, in the moral atmosphere that affects the vast majority of our contemporaries, marriage (and consequently the family) may be seen systematically sapped and sabotaged by the very motive in whose name it is still contracted.

In my opinion this is the principal, though not the only, reason for divorce and its ever-growing frequency. We are in the middle of attempting—and bungling—one of the craziest experiments imaginable in a civilized society: basing marriage, which is permanence, on romance, which is a passing fancy. Of all the motives for marriage that I enumerated, we retain in practice only the most unstable, the most ephemeral. Not for one moment would I deny that love or romance must play a role in a solid social order, but I do say that this is the minor and decisive role of a catalyst—which may disappear without any harm once the combination has occurred, thanks to its presence. We see, on the contrary, an entire body of family magazines hopelessly striving to give women ways for saving romance in marriage. Actually, this is an indirect confession that romance and permanence are not compatible. Instead of squandering energy in an attempt to resolve this contradiction of nature, would it not be better to face the facts and from the very beginning admit the two following propositions:

1. By its very nature, romance is incompatible with marriage (even if it provokes it), for it is essentially nourished by obstacles, delays, separation, and dreams, while marriage essentially must reduce or suppress these obstacles every day, must be realized in the immediate and in constant physical closeness.

2. The natural and logical outcome of a marriage founded on romance alone is divorce; for marriage kills romance, and if romance is reborn it will kill marriage for the same reasons for which the marriage took place.

Eros and Agape

When speaking of "romance," it is clear that I do not have love in general in mind, but, rather, a certain kind of love which has been cultivated by our period and which is too often confused with love itself.

Romance, the tender fever, the feeling that most of our successful novels and films discuss and exalt, represents a very special pattern of relationship between a man and a woman. To point out just wherein this pattern of relationship is scarcely compatible with marriage, it is proper first of all to discuss its origins.

"Romance" comes from the French word *roman*, which means both a novel and a story in the style of Provence, a district in the south of France. There, in Provence, the twelfth-century troubadours inspired a tremendous revolution in human emotions, and we must return to them to find the romantic theme in its purest form. A frequent phrase in the troubadours' poems will give a good clue to its nature: *l'amor de lonh*, faraway love, love at great distances; that is, love incapable of fulfillment because blocked by some obstacle, which helps to exalt it in the imagination. Geoffroy Rudel, Prince of Blaye, gives an excellent illustration of this love in his poems addressed to the Countess of Tripoli, the "faraway princess." The romance of *Tristan and Isolde*, coming a little later, fixes for all time to come the model of almost every romantic novel in the Western world: a man, a woman, and an obstacle between them, at the same time forbidding and inflaming a reciprocal but unfortunate passion. At first this obstacle is the legitimate husband, King Mark, and we have the familiar triangle. Then the obstacle becomes feudal and Christian law; later it is simply symbolized by separation in space; and finally it is revealed as integral to the psychology of the lovers when Tristan lays a sword between Isolde and himself— a sign of chastity, even though they are exiled in the forest and free to abandon themselves to their love.

What is the relationship between a man and woman gripped by this passion? It is essentially imaginary. It is not a real communication between being and being, but, instead, a double deception, a double fantasy, a kind of continual conspiracy to create obstacles and resistances exactly calculated to fan the emotions while rejecting the completion whereby they will be relieved. It would also seem that the violence of the passion is directly proportional to the insurmountability of the obstacle and not at all to any authentic quality in the lovers (who in the novel are extremely vague and conventional, as in the romance Tristan is merely the "strongest," Isolde the "loveliest and fairest"). In fact, we may say that Tristan does not love a real Isolde, nor she a real Tristan, but that they are both in love with love, with their feelings, with the burning emotion in their hearts—the burning itself; for the other person is simply an excuse for their emotions. Finally, the intoxicated nature of the passion must be made clear. The taste for loving, or even better, feeling one's self loved, for being in love, if suitable obstacles have been chosen, can go so far as to make its victims prefer "the delectable affliction" to health, social position, ambition, all forms of earthly happiness,

and, ultimately, life itself. *"Höchste Lust!"*—Supreme Joy!—cries
Wagner's Isolde, dying on Tristan's corpse; the supreme obstacle,
death, has brought the passion to its climax.

This faraway love is diametrically opposed in every detail to
the love of neighbor in the gospel. Distant love languishes and
suffers, while the other (according to St. Augustine) "runs,
flies, and rejoices." One is nurtured by absence, dreams, and
nostalgia; the other by presence, knowledge, and mutual exchange. One becomes exalted by struggle, pursuit, and failure;
the other is fulfilled in the daily building of peace. One is desire;
the other, gift and possession. One is passion, something that is
suffered; the other is action.

The love that is passion depends upon Eros; love that is action, upon Agape.*

We know that the troubadours' poetry, which spread the contagion of *l'amor de lonh* throughout the West, giving birth to
all our poetry and romantic fiction for several centuries, was
openly opposed to marriage. In current moral terms, *Tristan* may
be classified as a glorification of adultery. We have observed
that all the elements of erotic passion are appropriate for the
destruction of marriage, or will themselves be destroyed if the
marriage is happy and lasting.

To discover the secret reason for the crisis in modern marriage, all we really have to do is point out that romance in our
society is only the vulgarized by-product of the passion typified
by Tristan.

Like passion, romance is a poisoning that compels its complacent victims to say, "It's stronger than I am." But it has lost
its mortal virulence because social and moral obstacles have lost
their solidity and always end up by being conquered or deflected.

* To get a clearer view of this distinction, see my book, *Love in the Western
World* (New York: Pantheon Books, 1956), and Anders Nygren, *Agape and
Eros* (Philadelphia: The Westminster Press, 1953). A profound discussion of
both books may be found in M. d'Arcy, S.J., *The Mind and Heart of Love* (New
York: Meridian Books, Inc., 1956).

Therefore, instead of culminating in tragedy, romance gets lost in a happy ending. Like passion, romance ultimately is a form of narcissistic love, directed to an image of the beloved and not to a concrete being; it is a projection of intimate or unconscious nostalgia, not a real dialogue.

The big difference between passion and romance is that romance is, by definition, transient. It relies upon the strength or weakness of the obstacles that feed it. Tristan's passion established a kind of fidelity unto death. But it was a fidelity to a dream, a fidelity to its own desires rather than to the person who inspired it. It retained, however, two important aspects of valid fidelity: a sense that this is "for life" and the feeling of an imposed fate, "come what may." But romance, if it ever arrives at normal happiness, has every likelihood of disappearing. "This dream girl," Joe thinks, "who looks like my favorite movie star, who was so hard to get and so exciting to chase, is now a real person at my side, changing the baby's diapers day and night. I married her because it seemed romantic. But nothing romantic can survive the smell of cooking in our three small rooms."

And Sally herself thinks that she deserves more than this fate, that Peter might be the one who could make her life worth while. After two years both husband and wife are ripe for a new romance, which they will certainly find, since this is what they secretly want. If they hold on to the ideas on which they based their marriage, they will logically be led to divorce, and will be ready for new and futureless marriages. This has become society's most common situation, so much so that most people are convinced that "that's the way life is," that it has always been this way and always will be. But as far as the historian of social behavior is concerned, this notion is doubly wrong. First of all, if that's the way life is, it is because Western peoples have continuously adopted a more and more glamorous idea of love since the beginning of the twelfth century. Not clearly recognized, but all the more slavishly followed, this idea is the enemy of our matri-

monial institutions, benefiting from the unceasing propaganda of
books and movies. And second, it is hardly likely that, if that is
the way life is, it will stay that way forever, for no human society
could survive long if the rate of divorce (that is, broken families)
equaled the marriage rate.

Totalitarian Marriage and the Revolt Against Romance

On the threshold of the anarchy menacing us, it is only too easy
to offer a list of "remedies" which would re-establish a tolerable
order: To restore the meaning of the marriage oath; emphasize
the primacy of reason over emotion; reform the divorce laws;
prevent impetuous marriages; instill a sense of social responsibility into youth; in short, "go back to the traditional virtues."
Unfortunately, these pieces of advice would be in vain. People
never "go back" to anything, especially in the area of social
customs. In the unlikely event that modern society seemed to be
returning to some of the virtues affirmed by our ancestors, it
would not be because of wise advice, but because of powerful
defensive reflexes within the social body. I can see two of these
reflexes operating in this century.

1. The totalitarian reaction. It should also be called the reaction of the modern state, which cannot tolerate individualist
anarchy, since this tends to destroy its tax structure, the re-
cruitment of armies, and more generally, the collectivist disciplines of education. Nazis, Fascists, and Stalinists all agree on
this point: the family, the social unit, must no longer be exposed
to the assaults of the most antisocial of emotions—passion, or
even romance. Just recall the drastic steps Himmler took to regu-
late marriage in the name of the state, first for the S.S. Corps,
then for procreation in general. A racial "science" was charged
with the responsibility of progressively eliminating every form of
arbitrary, individual, sentimental choice, substituting in its place
a kind of marriage bureau, established by party functionaries on

the basis of physical measurements, pedigrees, and political certificates.

Russia has never gone this far. Having swept away every law relating to marriage, divorce, and children during Lenin's regime, it confined itself to re-creating a code that deceptively resembled those in bourgeois countries, but was enforced much more strictly. This was maintained by propaganda ruthlessly directed against romance, sentimental songs, and the idea of individual happiness, which was considered decadent. Bonuses were offered to large families, and obstacles were placed in the way of divorce; above all, general poverty seemed to have temporarily stabilized the situation of marriage in the U.S.S.R.

But it is the question of permanently mobilizing the state that characterizes every totalitarian regime, and from the facts mentioned we cannot infer anything from it for the future. Nevertheless, the initial totalitarian experiments have lent credibility to the idea of a time when marriage would be entirely controlled by some official eugenic science, giving the state the right to limit individual choice. Perhaps we would then see the social conditions reproduced which are most apt to breed secret and mortal passions, worthy even of Tristan, but infrequent, disparaged, and disgraceful, and therefore harmless from the collectivist point of view.

2. The decadence of romance. A much more normal and completely different evolution has been taking place in the democratic, middle-class countries. It is more normal in the sense that it operates freely, but surely it is even more revolutionary in its effects.

The extreme vulgarization of romantic values is, in the long run, much more dangerous for romance than any moralist's diatribes. The decline of sexual taboos and the emancipation of women both work in the same direction. Romance, like genuine passion, requires opposition or even official disapproval in order to be kindled. Lacking serious obstacles, the stream that carries it forward empties too quickly into reality, where it founders. "It is not Love that turns to reality," a troubadour wrote in the twelfth century.

Yet the general evolution of customs in countries where romance is most freely produced "turns toward reality" unswervingly.

Woman's acquisition of political, legal, and—most significantly —economic equality is probably the principal factor in this evolution. The very fact that a woman may have a profession, which means a life of her own, obliges man to consider her as a real and autonomous being, one who must be dealt with practically and whose initiatives must be respected. Such a being lends herself poorly to the nostalgic projection of the intimate dream of the lover. She is no longer an object for contemplation, but a subject acting on her own account. A true dialogue between man and woman will necessarily be substituted for mutual narcissistic reverie; in this dialogue considerations of social background, education, and general qualifications will be reintroduced, along with concern about character, life goals, and material resources for setting up housekeeping. Romance tended to believe it could surmount all these things and consequently gladly neglected them.

The commercialization of romance is a second noteworthy factor in this evolutionary process. We have seen that passion is heightened in revolt against the tyrannical and prosaic conventions of society, morality, and even life itself. But passion loses its intimate intensity when it is advertised on every magazine page and on every street corner. Today we have arrived at a point where romance, far from being an exceptional state, fascinating even in its torments, has become part of conformist behavior. The young man who is not in love tries to hide this disturbing peculiarity from his friends; he wonders what is wrong with him that he is not like everybody else—that is, like heroes in the films and short stories that are the models for his generation. But even the models themselves are beginning to undergo a change. The serious creative writing of the past few decades includes almost no great love fiction. It has practically abandoned this theme to the manufacturers of best sellers. The Hollywood requirement of a love interest in every film at any price—even in documentaries on the atom bomb—is undergoing a variety of attacks. A bitter, cynical, or simply realistic note is already replacing the formerly indispensable happy ending in many screen plays. This reaction may be developed forcefully in the years to come, and it certainly will not fail to influence social customs. For romance, the literary theme par excellence (since a happy marriage was dull and uneventful), had contaminated the Western world by means of literature long before the movies took up the banner. La Rochefoucauld wondered, "How many men would fall in love if they had never heard love spoken about?" We can ask ourselves how many men will still think about falling in love when people no longer talk about it.

In this regard, let me emphasize that passion and romance, artificial creations of the Western world, are linked to sexuality only in a dialectical and paradoxical manner. Desire is not the same as being in love, and the premature possession of the love-object often kills the possibility of romance. *"D'amor mon casticaz,"* chastity is born of love, a troubadour said. That is why the romantic periods of Western literature coincide with puritanism. (The Victorian novel is the best example.) At the moment we appear to be entering a period of easy or relaxed morals, comparable to the first half of the eighteenth century. The liquidation of Victorian and puritan taboos, influenced by popularized psychoanalysis, big-city life, rebellion against the middle class, and female emancipation, is about to poison one of the principal sources of romanticism.

At the mid-point of our century, everything is helping to undermine the taste for romance (at the very moment of its greatest audience) and is working in the cause of marital stability, the basis of family life.

Toward an Alliance of Equals

We must accept the facts: everything concerning passion is paradoxical. It is fed by the difficulties it encounters; it feeds on them in order to increase its torment, choosing passionate torment in preference to happiness; it compels a man to die for the image of a woman whom he might not love if he had to live with her. It enters Western history as a drive toward beauty and infinite love, but by negating real love it both exalts and depresses its victims; it has enriched our literature at the expense of our morality; and today, wearing a benign form, adulterated, vulgarized, it helps bring about millions of marriages that it will soon destroy. Should we mourn its decline or rejoice about it? It would be useless to try to give a single, forthright answer to this question.

If, by a defensive reaction of a society threatened with anarchy, romance is now rejected in favor of exclusively realistic attitudes in the relationships between men and women, our descendants will probably be bored. They will feel that something is missing from their lives, that there is a hollow place in their hearts. "We moderns," men of small faith and less religion, see the life of the emotions as a kind of ideal, or an evasion of choice; as the least harmful approximation of a substitute for the joys and cares of the spirit. (Elsewhere, in totalitarian states, political passion already has officially taken their place.) Killing romance, or what is left of it, will make us lose as much as we gain. Only an extremely intense spiritual life would be capable of appeasing the absence of "the delicious torment" of romance, elevating Agape above Eros, and we have no right to expect a collective miracle.

The fact is, we will be able to do something about the evolution I have described only by making people conscious of the real situation: by exposing the true nature of passion and defining the types of human relations it takes for granted and encourages—

in fact, the psychoanalytic method. Having done this, we can then suggest some new directions for the education of society.

Attacking romance in the name of morality would be a mistake, since it is fascinating to the same degree that it appears forbidden, and dies when universally approved. We could limit its dangerous qualities much more effectively simply by showing the young that, no matter how valuable, romance is inadequate as a foundation for marriage. Marrying someone "for life" because of a two-month fever is not an act of courage but of stupidity. We would probably do well not to be as harsh on films and novels called "indecent" by puritanical standards as on those that depict romance as an ecstasy and the supreme intoxication —an outrageous lie that, surprisingly enough, even the most skeptical of the young believe in. We should also ask our novelists to abandon their romantic triangles for a while and show us a modern type of marriage, no longer based on "love" alone, the *quid pro quo* of two dreams, but on a sworn alliance of two equals.

We can influence the realm of morality only by modifying or reversing certain standards of judgment, only by renovating styles in current moral attitudes as to what is acceptable and what is not. Freud's contribution lies in making it possible for us to discuss the unconscious mind and sexuality. The troubadours made a profound impact by making *joy d'amor* fashionable. Movies and cheap literature affect us by prolonging the rage for romance, even though it is condemned by new social realities. Those who discuss our times would be helpful if they expressed values that correspond to current social facts and the loss of romantic illusions. Their influence would be important if they described examples of pledged fidelity, a practical partnership, the thrill of a common and constructive enterprise undertaken at any risk, free of Proust's "intermissions of the heart" and the ever-shifting play of sentiment. For it is these positive values that are the century's true style and excellence, and perhaps even its heroism.

THREE
Christianity and
World Problems

10 The Challenge of Marxism

The Elusiveness of Communist Doctrine

If you oppose the axioms of Marx and Engels with Christian doctrines, the Communists will tell you, not without a certain apparent justification, that they are unimpressed: they operate on the plane of history, not of eternal truths. You try to place yourself, therefore, on this historical plane. For example, you go to the Soviet Union. Like a lot of other honest people who have gone there, you see for yourself that the Soviet dictatorship closely resembles a Fascist regime. But when you try to draw the conclusion that this is what communism is—if it is to be identified, as the faithful insist, with its historic results—you will be told that you are absolutely wrong, that you understand nothing about "dialectical evolution," of which today's dictatorship is only a necessary but temporary phase.

There you are, thrown back on the doctrinal plane. You bone up on this famous dialectic. You will see that it was first discovered by Hegel, who made the mistake of basing it on the spirit, which amounted to standing it on its head. The genius of Marx put it back on its feet, basing it on economics; thus ballasted, it could begin to operate on a realistic level. You learn that its original purpose was the destruction of the state for the benefit of concrete man. In practice, however, it first reinforced the state to the extent known as dictatorship, but ultimately this dictatorship is supposed to disappear by itself, of necessity, along with its last opponents.

You thought you were in history, in reality, but you are now asked not to believe your own eyes, which see the advance of world-wide communism, but to believe a prophecy. However, you are likely to remain skeptical: after forty-five years of central control the state is no less powerful in Soviet Russia, and no one bothers any longer to mention its future suppression. The party faithful will tell you that this is a necessary tactic, moreover, duly foreseen by the dialecticians. Then, perhaps, you begin to glimpse the real meaning of "dialectic." It is nothing more than obedience to the party, *blind* obedience to Lenin, Stalin, or Khrushchev, unique trustees of doctrine. Abandoning the plane of eternal truths to enter upon the plane of history means renouncing *the* truth, and from then on believing only in the tactics of a dictator, who may alter truth every six months.

But then what are we talking about when we talk about communism? How are we to deal with it? Just what is the identity of a doctrine that from time to time pretends to justify theoretically a Soviet democracy, which is quickly superseded by Stalinist dictatorship? There is first pacifism at all costs, then imperialism, now continued under the guise of "peaceful co-existence"; an assault on the state and, simultaneously, the capitalism of Lenin's government; the expropriation of holdings in 1918, and the restoration of property in 1935; the suppression of inheritances, then their re-establishment; antimilitarism and the enthusiastic creation of an army, abundantly provided with marshals; absolute social equality, followed by a race for salaries and ranks; the ruin of the family, then its systematic rebuilding; and equal contradictions in the Soviet attitude to international organizations. How can we come to grips with such a shifting doctrine?

All these changes can be explained, I understand very well, by practical and contingent necessities, and I am not making a judgment of a political character. But it is disturbing to see so many intellectuals defending these maneuvers in the name of doctrine and constantly justifying them (although slightly after the event) by supposed "dialectical" necessities. Will sincere Communists understand that this method looks like plain opportunism to those who are not of their faith? What, then, is the point of discussion or serious examination? "Nothing will be equitable on this scale," said Pascal.

We do not want to exploit this equivocal element, but at least we should remember that it is there or risk falling into the clumsy traps it sets for us, into which ninety per cent of the adversaries of Marxism have fallen, and countless Marxists themselves!

However, in the struggle to discover some identity and continuity in the Communist attitude, through all the violent contradictions in its successive manifestations, I discern ultimately a great, invariable will: *the will to change the world.* Such a will could only be inspired by the intolerable feeling of some defect inherent in the world.

Knowing that a *universal evil* exists, and that consequently everything must be transformed, is, I believe, not only the initial act, but also the constant passion of conscious and consistent Communists. In their eyes, at least, it is this profound impulse that legitimatizes the most tortuous detours, the dialectical shifts, of the Communist Party.[1] The "cause" justifies the means.

But then, it is surely impossible not to see that such a movement bears the most striking analogy to the movement of the Christian in his battle against sin.

Only on this plane, it seems to me, is a comparison possible.

[1] "For us, communism is not a state that ought to be created, an ideal. . . . Communism is the name we give to the movement which will effectively suppress present reality. The conditions of this movement are dictated by this circumstance" (Marx, *German Ideology*).

Does Man Come First, or the World?

Like the Christian, the Marxist has recognized that man does not exist alone, that he is linked to a society, that he is a "related" being.[2] Again like the Christian, the Marxist believes that present society has no right to determine the whole of man, is incapable of it. For society is divided against itself and turns the man abandoned to it into an antinomian being, "divorced" and "alienated" from what is most human in him. The discovery of this "self-alienation," which according to Marx is the truth about all societies in the past, including primitive communism, has its formal counterpart in the Christian diagnosis, the recognition of a fundamental corruption, which is called original sin.

It follows that for the Marxist as well as for the Christian, man can find his fulfillment and "regain himself utterly"[3] only by grace of a future and radically renovated economy.[4]

The Christian and Marxist share similar reactions, formally speaking, against all types of state; an absolutism against all speculation that is idealistic, detached, and unactual, and against all activities that do not help to transform, to change something in one way or another—to fight effectively against the universal evil.

This fundamental will to transformation is perfectly expressed and summed up, for both sides, by two propositions that vigorously affirm the need for a "change," a concrete, visible, practical change. They differ, however, in a significant manner in regard to the means they prescribe.

The eleventh of Marx's theses on Feuerbach states that "the philosophers, until now, have merely interpreted the world in

[2] "We are every one members of one another" (Rom. 12:5). On the other hand, Marx never stopped criticizing the "isolated and abstract individual" (cf. VI and VII of the *Theses on Feuerbach*).

[3] Marx, *Criticism of Hegel's Philosophy of Law*.

[4] In the broadest meaning of the term, which could refer to Marx's "classless society" or the Christian "kingdom of God."

various ways: the point now is to transform it." The Apostle Paul writes in the Epistle to the Romans (12:2), "Do not conform to this present time, but be transformed by the renewing of your sense, so that you may discern the will of God, which is good, agreeable and perfect."

In both cases there is the same word "transform," and it is a matter of transformation to the extent that one is specifically human. For Paul, transformation means obedience to the Spirit; for Marx, it means creation of a revolution. Hence it is a matter of action. It is a matter of attesting to faith through a realization of the will of God, in opposition to the will of the period; or attesting to thought, through a social act which can only be revolutionary.[5]

Nevertheless, the difference between Marx and the apostle is extremely obvious. Paul wishes to transform man first, and the world through him; whereas Marx wishes to transform the world first, and then man by means of it.

It is important that we be very clear about this central opposition if we are to understand why the practice and ends of communism radically contradict the practice and ends of Christianity, from which also they obscurely derive, although they have been severed from their links with eternity and are abandoned solely to the laws of time.

From Anti-Religious Polemics to Marxist Doctrine

That Marx's original doctrine is in polemical form can never be said often enough. It is very consciously conditioned by the circumstances of Western Europe in the middle of the nineteenth century, and by the desire to change those circumstances.

---

[5] "In practice, man must prove the truth of his thought, that is, its reality and concrete power. A dispute as to the reality or nonreality of thinking which is isolated from the practical world, is a purely academic quarrel" (second thesis on Feuerbach). The same applies to the Christian: faith without good works is not faith (James 2:26).

In particular it is "materialistic," in the common meaning of the word, only to the extent that the mentality of the period may be described—and describes itself—as "spiritual" in the most debatable meaning of the term.

From the religious point of view, just what were the circumstances Marx had to cope with? It was the period of restoration, of liberal professors and the bourgeoisie, the age of the giants of capitalism which was developing in England and Germany, of Hegelian theologians or other opponents of Christianity. All stood on common ground in teaching, or letting it be known by their example, that religion is concerned only with the "inner man." Religion was a "private matter"; this was so well understood that all Marx had to do was to assert it. Religion did not put a stop to financial speculation, or the oppression of workers, or to calling "just," if necessary, what was useful for the owners. Religion no longer seemed to inconvenience anyone.[6] It sanctioned and protected the established order. It even interpreted this establishment, and was no longer a means of judging it.

Marx did not waste time denouncing the error at the root of such a fakery. He knew it was too deeply ingrained in man to be touched by simple philosophical criticism.[7] But philosophical criticism was the only weapon he could muster on the plane of the "spirit," for he was an unbeliever. Besides, it was not the "spirit" he wanted to save but man, whom the spiritual thinkers of the day had abandoned to an increasingly inhuman fate. Consequently, he had to resort to an entirely different sort of argument, supposedly "materialistic." On the one hand, he employed the violence of the proletariat; on the other, the infallible "science" of the laws of economic evolution.

[6] I am speaking of religion as Marx saw it, as it appeared in the social body. I have not forgotten that the same period witnessed the great revival of pietism.

[7] "The weapons of criticism obviously cannot replace the criticism of weapons" (Marx, *Criticism of the Hegelian Philosophy of Law*). They had to be used, of course, but they were not enough. "To be radical consists in attacking the evil at its root. For man, the root is man himself" (*ibid.*). That is to say, actual man is a social product, according to Marx, and not a spiritual and carnal creature.

The process may be summed up and simplified as follows: those who pretend to reform the "inner man" carefully keep themselves from contact with the exterior world. In opposition to them Marx says the exterior must be transformed first, and the rest will follow necessarily. To save the rest—culture, mind, and soul (if you insist on it)—we must begin by denying its existence. The "spirit" invoked by the middle class is only a caricature, but the harm it has done is so widespread that we can no longer dream of re-establishing truth by purely spiritual means. The striking arguments of polemical materialism must be placed in opposition to the "spiritual" lie: we shall call it dialectical materialism in order to indicate it is only temporary, instrumental, that it must be in the service of truth in the long run—which also contains the "spirit." In short, it is only a matter of strategy. Let us make a virtue of necessity. Things and their relationships must first be changed; let us attempt to change the world—that is, economic and social relationships. If there is time left over, we will change man. Perhaps all we have to do is change the material frame in order to transform the contents? Have we not already shown that culture, for example, is merely a "reflection" of an economic process?

Thus we see how Marx himself is trapped by his own polemic. It was only at the end of his career that his friend Engels discovered the danger of it. "Marx and I," he wrote in 1890, "were perhaps responsible for the fact that our disciples sometimes insisted too much on economic factors. We were forced to insist on their fundamental character in opposition to our adversaries who denied them, and we had neither the time nor the occasion to do justice to other factors."

From Marxist Doctrine to Soviet Tactics

In fact, it was from the opportunistic "lie" of polemical materialism, inevitably turning into party doctrine, that there developed the tactical "truth" of that vulgar materialism which

the bourgeois press has such fun attacking today. (Such news-
papers, of course, practice their own kind of materialism while
denying it for the purposes of their cause.) This materialism,
which was attacked from the very beginning by Marx,[8] has become after him an absolute lie, exactly symmetrical to that of the
idealists: the belief that changing the order of things will auto-
matically change human reality. Marx was compelled by his opponents to declare the primacy of the material, and he did not
realize that he was unleashing an absurd prejudice, an error no
less grave than that of the defenders of pure spirit. The error,
of course, is the belief that the cause of all man's misfortune lies
in things and not in himself. (Marx was not conscious of this,
but he is nevertheless responsible for it, a point to which we shall
return.)

People, especially the middle class, like to parrot the old saw
that clothes do not make the man and that money does not bring
happiness. But in practice they desperately believe that clothes
do make the man, and money *does* bring happiness. Marx came
and explained to them in fifteen volumes—which have been sum-
marized—that they are right to believe it. What is more, he
demonstrated that those who pretended to doubt it, who preached
that money did not make for happiness, were simply exploiters who
had plenty of money and wanted to hold on to it—precisely because it *had* made them happy.

Therefore, there was just one road left to follow: establish
a Five-Year Plan, create a powerful heavy industry, compete with
America, and accumulate still more riches, since money dis-
tributed among the masses never fails to produce happiness. Suc-

[8] In the *Theses on Feuerbach*, in particular. There one may read a sentence
which proves that Marx in no way pretended to neglect human, personal factors,
without which the materialism would not be "dialectical." "The coincidence of
the modification of circumstances and of the modification of human activity, or
personal transformation, can be rationally understood only as a revolutionary
activity." What an extremely important sentence! But how forgotten in today's
Communist activities.

cess requires discipline. Continued success requires a dictator. Who cares if the middle class is infuriated? Let the scrupulous be indignant; let the overly sensitive weep for "the God that failed." What must be done, must be done. Does the dictatorship of the state contradict Marx? What difference does it make, since the goal is wealth, mother of happiness? Isn't that what Marx wanted?

To sum up: Marx did not want vulgar materialism. But polemical necessities on the one hand, and his definition of concrete man as purely social on the other, led him to emphasize material factors. It is this emphasis that "the masses" have sensed, because everything predisposed them to it. The result is Communist imperialism, which hardly differs from Fascism in its oppression of man and his freedom.

The Christian Attitude to the World

There is good reason to talk of Marxist "doctrine," of Communist "ideology" and "tactics," but it would cause irremediable confusion to speak of Christian "doctrine" in the same way. The Christian, and especially the Protestant, absolutely rejects the idea that theological dogmas represent the theory of a practice.[9]

Christianity is not a program, nor an "ideology," in the meaning used by certain Marxist primitivists, nor simply tactics —which goes without saying. Rather, it is an attitude, a total attitude. (I would prefer to say "totalitarian," but the word has

[9] According to Karl Barth, for example, theological dogma is only a perpetual questioning, a self-criticism, if you prefer, that the Church addresses to itself, and whose function is endlessly to correct, to rectify the message announced by preaching the sacraments. It is an act of obedience, and it is also an act of humility. Any human word on the subject of God must be inadequate and can only be a return to the one perfect revelation, to Jesus Christ. "Doctrine" is thus only a critical measure that the Church takes of her message in relation to her fidelity to her foundation, her content, and her purpose. Doctrine presents nothing, even at the most superficial level, that can be compared to a theoretical program intended to become a matter for action.

been perverted by secular caricatures of the Christian revolution.)

Christian life and thought refer at every instant to what determines the whole of man: his beginning, his end, and his present mission. The Christian knows that he comes from God, the Creator, and that he is going toward the kingdom of God, the Reconciler. He knows that his mission in life is to obey the Word, which is Jesus Christ, the Mediator. But the Word judges "the world," which rejected it. It saves only those who utterly reject this world while living in complete expectation of the kingdom. This denial and active expectation constitute the most radical possible revolution—or, rather, the only radical revolution. In our Western world, troubled by a message it misunderstands, all other revolutions are only enigmatic shadows of this primordial event—its temporal substitutes, drifting rudderless toward the abyss.

"Do not conform to this present era, but be transformed. . . ." For the Christian, this does not mean that the world should be abandoned, that when conversion has been achieved, he has nothing to do but wait and submit mournfully to the laws of a world he condemns. In that case, what would his rejection mean? What proof would we have of his transformation? An irritable resignation? Mere reticence or mental reservation amid triumphant conformism? This is certainly what the Marxists think, but it again clearly reveals their initial error about man, their ignorance or blindness in regard to the duty and the power of man transformed by faith.

According to the gospel, the new man is someone who has direction. He has found a new orientation, as the word "conversion" implies. Obeying the Word that God speaks to him, he simultaneously recognizes the origin and purpose of his life; from that he becomes aware of his sin and of everything that led him astray. For if the world is delivered up to injustice and chaos, it is man's fault, who was the world's king and has betrayed it.

Every individual sin repeats and aggravates that fault. Therefore the consciousness of sin, the knowledge of origin and purpose, and the obligation to act in order to redeem the evil that has been done—these are three indivisible moments of the "transformation" spoken of by Paul. One is not conceivable seriously without the others. "Every direct knowledge of God gives birth to obedience," Calvin wrote. What kind of obedience would it be that did not manifest itself? Personal transformation, in the fullest sense of the gospel, can only be expressed, if it has been achieved, by some action on the part of the Christian: against the world, as it is presently constituted, and on behalf of the world, as restored in the Promise.

We must go further than this obvious affirmation. Not only does the convert become a transformer of the world (otherwise he is not converted), but every transformation of the present form of things which does not result from a conversion of men must appear to a Christian as a "reformation" of little significance. This is the thing that really seems outrageous. But the gospel is explicit: "What does it profit a man to gain the world, if he loses his soul?" His soul—that is, the consciousness of his origin and purpose, of the very meaning of his action, his thought, his whole earthly life! To be more precise—for we are not speaking of "purely theological" truths as the unbeliever would call them—what would it profit a man, as the Christian sees him, to save his material and moral life, to escape war, poverty, and oppression, if he ignored or refused "the one thing necessary," the only guarantee of salvation? If a man is converted, should he then let the world go its way, allow war to break out and the unemployed to die of starvation? That would prove that he is not converted. Consequently, I will act, but not for the world, and not to preserve some good, but because I know myself to be personally responsible for the established disorder. I will act in gratitude to God who has transformed me. If I did not have this gratitude, I would be ignorant of my salvation. But if I know

my salvation, I cannot tolerate my sin and its effect upon the
real world where men live—and die.

Mutual Reproaches between Christians and Marxists

Since the Christian conception of man is that he alone is responsible for the evil in the world, it is understandable that the
Marxist state of mind seems extremely limited to him. A comparison may be useful. The child who loses a game, or bumps
against the furniture, becomes angry with objects and holds them
responsible. He beats the table, just as Xerxes had the Hellespont
beaten. This is the childish prejudice that Marxism was to con-
solidate in the proletarian consciousness. A gross deviation, it
will be said; but could it be avoided? Did not Marx say the order
of material things must first be changed, and that men thereafter
would become more adept at understanding each other and living happily? "Change life!" cried the young Rimbaud, and
leftist intellectuals adopted this motto in opposition to both vapid
spirituality and the routine and cynicism of conservatives.

St. Paul does not possess this tragic naïveté. He is not angry
with the Roman Empire and does not plan its destruction as the
primary objective of Christians. Nevertheless, the Empire deprived them of all freedom, and soon even of their lives! Isn't it
necessary to do the most urgent thing first, to save your own
skin, to overthrow the despots? That is what good sense and Marxism tell you to do. But if the apostle had placed the battle on
that so-called realistic level, even supposing that the "Christian
party" had triumphed, nothing would have prevented it from
suffering the common fate of political rebellions: it would have
reshaped the forms of power it had overthrown,[10] and, postponing

[10] My supposition is not completely gratuitous; it was realized later under
Constantine, through legal means, it is true, but with the same inconveniences.
There are surely laws of history, in the sense that we find the same mechanisms
again wherever the spirit resigns.

evangelism (its *raison d'être*) to more peaceful times, would have devoted itself to more urgent tasks—giving bread and circuses to the masses. But Paul was an apostle and not a dictator. That is why his message is still preached to us. He did not preach hatred and cynicism—which belong to the form of the world— but the news (absolutely new, coming from elsewhere, from beyond this world) of man's transformation in Christ, who had come into the world. He did not announce a hypothetical future in the name of a difficult theory, but an immediately active and totally salutary Presence, in the name of a living Person and his love. He proclaimed man as changed.

All this is really too good. Too beautiful to be true, say the Marxists. (A Christian, supposedly a changed man, I still have enough of the old Adam in me to understand their difficulty.) On what is this transformation you are talking about based? On faith which my intellect denies, which it orders me to ignore. I cannot see the results of such a faith in our Western world.[11] If I do not have your faith, I simply do not see them. I see an established Church oppressing all dissidents, in collusion with the powerful, always supporting reactionary regimes and preaching resignation. It is really too easy for it to justify its bad conscience, pretending that the inner world alone matters and that "bread of life" is sufficient to feed man! Perhaps it is sufficient to feed you personally, but that is not what will abolish poverty, prevent war, and change the world!

We Christians must admit, to our shame, that for the great

---

11 "I can never see Christianity becoming revolutionary!" Jean Guéhenno once exclaimed (*Union for the Truth*, March 22, 1930). To which Prof. Hans Mühle- stein, a German Socialist, replied, "Every revolution in Western history is a re- sult of the Christian religion. Every other cause is secondary." And Henri de Man: "I believe that there has been no attempt at revolution that did not have a Christian origin. If socialism does not exist in Asia, this is because Christianity does not yet exist there." In support of De Man, it may be mentioned that the syndicalist movement in Japan was founded by a Christian, Kagawa.

mass of workers these reproaches seem justified. If Marxism has provoked an uprising of hope among the exploited and raised such waves of enthusiastic support, it is because it found itself alone in protesting against the way of the world. You may say that this was primarily because it was intelligent enough to blame capitalist oppression, only too real, for all the evil in existence —all the evil for which, as a matter of fact, the sin of each of us is responsible. (The reign of capitalism is only the most urgent and obvious aspect of this sin.) The objection is accurate but inadequate. What finally explains the "religious" success of Marxism is its avowed desire, concrete and immediate, to change everything, not just the "spirit" or the "interior." If Marxism has been able to achieve this, it is precisely to the extent that Christianity, in the eyes of the masses, has no longer dared to show itself Christian. The salt has lost its savor and its salutary bitterness. The only true and certain hope is no longer preached to the world with a sufficiently embarrassing and overwhelming force. Marxism offers the hope of change, because the "spirit" which should have been the agent of total change, the perpetual and only real change, has become the guardian of conformity; or at any event, because of excessive prudence has not known how to prevent the masses from seeing it as such.

Christians are more responsible for the success of Marxism with the crowd than Marxists are responsible for the decline of the Church in the modern world. That is why the Marxist's complaint to the Christian is more humanly valuable than the Christian's of the Marxist. On the whole, if Marxism is a self-deception and nevertheless succeeds, it is because Christ is poorly preached by his disciples—whether in words or in actions.

If Christians returned to a more faithful—and therefore more painful—consciousness of this fact, I think they would refrain from attacking Marxism in reactionary terms. But once this is said and maintained, it remains true that in doctrine, and independently of all our faults, the Marxist objection is worthless, while the Christian objection is irrefutable.

When a Marxist reproaches me for being satisfied with a completely spiritual change, which does not affect anything in the course of things, I am justified in replying to him, "Your reproach applies to my hypocrisy, my cowardice, my lack of faith, but not at all to faith. For faith, as Luther said, is 'an anxious thing.' You don't have it with impunity, and if you do, it will be seen, things change. What you reproach me for, actually, is not being Christian enough! You are urging me to be even more Christian, when you think you are refuting my religion. Your atheism becomes a kind of sermon. It is crazy luck for a dialectician. If you say that the Christian is someone who does nothing, you prove you know nothing about Christianity." (I repeat that this is not the Marxist's fault, but our fault, and first of all mine.)

On the other hand, when I reproach Marxism for its present-day materialistic deviation, I am leaving out what is essential in Marx; I am not criticizing a contingent error. I don't say: "You are not Marxist enough!" I maintain that from the very beginning, from the original doctrine, intrinsically, and in so far as someone is a convinced Marxist, not in so far as he is false to Marxism, he commits a fatal, irrevocable error that is today very apparent. It is an error about man and his cosmic mission, about the *person*, as defined in my vocabulary. My criticism goes to the very core of Marxism, while the Marxist criticism merely applies to a denatured Christianity. I repeat, the core of Marxism is its will to change the world first, not man first and the world through man. Such a will can only lead to excesses of materialism, not because Mao and Khrushchev are wicked men, but because of the effect of elements in the spiritual and physical conditions of man which are not reducible to any imaginable social or historical determinism in the past, present, or future.[12]

---

[12] I do not say "what is permanent in man's physical and spiritual circumstances," for then the Marxist would make me admit that even extremely essential aspects of being may vary, according to the society and the nature of its institutions. (Thus the pretended primordial need for property may very well be annihilated in man by a Communist regime.) What, then, remains in man

The Problem of Final Ends:
Kingdom of God or Earthly Paradise?

We have now arrived at the point of real decisions, since in principle all gross ambiguities have been eliminated.

Like me, there are many people who are struck by indisputable formal resemblances between the will of the true Christian and the militant Communist. They have attempted a practical synthesis of these two beliefs, seeing them as complementary. Others, more numerous than is imagined, would like to see such a synthesis, apparently fearing for their faith, or its "success," if the synthesis is not achieved. Only a specifically theological criticism can determine the limitations that exist in fact, and make the decisive distinctions.

The practice of communism is amenable, in itself, only to political, economic, and historical criticism.[13] I do not see that the Christian has any specific light to shed on these subjects, which require technical knowledge. But the final ends of communism and the postulates it presupposes do properly fall within the province of a theological criticism.

Just for a minute, permit me to be a bit schematic in order to be more clear. It seems to me that the ultimate opposition between the Marxist belief and the personal faith of the Christian

---

that is irreducible by any social transformation? Physical death and sin. And also the quality, the creative function of the mind. In short, everything essential. I say that every doctrine that does not take one of these conditions into account necessarily leads to idealism, or its obverse, materialism. Totalitarian communism necessarily results from a purely social conception of man which rejects the spiritual, creative functions, and the burden of sin. On the other hand, it could hardly be shown that the secularization of Christianity necessarily results from the gospel.

[13] As made, for example, by Werner Sombart and De Man in Germany, and in France by the Ordre Nouveau. In particular, see Robert Aron and Arnaud Dandieu, *La Révolution Nécessaire* (Paris: Grasset, 1933) and its criticism of Marx's idea of exchange.

is sufficient to explain everything else. Communism prepares for an earthly paradise, the temporal paradise of man; Christianity prepares for an eternal kingdom, which is God's and may not be found on earth. Both are eschatological in the sense that they defer their accomplishment to a final and invariable state, to a future and complete term, attainable only after a long tribulation, a long temporal passion. And it is the "faith," the substance of things hoped for, that alone makes the evil of the world bearable during the journey toward the final goal. (The Christian sings at the stake, the Communist accepts a starvation wage if it will help save Russia.) But the Christian *eschaton* is beyond this time; it is eternal and is also immediately present in our hearts.[14] The "last things" of Marxism, however, are temporal and disappear into an indefinite future—a hundred years, a thousand years, two thousand years—and cannot exist *hic et nunc.*

How will the radical difference between these two ends— temporal and eternal—manifest itself in our century? The phenomenon of conversion provides a clear answer.

A man converted to Christianity is someone who receives and grasps revelation in terms of Person. Suddenly the kingdom is within him. This man is no longer master of his life. He is the agent of a vocation coming from beyond him, but intended for him alone and existing here below, and which henceforth animates all his acts and most intimate thoughts. Beginning now, his person is re-created. Beginning now, he enters into battle with the world and its wickedness. His person bears witness in favor of the *fait accompli* of a human revolution. The Christian convert, therefore, begins at the very end to which Communist aspirations looked forward. What Marx saw only at the end of an historical process, he already possesses: the *person.* And then he proceeds to attack the world.

But a Communist convert is not attached to an actual Presence. He places a bet whose object is not attainable today. He directs

14 Luke 17:20–21.

his action toward something that has not yet been achieved, since history has never known a true realization of communism. Of the two, it is then the Marxist who is utopian and the Christian who is realistic (I mean, of course, the genuine Christian).

The Marxist replies, "I don't depend on a faith in the invisible, but upon concrete facts that we must alter. Each reform achieved, each claim realized, brings me a little closer to my goal." But the final goal of communism is the liberation of man. And *I* have shown man liberated, while the Communist only shows me some preliminary conditions for an endlessly deferred liberation.

I will point out yet another difference no less radical and urgent. The Christian convert already possesses the essential; because of this, he sees himself constantly constrained to change everything about him that is opposed to his good. If he is Christian, he knows he is part of a body that bears all the marks of sin. As a result, in the name of his faith, he faces the world from the position of a permanent revolutionary. Not only does he see himself called upon to come to his neighbor's help, but he cannot be satisfied by his efforts if he compares that relatively improved condition to the perfect gift he has received in Christ. Within himself he possesses the capacity for a perpetual transformation, necessary in every single area where it may be developed.[15] The Marxist, on the other hand, who certainly feels anger at the spectacle of current injustice, since he thinks only man's interests are involved and conceives of man's entire being as socially

15 Here I am talking about what being consistently Christian would involve. Obviously, most of us fall far short of our vocation. A good many of our betrayals result from the fact that we do not agree to submit everything to God's will. We brush aside certain activities, in which the Marxists have become specialists because of our abstention: politics, business, our material interests and those of others. Here is a typical example: Sir John Browning, author of one of the most devout English hymns, is the same man who compelled China to open her ports to the opium trade, under the threat of bombardment. Such a fact seems to justify much of Marxist criticism. Actually, it merely condemns the man, not the faith whose demands he ignored.

directed, will see himself fatally neutralized in the gradual gains he achieves. Present social interests are balanced against the desire to go on to the ultimate achievement, since this fulfillment is never anything more than a theoretical future—however intense the individual Marxist's expectations—and not a demanding and thoroughly animating presence.

This is the real reason for the so-called reformist or totalitarian deviation of the materialist revolution. If this is not to be the constant fate of the revolutionary upheavals that stir humanity (as in 1789 and 1917), man must be delivered from his sin, he must be "converted" and pulled out of the very level at which Marxism keeps him.

Christian and Marxist Means of Action

Preparing a kingdom of man, or testifying through visible acts on behalf of the return of a kingdom already realized in Christ, both take for granted a will to change everything that can be changed. They also take for granted certain means of action that may not be the same in both cases, if the end alone justifies the means.[16]

The end, or *telos*, of Christian action is the kingdom of justice and love. Every act which could contradict, in the present, the law of justice and love, even if committed in the interests of the Church, would destroy the Church to the extent that it lives in each of its members and not in an abstract heaven.

For the pledge of Christian action is not future, but eternal— and therefore present. If, in order to safeguard the future of the Church, I am disobedient in the present, I lose everything at once: present, future, and all eternity. I crucify Christ and set

---

[16] I am not using this expression in what is commonly called its Jesuitical meaning, but rather to emphasize that the end also should indicate the right means to prepare for it. This would not justify means in themselves contrary to justice or to the essence of the end desired.

myself against his return. Christianity can make no use of opportunism; the means employed by a Christian must be as pure as his end.

It is just the opposite with the Marxist. Having no accomplished model behind him, nor sovereign Presence within, he feels free to use any means possible to achieve a momentary gain for his party and his class. Whoever is the current master in the Kremlin feels he can justify his negations of Marx's goals as good "dialectical" doctrine. Totalitarian statism is defended by the argument that it is the only means of achieving an economic structure favorable to the development of socialism. Many Marxists are indignant with this, but I question their consistency and wonder whether the indignation interprets the true will of Marxism, rather than a residue of liberal humanism. Tension between Communist nations does not alter the fact that the vast majority of Communists follow the party line. It is obvious, then, that for the great majority of Communists, lies, hatred, oppression, the supreme hypocrisy of *raison d'état,* and even war if necessary, are perfectly acceptable means to the degree that they serve the progress of the proletariat and prepare for a future in conformity with doctrine. What does a personal and actual "fault" mean to them, since there is neither present nor eternal salvation, and since salvation is not *for them* in any case, but for the descendants of their descendants?

Let us imagine that a good Christian thinks it proper to join the Communist Party or agitate in its favor. He will find himself trapped. If he accepts the disciplines of action imposed upon him by the party, which include hatred and lying, he saves the world but loses his personal reason for existence and denies the faith he thought he could serve better in communism. If he tries to act only as a Christian, he becomes an enemy, a Trotskyite, or a saboteur.

All this is based on a single fact, which can be expressed rather simply: the final goal of a Christian is either present in every one of his actions, or absent; but the final goal of a Marxist is in a future absolutely irrelevant to the actions he can perform today in a nonsocialist order. Hence we see that, in spite of language, the transcendence of Christian faith is apparent here and now, and engages the whole of man; while the immanence of Marxist belief endlessly refers the whole human fact to an indefinite future and absorbs only certain human tendencies—precisely those that the classless society of the socialist future must suppress! The Marxist believes that good comes out of evil; the Christian believes that good is born of perfection.

On the Political Consequences of Faith

I now want to speak to professed Christians. Many Christians seem to think that only man's transformation is important, since it is truly essential and the goal of all other changes. Others believe personal sacrifice and charity for the sake of one's neighbor are the fulfillment, so to speak, of specifically religious activity. I well understand that the sacrifices made are not simply "spiritual," but often involve financial risks and sometimes the surrender of earthly goods and cherished interests. But I ask these "changed" Christians if they are sufficiently concerned about the social and political consequences that their attitude implies. Why do they refuse to take any part in politics? How is it that in practice so many of them are completely disinterested? They may want to say, "You can't do everything. When more men are converted many problems will be posed differently. . . ." I want to believe them, but cannot help realizing that the Marxist offers this same excuse to justify a completely opposite course of action.

The Marxist materialistic deviation must not lead us only to simple theoretical denunciations; it must be a warning to us to be relentless in correcting the false spirituality that threatens our Christian life and is the undoubted reason for the success of

Marxism. As long as Christians do not understand that their faith must manifest itself in every action of their lives, including politics, they will not be able to answer the Marxist challenge, which to that extent will be justified.

I do not believe in a Christian politics, deduced once and for all from theology. But I believe that as soon as Christianity truly shows itself, it enters into conflict with certain political structures and contributes, by its most intimate action, to the creation of new forms. It is important to know which forms, and to prepare for them consciously. Otherwise we yield the field to all kinds of desperate enterprises that arouse the unbelieving masses. It becomes, so far as I can see, a question of solidarity, which is a kind of charity. Occasionally, Christian duty can also appear more historically defined and localized. Let us look at a contemporary example of this.

Everybody by now has been forced to see something of what the totalitarian threat represents: the offering of everything in our lives, both spiritual and material, to the deified state, a situation which recalls the Roman Empire at the beginning of the Christian era, as we have already noticed. However, at least one of the factors is different: Christians no longer congregate in hidden groups. They have established churches which are visible (sometimes even too visible) and organized (sometimes too well organized). Rightly or wrongly, we speak of Christian states, Christian nations, Christian civilization. All of this is challenged by the demands of totalitarianism, as the spectacle of Nazi Germany demonstrated. The new state wants to be worshiped, and if not in specifically religious terms, at least in forms that are hostile to the Ten Commandments and the duty of Christian love. The conflict is inevitable.

Is it enough to allow one's self to be persecuted? Is there nothing to be done except submit to martyrdom? Or must we become conscientious objectors as regards the state? Have we only ourselves to save, when our past errors have had a part, perhaps the key part, in the coming universal misfortune? Any passive wait-ing, however courageous, becomes complicity in the present situ-ation. A totalitarian state could not establish itself against general public opinion, which only follows those who put forward con-structive ideas. But what constructive point of view can the Christian propose if he does not want to remain the kind of con-scientious objector I have described?

A Protestant, more precisely a Calvinist, should be capable of answering such a question. Of all the Christian churches, the Calvinist Church is in fact the most antitotalitarian. I shall only briefly refer to the persecutions in France conducted by the dragoons, and the wars of religion that preceded them. It is obvious that this was a war between an already "totalitarian" crown and groups which, though loyalist, refused at a certain point to conform. It would be going too far, perhaps, to argue from a situation determined by brutal persecution that Calvin-ists were acting on principle in support of a federalist regime. But if we go back a little further to the reign of Francis I, that is, to a time when totalitarianism had not yet become so rooted as under Louis XIV, we perceive that the first discipline the Calvin-ist churches laid down was clothed in a consciously federalist form. This is not just an accident of history. The very basis of Calvinist doctrine is expressed in this way. The importance Cal-vin attached to the idea of personal vocation is enough to ex-plain this process.

A charismatic ethics finds its necessary counterpart in a feder-alist organization of the Church and even of the state. Despite what the textbooks say, Calvin did not establish a theocracy, but a federalist society, respecting God-given diversity within spiritual unity. The consequences of this creation are visible today: nowhere has the totalitarian spirit found less assistance and more open resistance than in Calvinist countries where the notion of group autonomy remains alive (England, Scotland, Switzerland, Holland). In Nazi Germany the struggle of the churches against the moral domination of the state was led, as everyone knows, by Karl Barth, a Calvinist.

It would be easy, but wrong, to minimize this fact by opposing it to the unitary and imperial spirit that animates the Church of Rome. The great ecumenical concern that we see arising in all churches is a promise in which we must believe with the full force of our faith. I would like to draw simply one conclusion, which should be valid for all Christians, no matter what church they may belong to. We have all received a strictly personal call from God, a charism, for which we are responsible. Consequently, we cannot approve of any form of government which by definition opposes every diversity and all spiritual autonomy in the midst of the community. Our whole personal being is at stake, as well as everything of value in the community for all the men who compose it. If for no other reason than this—and I have already given others—a Christian cannot approve of the political form of communism.[17] The Christian must, therefore, prepare another form of government, and finally take a positive position in the immense battle between state absolutism and free federalism.

Christian Responsibility and Marxism

We are all familiar with the "anti-Marxist crusade" that has been organized throughout the world because of capitalist panic. The real motto of that crusade is "Profits come first!" but it is very skillful in using the spiritual as a mask. In this way it enlists many fine people in the service of a cause which is presented as a gilt-edged security. In fact, this is a crusade of hypocritical materialism against generous materialism, a war of religion— like that between Fascism and Stalinism—which is not ours. I oppose such an undertaking for the same reasons that made me

---

[17] "Soviet Russia is the only completely totalitarian state," said Victor Serge, a Communist opposition writer, when he returned from exile in Siberia.

oppose communism—and even more strongly. We are asked to choose between two kinds of materialism, but communism at least wanted to change the world. . . .

Against the demagoguery of our modern crusaders, I repeat the statements of Berdyaev and Gide that the "truth" of communism comes from the betrayal of Christianity by Christendom. All the valuable and generous aspirations of Marxism are so many attempts to salvage Christian truths which have gone astray or been distorted or "hidden under a bushel" by Christians. This is even true of its totalitarian aspirations, which are monstrous in their contemporary form, but which obscurely interpret the aspiration of the once-Christian West for an economy that has been saved: the kingdom in which God is "all in each." If the Christian churches have suffered in our time—and may yet again—at the hands of a tyrannical state, they should realize that they themselves are responsible for this, to the extent that they formerly succumbed to theocratic and secularist temptations. If our culture and civil liberties are persecuted as the result of "materialist" doctrines, we should know that we ourselves are to blame, because we have cultivated a spirit that was detached from reality, a detached and unfruitful liberty.

The whole trouble comes from our spirit. It must do penance, for it should have given testimony of its salutary primacy. And a fresh start must be made.

The tragedy of Marx and Marxism is that they did not know how, or were not able, to distinguish between the truth of the spiritual and its caricatures.

We do not have to rebel against Marx's orphaned truth, cut off from the living bonds that linked it to God in its purpose and origin. But we must proclaim the perfect truth from which we ourselves were the first to stray. "Woe unto me if I do not spread the gospel," the apostle said. Woe to me if I refuse to realize the gospel in every sphere of life. The only effective struggle against materialism is the struggle we must wage against our constant temptation to spiritual fakery.

11 The Hungry Whale

Why is the need to seek so vital in the Western world?

As far as seeking in general goes, the answer seems easy. The seeker is not content with what he already has. Such an answer applies only to the man who is occasionally looking for something: the moment the right job is found, a job-hunter will stop thumbing through the want ads. The quest I would like to talk about is really quite different. It is a passion, which means it can be satisfied by no concrete or circumscribed conclusion. Characteristically, such a search is endless, tireless, and always eagerly pursued. Whatever nourishment it finds, it is not satisfied—its appetite merely increases. It is clear, therefore, that at the heart of the quest there is no crude animal instinct but a spiritual passion. I could not define it better than by relating a legend taken from mystic, orthodox Russia of the old days. It is the legend of the Great Whale.[*]

Once there was a great whale that was captured alive by the people of a small village. The whale was hungry, so the villagers brought her all the food they could find. Soon she ate everything up, but she was still hungry. Since they had nothing more to give her, they carried her to a neighboring village that had an even greater supply of food. There, in the public square, she was fed enormous quantities of food, all of which she devoured. But

[*] I owe this story to the great Russian writer in exile, Alexis Remizof.

134

she was still hungry, even more so than before. The people wanted to keep their whale, for they loved her very much; but they hardly knew how to satisfy her. Finally, they asked, "What do you want from us?"

"I'm hungry."

"But we've given you all the food we have."

"Even when you have given me a hundred and a thousand times more food, I shall still be hungry."

"Then what do you really want?"

"I want God."

This legend reveals the ultimate goal of all human seeking. The whale wanted the absolute, the Whole, the final and definitive reply. She wanted something that goes beyond any partial response, precise and useful; beyond anything that could be had or known, even beyond our fundamental agonies before life, the world, and the unknown. That is why her hunger was insatiable.

Only the greatest mystics go straight to their goal, by-passing all the stages of man's quest. Some of the greatest scientists—a Newton, an Einstein—are goaded on by their mathematical intelligence alone, not by their entire being. The rest of mankind, on the other hand, halt on the road, still more or less far away, whether they seek security, wealth, power, or, looking higher, pure knowledge or beauty. Most of them, however, would hardly be able to say exactly what they are looking for, which is never simply this or that, but rather a mixture, whether conscious or unconscious, of the goals just mentioned. Unlike animals, what men all have in common is the profound need to transcend their present condition, with its inherent and social limitations. But the distant horizon of all human seeking, from the mystical to the technological, remains the same, no matter what name it is given.

I have attempted to define the ultimate meaning of man's search in general terms. Now I would like to take up the particular problem of the Western quest.

European civilization has dominated the world for centuries. In our time it is still the civilization imitated everywhere, even by those who are fighting it; therefore it is still the strongest. Moreover, comparing it with other civilizations, past, present, or those now in development, we perceive that ours is distinguished by two great traits, generally held to be causes of weakness: *uncertainty* or *unrest*, and *permanent disorder*.

The ancient Chinese and Egyptians, the Sumerians and the Romans, the Aztecs and the Mayans, all created stable orders. Their priests and princes had solved their basic problems. Today Soviet Russia offers (or imposes on) its citizens more security and fewer problems than our free democracies do. (This is the secret of the temporary success of totalitarian regimes: they offer and impose overwhelming certainties.) But we in the West—although more in Europe than in America—suffer from general unrest; we never stop speaking of the disorder of our time. We feel as if we were living in continual chaos, in a jungle of moral contradictions, both intellectual and practical. Just where does this fundamental anxiety come from? And what is the ultimate reason for our permanent disorder, which has been deplored by our greatest minds for centuries?

I think that this unrest and disorder are not accidental. I think they stretch back to the very source of our civilization, that they are inseparable from it. I associate them with our greatest traditions: Christianity and the scientific spirit. Our unrest springs from our faith, and our uncertainties are created by the very nature of our certainties.

This paradox can be easily explained. Let us take the Christian as an example. The Scriptures tell him that there is not a single just man; moreover, that a just man would have to be a saint. The Christian knows that sin consists in being divorced from the living Truth, and that all men are sinners. He is seeking to draw closer to truth and holiness. In his unending effort he is sustained only by his faith in grace. He is, then, always restless but aware of the reasons for his unrest. He knows that it is normal and not hopeless, because it is inspired by his faith—that is, by his certainty in God.

Let us now consider the scientist. He has read scientific history, and from it he has learned that all truths established by successive schools of thought are relative and provisional. They have been superseded, one after another. And yet the very reason for the existence of science is to hold on to established truths. Here again, in the endless effort to reach a fleeting goal, the scientist is sustained by his confidence in reason and corroborating experience. The same scrutiny that questions all previously acquired fact is, on the other hand, an assurance of progress toward the truth. Hence science advances from disorder to a certain order, then toward a new disorder, then toward a new and larger order.

This perpetual anxiety, which is determined by the two principal forces that have produced our civilization, is precisely what best defines Western culture. This is how the West distinguishes itself from ancient and Asiatic civilizations, which are examples of totalitarianism. Against the idea of a sacred and intangible truth governing every detail of life, a total and definitive order decreed by a king-priest or a dictator, the West offers the idea and the practice of continually questioning everything, of endless dissatisfaction, of an unrest which creates disorder and revolution, certainly, but also freedom.

Uncertainty and dissatisfaction, contradiction, disorder, and chaos: so many causes for weakness and ruin, it would seem. Nevertheless, it is all these things that have made Europe possible. And Europe has dominated the world, not in spite of these qualities, but because of them.

It was insatiable curiosity that led Renaissance navigators to discover the other peoples of the earth, to convert and conquer them—whereas we Europeans have never been discovered by anyone. This passion to verify man's power over nature was also at the origin of all the physiological, physical, and mechanical experiments in the Renaissance. Beginning with those courageous pioneers, the development of chemistry, physics, and mathematics has moved forward rapidly in the nineteenth and twentieth centuries.

Considered as a whole, where is technology leading us? Already we can foresee that, by the end of this century, the application of solar and nuclear energy will reduce the labor of ordinary workers to several dozen hours a year, with production increasing tenfold. The advancement of technology will, in fact, lead to the liberation of man. But what will man, emancipated from work, do with all the free time in his life? This is an enormous and utterly new problem. It will make today's economic and social dilemmas outmoded, giving greater importance to the vast questions of education, culture, and, in the long run, religion. Hence each new success of the Western quest creates new uncertainties, calling for new progress—and, indeed, new research.

I have indicated that the genius of searching and investigation is also the genius of the West. Let me say, too, that the very survival of our Greco-Roman-Judaic civilization depends upon the genius of pure research.

In point of fact, it is technology and its constant progress that have allowed the West to dominate the earth. We can maintain our position only by means of technological progress, in the face of the burgeoning concurrence of new empires, all of which have adopted and developed our techniques and methods. But technological progress depends upon pure research. And pure research in its turn depends upon the whole cultural and spiritual harmony of our civilization.

Nothing could be more false or more dangerous for us than to encourage an absolute divorce between culture and technology. I have just shown how technology enters the stream of popular culture. But let us not forget that pure culture, pure research, is the real origin of technological progress.

Here is a perfect example. Four or five years ago I was looking for some money for a cultural project. I went to see a manufacturer of large turbine engines. He listened to me, at first inattentive, then impatient. Finally, he said that the way things are today, turbines are important, but culture is only a luxury. The first thing to do, he went on, is to fight communism, which he confused with social reform. I left him empty-handed, saying to myself, "This man gets his power from turbines, but he certainly didn't invent them. Who did?" I opened an encyclopedia and found that the turbine engine was invented by a great eighteenth-century mathematician named Leonhard Euler. Born in Basel, Euler grew up in a studious and religious atmosphere. Influenced by pietism, he felt abstract science ought not to prevent his being useful to mankind. Thus, long ago, he designed plans for a new machine, which he christened the turbine.

Hence it is thanks to Euler's genius, which was immersed in the cultural environment of Basel and influenced by pietism, that thousands of workers and engineers earn their living today, great liners cross the oceans, and enormous wealth is amassed.

12 The Ecumenical Movement and Federalism

The ecumenical movement will become effective in the eyes of the nations only when it is capable of answering with force and authority the political questions of our time. The fact that it has at least a presentiment of this mission was shown by the Geneva Memorandum, virtually an "encyclical letter" which it improvised on the eve of the last world war.[18] Even the more recent declarations—at Lund, Evanston, and New Delhi—suggest that the ecumenical movement is still far from having a dynamic vision of immediate action. They suffer above all from a lack of *ton*, which reveals the absence of any internal necessity. They express the agreement of a certain number of persons of good will, not the impulse of one precise and militant will. They were a respectable result, not a starting point. They probably have an historical value. But like many documents which eventually acquire historical value, they will have passed unnoticed in their time.

This lack of effectiveness on the part of ecumenical messages on the political level arises, no doubt, from the fact that they are

[18] *The Churches and the International Crisis* (New York: Federal Council of Churches of Christ, 1939). See Bishop I. L. Holt, "The Church's Effort on the Brink of War," *Christendom*, Winter, 1940.

compromises, minimum agreements, not easily obtained and perforce too general. Futhermore, the error committed so far has been an attempt to choose a prudent political attitude, more or less opportune on the one hand, more or less acceptable on the other. It was probably not possible to do more at the moment. Actually the world situation was examined and an attempt made to ameliorate it according to the incontestable principles of Christian and natural ethics. But moral reformism has never been able to influence the course of events. History is made up of initiatives, not of revisions, resolutions, and amendments. To succeed, an initiative must represent risk as well as prudence. It must be carried away by a passion springing from creative faith. The men who have made history are those who had an impassioned vision of their goal and who knew how to turn circumstances to their purpose. In a certain sense it might be said that they found their starting point in themselves, in their faith, or in their most profound ambition, and not in the data and aspirations more or less expressed or assumed in their age. Their action was effectual to the exact degree that it was the direct expression of their being.

If the ecumenical movement wants to act—and it must—it will first have to recognize this fundamental law of action. In other words, its political action must emanate from itself, from what it has, from what it is, and from its constitutive faith. It does not have to borrow here and there in order to compose a mosaic of desirable resolutions; on the contrary, it must affirm itself according to its being and its law. Its political position must necessarily express its very nature, that is to say, the essence of the ecumenical hope. Its declarations must *translate in terms of practical organization the principles which are implied in the definition of ecumenicity.*

To summarize, it is not a matter of adopting an accidentally or indirectly "Christian" policy. It is rather a question of *developing* logically the policy implied from the beginning in the ecumenical

will and hope. The following pages will be only a working outline
of this development.

Certain permanent conflicts of history have taken a character
of unprecedented violence in our time. Above the infinite com-
plexities of our economic, social, political, and religious difficulties, they stand out the more clearly because they have attained
an almost deadly point of tension: political and economic conflict
between the totalitarian state and the rights of men; moral conflict between the oppression of collectivism and the anarchy of
individualism; ideological and religious conflict between an imposed unity and a thoughtless division, between a rigid centralization and an endless scattering. It is to be noted at once that
these various conflicts are in reality aspects of one and same
fundamental opposition, viewed from different standpoints. It is
next to be noted that each of these opposed terms is equally false
in itself; that is to say, at the same time excessive and incomplete.
It follows that, on this level, no solution is possible. They are
irreconcilable because the combination of two errors cannot
make a truth—it makes only two graver errors. The practical result of political and economic conflict is war and revolution. The
result of moral conflict is tyranny and anarchy. The result of religious conflict is narrower orthodoxies and more schisms.

In order to resolve the opposition between unity and division,
it would be useless to seek an intermediary solution. One must
change levels and find the *central* attitude from which these two
errors are only morbid deviations. Between the plague and
cholera neither a "happy medium" nor a synthesis is possible.
One must return to health. And, first of all, one must know what
health is.

Political and economic health I shall identify with federalism;
moral and civic health with personalism; religious health with
ecumenicity. I shall define these three terms with emphasis on
their fundamental relationship and on their necessary hierarchy.

For me, the theology of ecumenicity implies a philosophy of the person, the application of which is the policy of federalism.

Theology of the Ecumenical Movement

Let us first clear up a misunderstanding which the title might suggest. I do not mean by "ecumenical theology" a utopian synthesis of existing theologies, or a new doctrine which would risk not being compatible with any of the existing theologies. What is needed is a doctrine concerning the universal Church, such as is implied in the very fact that an ecumenical effort exists. We presuppose this doctrine whenever we say, "I believe in the Holy Catholic Church," I shall emphasize here only a few of its important features.

The principle is this: the theology of ecumenicity depends upon the *faith of the union of Christians in Christ,* this faith being distinguished negatively by the rejection of the heresy of uniformity.

Certainly there is no worse threat for the ecumenical movement than the utopian temptation of a formal unity, humanly verifiable, assured, and definitive. For it is precisely the desire to achieve such a Utopia which has produced the schisms and oppositions that the ecumenical movement proposes to surmount. In the exact degree to which the churches have attempted to transform their faith in the *Una Sancta* into a visible assurance, a restrictive unity of organization and of doctrine—in this exact degree they have doubted their inherent and humanly uncontrollable union and have lost their real communion. We might recall the story of the tower of Babel: the desire to build a visible monument to the glory of man's unity led to the division of language.

It is fitting to leave to the theologians the task of defining the positive doctrine of union in the name of which the heresy of uniformity must be condemned. The doctrine of the multiplicity

of gifts bestowed by the one and same Father; the doctrine of
the plurality of mansions in one and same heaven; the doctrine
of the diversity among members of one and same body: whatever the name given to it, in no case will it be lacking in indisputable biblical foundations. (For my part, I see no better biblical foundations than the First Epistle to the Corinthians. It is
precisely in his appeal for union that Paul establishes with greatest force the legitimacy of diversities. This seems to be an excellent method.) Is it also permitted to recall the precedent of
the *seven* churches of Asia, each one possessing its own angel; or
the verse, "that they may all be one; even as thou, Father, art in
me, and I in thee," which establishes the pattern for union in the
distinction of the divine Persons? Let us ask the doctors of the
Church. Yet here is what we should affirm from now on: the
theology of ecumenicity implies that *the diversity of divine call-
ings is not an imperfection in union, but its very life.*

A second, complementary feature must at least be recalled
here: the theology of ecumenicity does not aim at dismantling the
existing orthodoxies in the various churches. On the contrary,
its first effect is to strengthen them by making them more conscious of their real value, and precisely by this detour it hopes to
attain a profounder communion of spirit. In other words, the call
to union is not addressed to the virtual dissidents of each church,
but rather to its faithful members.

Nevertheless, this method is only compatible with the orthodoxies which I shall call *open orthodoxies.* It cannot embrace an
orthodoxy which would consciously yield to the temptation to
uniformity; that is to say, which would tend to isolate itself and
no longer admit direct recourse to the Head of the Church, who
is in heaven and sitteth on the right hand of God, and not on
earth, in a certain city, or in writings, or in a local prophet. Certainly no church or sect has ever been able to close itself totally
and to bar the door against the inspiration of the Holy Spirit.
No church or sect has ever denied that its real Head is in heaven,

though more than one has acted as if he were on earth, that is to say, at their disposal. More than one has identified the *Una Sancta* with its organization or with its particular doctrine. To the transcendent principle of unity which assures the permanence of the universal Church, many churches or sects have added, and actually substituted little by little, an immanent principle of unity, namely, a principle humanly controllable. That is the very formula of tyranny, for, against an immanent principle of unity made absolute, there is no possible recourse or appeal on the part of the church member who feels himself unsatisfied. This man must submit or leave. If he submits, he runs the risk of obeying men rather than God. If he leaves, it is with bitterness, and the church which he perhaps founds will be opposed to the former one instead of being merely different.

I have nothing to say here about the unity of Roman Catholic organization, considered as necessary for salvation; but I shall recall the criticism which Karl Barth made of Protestant ortho-doxy of the eighteenth century: a certain manner of proclaiming the dogma of literal inspiration of the Scriptures, for example, is tantamount, he said, to disposing humanly of the Scriptures. For as soon as the principle of unity appears humanly verifiable, the orthodoxy of the Church "closes" upon itself. From this circum-stance came the numerous schisms of the Calvinistic churches during that period.

A church which pretends to be self-sufficient and to *possess* its own principle of unity, a church which tends to close itself from above in order the better to assure its human cohesion, at once becomes isolated and generates schisms. Its attitude is thus doubly anti-ecumenical. Its will for uniformity opposes union. It trans-forms diversity into division. Then there is scandal, and then the body suffers both in its Head and in its members.

The normal life of the body depends upon the vitality of each of its members, and the life of a member depends upon its har-mony with the other members, assured by the fact that it belongs to the same head. We shall find below and repeatedly this theme of organic harmony opposed to the theme of systematic unity.

It is to be noted that this in no way entails praise of mere liberal "tolerance" based upon dogmatic indifference; for harmony of members is not tolerance but a vital necessity. The lung does not have to "tolerate" the heart. It must be a true lung, and by this very fact it will help the heart to be a good heart.

It is also to be noted that churches which do not represent a distinct spiritual function, but only the accidental division of the same organ—that is, churches of the same family and within one country which formerly employed different languages but now both use the national tongue, or were divided by issues which have now passed away—have nothing better before them than to fuse as soon as possible.

A Philosophy of the Person

The ecumenical positions I have just outlined imply a doctrine of man. To the conflict that opposes unity and division in the plan of the Church, there corresponds, term by term, the conflict that opposes collectivity and the individual in the plan of society. And in the same way in which ecumenicity returns to the central spiritual position that founds union upon diversity, we must look for the central philosophical position that founds human fellowship upon freedom. I call this personalism.

Let us try to illustrate by historical examples notions of the individual, of collectivity, and of person.

The *individual* is a Greek invention, and his birth marks the birth of Hellenism itself. He is the man of the tribe who begins to think for himself and who, by this very fact, distinguishes and isolates himself. To reason is first to doubt, and next it is to revolt against the taboos and sacred conventions of the group. Then the group expels the "nonconformist." It is the men ejected from various groups who founded the first Greek *thiasoi*, communities comparable to the modern city and based no longer on the *sacre*, blood, and the dead, but on contracts and common interests. All the members of the tribe had to act in the same manner minutely prescribed by custom, and all dissidence of conduct entailed execration or death. In the city, on the contrary, each man tried to singularize himself. Competition, originality, private rights, self-consciousness, replaced the respect of taboos and of strict observance of the collective *sacre*.

But this centrifugal movement in relation to the original community, while at first identified with intelligence and reason, soon results in a dissolution of the social bond. It leads to anarchy. Now follows a feeling of social emptiness. It is a sort of dull anguish out of which emerges the call to a new and more solid community in which the isolated individual will again find reassuring restraints and in which the state will recover its power.

It is Rome, then, that serves as the eternal symbol of *collective* reaction. The triumph of Rome over Greece is the first fatal totalitarian victory over an individualism which has become anarchic. Between individualism and dictatorship the opposition is not so great as one would imagine. It is rather a question of the inevitable succession of events. The individual opposes the state only in the same manner as emptiness opposes fullness: the greater the emptiness, the more powerful the appeal. In many respects, indeed, totalitarianism does no more than complete the process of dissolution begun by individualism; it liquidates existing groups in order to accomplish unification by a *mise au pas*. It is with the sand of individuals that the state makes its cement. But this centralized state, this rigid and too highly controlled unity, soon crushes all individual initiative by refusing recourse to a power beyond its own. It deprives itself of any creative inspiration. Man becomes no more than a social function, a *politischer Soldat*, as one would say today. And the spirit is jeopardized for lack of liberty.

Individualistic Greece triumphed over the barbarian com-

munity of blood relationship. Later, however, she sank into anarchy. Rome triumphed over the anarchy and then sank under
the weight of her collectivistic apparatus. Again the social emptiness occurred. What was the new society to be?

At this crucial point in history, in a situation which recalls
strangely the present struggle between individualistic democracies and totalitarian states, the unique event of the Incarnation
took place; and it brought to the question of the ages the eternal
answer of the Church.

From the sociological viewpoint we take here, what is this
primitive Church? A spiritual community formed of local communities, or "cells," which are not based upon the past nor upon
common origins. "There can be neither Jew nor Greek." These
communities are founded on neither class nor race, nor on any
other collective reality. Their bond is not terrestrial nor is their
Head; he is seated in heaven on the right hand of God. Neither is
their ambition terrestrial. They await the end of time. And mean-
while they constitute most assuredly the germs of an authentic
society. They have their social organization, local heads, hierarchy, assemblies. The convert, assimilated by one of these
groups, finds in it, on the one hand, a social activity which
binds him to his "brothers" and saves him from solitude; on the
other hand, he attains a new human dignity, since he has been
redeemed and has received the promise of his individual resurrection. He is at once bondman and free, and he is this by virtue
of one and the same fact: the calling he has received of God.

This reborn man is not an individual of the Greek type, since
he is more eager to serve than to singularize himself. He is not a
mere piece of machinery either, a mere function of the state as
the Roman citizen was, since he possesses a dignity independent
of his social role. What name is to be given him? A new word is
needed. Or rather, an already familiar word may be used with a
new meaning.

In order to designate the relations constituting the Trinity, the

Greek Fathers had adopted a Latin term, *persona* (social role). This same term was to be used by the early Christian philosophers to mean the reality of man in a Christianized world. For this man is at once autonomous and responsible to others. Thus the word *person,* with its new meaning and the social reality it signifies, is certainly a Christian creation, or rather a creation of the Christian Church.

In the *person* thus defined, the eternal conflict between freedom and collective responsibility is resolved. It is the same God, who, by the calling which he addresses to man, distinguishes this person among all others and restores him to concrete relations with his fellow men. Freedom is assured by the constant possibility of recourse to God, above and beyond the community. And the community is bound together by its fidelity to God. Thus the rights and duties of the individual have the same foundation as the rights and duties of the whole. They are no longer contradictory. That which liberates a man also makes him responsible to others. That which unites the community also obliges it to respect individual vocations.

The freedom of the present century advertises itself by the utopian slogan: To every man his chance. But the freedom and obligation of the Christian person are defined at the same time by the formula: To every man his vocation.

We have found again in this doctrine of man the same structures as in the doctrine of the universal Church previously outlined; the same central position defining at once union and diversity, obligation and freedom, the rights of all and the rights of the individual. In the same way as the theology of ecumenicity prevents, on the one hand, a closed orthodoxy and, on the other, obstinate dissidence, so the philosophy of the person prevents, on the one hand, oppressive collectivism and, on the other, individualistic anarchy.

Yet here again we must insist on this point: *person* is not a middle term between the too-free individual and the too-much-en-

slaved *politischer Soldat.* The person is complete, and the other
two are only diseases. At the immanent human level, no balance
is possible between anarchy and forced unity, the individual and
the totalitarian state. But as soon as transcendence intervenes,
there is something better than balance—there is a living principle
of union. "Where the spirit of the Lord is, there is liberty," but
there also is the true communion.

It remains now to develop the political implications of this
theology and this philosophy.

Federalism as a Policy

I have said enough to make it easy to see that only federalist
organization in politics can correspond to the ecumenical attitude. As for the philosophy of the person, it will be normally that
of the good citizen of a federation. The paradoxical motto of
Swiss federalism, "One for all, and all for one," is equally ap-
plicable to these three levels.

Ecumenicity excludes closed orthodoxy (creator of schisms)
and obstinate dissidence. Similarly, federalism excludes imperialism (instigator of wars) and shortsighted, selfish regionalism.
(Let it be further remarked that imperialism is nothing other
than the individualism of a group, and individualism is the imperialism of an isolated man. As the state ceases to be a real
state when it wants to become absolute sovereign, so man ceases
to be complete when he makes his freedom absolute.)

Federalism begins with local groups (region, community,
public projects, and so forth), and ecumenicity equally recognizes
their value (various churches, parishes, orders, and so on). It is
indeed in the local group that the person can realize himself. For
in it civic tasks are presented on the scale of the individual, and
actual enrollment in the community becomes possible. In the
small congregation people know each other and what men and
problems they must deal with. If one is in opposition to the group,

he is free to voice his opinion. If that is not sufficient, he may change to another group. He is not isolated as an individual is isolated in a large modern city or in a vast centralized state. On the other hand, one is no longer tyrannized by a rigid, uniform law, since in a federation one may always belong to different groups—one religious, another social, and a third cultural or political or professional. This plurality of memberships, whose equivalent would be ecclesiastical ecumenicism, is excluded by the totalitarian regime, which claims to make the frontiers of the state coincide with those of all social or spiritual or private activities.

Federalism, like ecumenicity, recognizes that regional diversities are the life itself of the union. However, by the central organ which links all the regions, it preserves for the citizen the right to appeal against abuses of local power. It asks for the organic cooperation of its members and not that caricature of order which is unity in uniformity. Instead of petrifying the frontiers of the groups that make up the federation, it tends to enliven their nucleus. Thus, for the static balance of powers it substitutes the emulation of living values. Spinoza defines peace as "the harmony of strong souls, not the spineless impotence of slaves." We might define ecumenicity and federalism by the same formula, substituting for souls "churches" and "regions."

Our object so far has been to establish the following relations: ecumenicity, personalism, and federalism are different aspects of a one and same spiritual attitude. They spring from one another and are interdependent. They have the same structures and the same ambitions. To the notion of rigid unity they unitedly oppose one of communion; to the Empire, the Commonwealth; to uniform and geometric order, pluralistic and organic collaboration; to the pair of *frères ennemis* which the uprooted individual and the totalitarian masses constitute, the pair of *frères amis* which the person and the federal community constitute.

To desire federalism without accepting ecumenicity would be

depriving political organization of its spiritual foundations. But to accept ecumenicity without at the same time desiring federalism would be not really to accept ecumenicity with all its consequences. For faith without works is not faith.

Federalism and the Ecumenical Movement

We now find ourselves within the drama of the struggle between East and West. We realize that the present conflict is insoluble in its present terms. If totalitarianism is finally triumphant over the democracies, it will mean not only the death of a culture and an economy, but will at the same time suppress all possibility of ecumenicity and subvert the universal values created by the evangelization of the Occidental conscience. On the other hand, if the capitalistic and individualistic democracies are victorious, this fact alone will solve none of the problems. Besides, everyone feels or suspects that the two terms of this alternative are equally improbable and that a future holocaust would prevent all possibility of a real victory on either side. An objective examination of opposing forces makes us see the world of tomorrow only as a period of increased statism and chaos. I do not say "revolution," because to start a revolution vision and a new doctrine and tactic are needed. But where are they? Who is preparing them?

The only hope and also the only possibility that remains is the federalist organization of the world. This alone can bring something new. This alone can satisfy both the confused aspirations of the nations and the practical necessities of peace. This alone is opposed both to individualistic capitalism and to totalitarianism.

But who, today, can propose this answer?

Even before we ask whether the churches *can* respond, we should understand that they *must*. But are not the two terms— *must* and *can*—fused in the reality of faith? Certainly! If the churches are loyal to their Head, they know that he reigns and creates, for those who believe, the possibility of doing what he requires. In the state of apparent impotence in which the churches find themselves today, this faith alone will be sufficient.

Likewise there are certain reasons which I shall enumerate for believing that the Church can intervene in the present crisis.

1. The history of the Christianized world shows that the ecclesiastical structures have often preceded and predetermined the political structures of a nation.

I shall indicate three groups of examples of this precedence of religious factors. First, has it been noticed that there exists a form of totalitarianism corresponding to Russian orthodoxy, another which corresponded to a German Lutheran majority, and another, to Roman Catholic Italy and Spain; whereas none has developed in Calvinist countries or in the countries influenced by Calvinist elements, even the laicized, as was the case of France during the Third Republic? How can this fact be explained? Without making a detailed study, of which I can give only the main point, I shall say this: in Russia, in Germany, in Italy, and in Spain, the distinction between church and state had never been satisfactorily established. The result was, among the people, a feeling that church and state formed a whole and that both of them constituted *the Power*. If one was overthrown, the other was fatally attacked. And since a revolution always imitates the form of government it overthrows, a Stalin, a Hitler, and to a lesser degree a Mussolini found themselves obliged to adopt for their own use the caesaropapism or theocracy which they had conquered. They claimed at once temporal power and spiritual authority, and thus became totalitarian. On the contrary, in the Calvinist countries the separation between church and state had always been real—even when it was not strictly established by law. Likewise, the duties of personal vocation have always been placed above duties toward any political power. Thus, when faith weakened in these countries, its lack was not revealed by the

outbreak of a totalitarian antireligion, but by a contrary phenomenon of individualistic dispersion.

A second example: England and the Scandinavian countries in
the sixteenth century brought about their reformations within
the traditional Church, without violent rupture (especially in
Sweden). A new content, Calvinistic or Lutheran, was introduced into the old ecclesiastical frames and under their aegis.
Today we are seeing this phenomenon repeat itself in the same
countries—this time in the political and social orders. The traditional frames subsist (monarchy, social hierarchies), but a
socialist content is introduced into them (here again with less of
a shake-up in Scandinavia than in England).

A third example: Calvin always refused to establish uniformity
of government for the various churches which acknowledged his
reform. The *Una Sancta* appears to us on earth, according to its
own terms, in its diversity "of churches and of particular persons." It must be organized in the federation of parishes and of
provinces by synods. This type of ecclesiastical organization was
to find its political equivalent in a federalism which was more or
less marked according to the nations involved: Swiss Confedera-
tion, the United Provinces of the Low Countries, the British
Commonwealth, the United States of America (the form of individualism in this last country being predetermined by the fact
that it was founded by seceders). And it is known that the Protestants of France, in the sixteenth century, looked forward to a
federative organization of the kingdom, while Sully, one of their
leaders, conceived his "Grand Dessein," that is, the plan of a
confederated Europe.

It would be easy to multiply such examples. I indicate them
here only to show: first, that intimate knowledge of the religious
processes in a given country is a key to the political processes
which will be manifested sooner or later; second, that the action
which the ecumenical movement can and must exercise over these
religious processes will prepare the ground for a realistic political

action, taking into account the empirical data and spiritual diversities on the knowledge of which all serious federative effort is necessarily based.

2. The theology of ecumenicity and the philosophy of the person which it implies are the only *conceivable* bases at the present moment for a new order of the world. (The "religion of man" that has been proposed by some is a contradiction in terms, unless it be a formula of totalitarian religion without transcendence, which, precisely, its proponents intend to combat!) On the other hand, the theology of ecumenicity and the philosophy of the person are the only bases now *existing* on which one might build, beginning today. (The "religion of man," or of the superman, is yet to be created, and time presses!) Rich in traditional elements, condensing all the experience of peace that we have, they convey and contain at the same time an incontestable revolutionary dynamism.

3. The organization of the World Council of Churches is in fact *the most truly international organization in formation.* It is well known that the ideological and political *Internationales* have disintegrated in the course of recent decades. (The socialist groups that exist in various countries tend toward divergence and not convergence on the international plane. The English socialists collaborate with the English conservatives, not with the Russian syndicalists, nor even with the American—to give only one example.) Apart from the United Nations, which is inevitably an artificial creation, however necessary its continuance, there are few opportunities outside the ecumenical movement which provide serious and regular contact among the national groups. This simple fact offers to the ecumenical movement an historical possibility without precedent, a heavy human responsibility, and, let us not hesitate to say—a vocation.

4. The liturgical revival, which in all the churches accompanies the ecumenical effort, is going to re-create a *common language,* an ensemble of common spiritual rules. This language-above-

languages answers exactly the legitimate needs of our time. It gives back to us the true formula of the living community, the one which unites men and not the one which melts into a formless mass individuals deprived of their normal consciousness. From the sociological standpoint the liturgical revival, favored by the ecumenical movement, marks the advent of a personalistic attitude beyond the antinomy of "isolated individual vs. militarized mass."

5. The theology of ecumenicity, the philosophy of the person, and a policy of federalism are alone able today to synthesize the deformed and disjointed truths that subsist either in the democracies or in the totalitarian movements. This results, theoretically, from what I have already explained. Only the ecumenical movement is, therefore able to prepare *the reconciliation of present adversaries*. It is not founded upon a compromise between opposing wrongs, but upon a central attitude which surpasses these wrongs at the same time that it realigns the truths scattered in the two camps.

The picture I have just sketched is ambitious. This is intentional; it ought to be ambitious.

The action of the Christian never begins with prudent consideration of the forces he believes he can muster, but with what God wants him to do. It is always an apparent Utopia; in reality it is only an answer. If I start to move, I soon perceive that I was weak because I had been motionless in my prudence, but that the action risked brings me the strength I needed.

From all sides a call is heard. I might name it the federalist nostalgia. Isolated authors have proclaimed it. Intellectual groups have attempted to formulate partial replies. To become a will, the obscure sentiment of the nations awaits only clearer and more convincing answers.

What is lacking for these scattered attempts is a common spiritual background and a precise vision of the necessary bonds uniting this background to the moral and political realities. There is no constructive action without an ideology. Yet there is no valid ideology without a theology, and no theology is efficacious without the support of a real catholicity, of a human community based upon the communion of saints. This community will not be revealed in congresses, but will be manifested in action and risk. In the same manner as we have seen churches born of missions take the lead in the movement toward union, we shall see ecumenicity realized with power only in the test of the world mission which it must now face by taking the initiative in federative action.

13 The End of Pessimism

> *The famous meaning of history, the key argument for the attraction of progressivism, seemed to be headed, once and for all, toward 1984 and its ant heap; now, all of a sudden, it has turned around in horror and is tacking, to the rhythm of the Marseillaise, toward 1848.*
> —André Fontaine in *Le Monde*, the day after the Hungarian Revolution

Fifty years of pessimistic analysis of our society and its destiny culminated a few years ago in George Orwell's *1984*.

As the century began, there was a book by Georges Sorel subversively titled *The Illusion of Progress*. Then Bergson arrived on the scene, demanding the injection of some soul into the mushrooming specter of the technological world. Two world wars, which ruined Europe's prestige and power, and three revolutions, which brought to power totalitarian tyrants who laid claim to both body and soul—let us admit that there was enough to justify the bitter skepticism of the best of us about the idea of progress. To continue to believe in progress was an immediate disqualification of the intelligence, and the idea quickly emigrated to the U.S.A. and the U.S.S.R.

Almost unanimously European thinkers became the opposition and prided themselves on denouncing the modern world in every possible tone of voice. Piously or angrily, objectively or cynically, they spoke to us of nothing but a spiritual crisis, a decline of the West, a betrayal by the intellectuals, a soulless world; of France against the robots, of machines against man, of man against the human, of the end of illusions, of the end of all. Maritain's *Anti-Modern,* and Chaplin's *Modern Times,* pure metaphysics and elementary clichés, powerless denunciations and ignoble justifications of totalitarian dictatorships—everything foretold an unprecedented human catastrophe, a merciless human bondage in the hands of anonymous powers: the machine, the police, and the state. Orwell had only to push it a little further. He had only to use the Soviet Union as his example, extend it to Western Europe, suppress the factors of human resistance, and despair in an exemplary manner, convincing his readers that he would like to be a rebel. European masochism had found its supreme expression. And Kafka was no more than the John the Baptist of a kind of gospel in reverse, "the bad news" of future resignation.

The Poznan riots, the Warsaw resistance, and the revolution in Budapest reversed the course of this vast drift and simultaneously restored hope to the world.

Human nature, denied by Sartre, triumphed in a generation that had learned only lies. Its powers to resist Big Brother, denied by Orwell, burst out on the streets of Budapest. Its faculty for claiming and imposing a positive meaning upon life, denied by Kafka, united writers with peasants, workers with students, in the sudden uprising.

The Western intelligentsia had been watching the approach of '84. And suddenly the East responded with '48, which is '84 backward.

Numbers had never been more symbolic. Let us try to interpret them.

For more than half a century everybody who mattered in European writing, art, and philosophy knew that we must be subversive or pessimistic, or both, at the risk of being considered out of date. It is useless to mention names; all the well-known ones would be there, a complete list of the very best people. You might say, "Valéry won't be there; he's a hedonist committed to order and convinced of the value of convention." But was it not Valéry who unleashed the great flood of European pessimism in 1919, in that famous letter which first reminds us that our civilization is mortal like any other? Does not the end of that letter predict that we are heading for the "perfect and definitive ant heap"? You might protest, "Claudel won't be on the list; he's an optimist in the baroque style and a civil servant of the highest rank." But Claudel's works are more subversive than anything that passes for such in the cafés, and his faith has the appearance of a challenge. If someone mentions St.-John Perse it must be recalled that he has chosen exile itself. All the others are in conflict with the times in an even more obvious fashion, whether they wage fierce attacks against middle-class morality or the rules of art, or oppose the flagrant intellectual anarchy by some restored orthodoxy, which by its very failure also serves to justify the discordant thinking of the modern world.

From 1919 on, the dominant influences on our best creative minds have been Nietzsche, Rimbaud, Kierkegaard, and Dostoevski. It is remarkable that this century has retained only the antisocial heroes of the preceding hundred years, the heroes of individual denial, the rebels against the modern world, those who insist upon questioning all the great commonplaces: democracy, the social state, atheistic morality.

And so everybody who matters in Europe is anti-middle-class, both ethically and spiritually. But in fact nothing matters except the middle class. It is the middle class alone, by means of its most cultivated and aware members, that has contributed to the posthumous success of the great geniuses who were damned, ignored, or rejected by its ancestors. And today it is the middle class that is agonized by those very things that earlier geniuses denounced in vain. It is the middle class that believes in the coming calamity they prophesied in the wilderness, and that has lost its faith in progress. Finally, it is they who yield to the infatuation of history, imagining that their hour has passed, that the proletariat must dispossess them as they once dispossessed the nobles, and that a Soviet regime is inevitable. In spite of himself, Orwell told the truth.

What a curious power the pessimists of one century hold over the descendants of their enemies in the next!

In the nineteenth century the middle class was optimistic, despite the dreadful suffering endured by industrial workers whose efforts made it rich. Today, the factory worker is jealously cared for by the state. In a few years technology will have set him free completely. But it is the middle class that fears the inevitable tyranny of machines. It is the middle class, a hundred years behind the times, that entertains a fatalistic and resigned pessimism. In this century-long lag of consciousness behind the real world, there is born the idea of a powerless thought, a terrifying reality, and a fatalistic sense of history, of which Big Brother will be the inescapable end.

There are two names I have not yet mentioned in this chapter, but which actually dominate the whole scene.

They are Marx and Freud. Their influence upon the ruling classes of the West is much more profound than is recognized. It goes much deeper than popular scraps of information taken from *Das Kapital* or *The Interpretation of Dreams*, or the judgments that have been made upon them.

Marx and Freud have much in common—especially their success among those whom they "unmasked" with a bitter and almost sadistic enthusiasm. This success is not the result of readings in their difficult and complex works, but of the polemical intention that inspired their writings. They actually imposed their way of seeing things on people who refused to accept their theses, or who contested their arguments. It is a perfect example of *succès de scandale*, of shock value, of the upsetting of taboos.

Sex and money were forbidden subjects of conversation at the family table and in the salons of the nineteenth century. Everything had to have the appearance of being conducted in the world as if they did not exist. The great industrialists considered themselves "philanthropists," children were born under cabbages, and the language of a man like Victor Hugo (except in his intimate notebooks) remained very proper. All of a sudden Marx shouted in his thick voice, "Let's talk about money; it's the secret of our social drama." A little later Freud yelled out, "Let's talk about sex; it's the secret of our personal drama." Then came the shock of recognition, the dazzling illumination, the illusion that the forgotten factor—rejected and denied despite good sense—as soon as it is dragged into the light will explain everything.

Several decades had to go by to relate these two propositions, explaining one in the terms of the other. At the beginning both seeemed "unique"—exclusive and total. Applying Marxist analysis to Freud's social milieu, psychoanalysis to the individual case of Marx, and both Freudian and Marxist criteria to the middle class, even to the working class (that frightening reality kept suppressed in society's subconscious)—all this shed light on the polemical intentions which animated these systems and made them succeed, but which also limit their scientific value.

Of very few systems can we really say they "made their time," as we can of these two. Even if Freud is outdistanced in his own field, and above all overrun by a resurgence of religious realities which he considered illusions; and even if Marx is proved wrong in everything he foresaw, except the future of Russian despotism—nothing can detract from the fact that these two tremendous geniuses shaped the twentieth century, drastically modifying our approach to the real. However, the determinisms they believed they had "discovered" have today been refuted. (Actually, it was the influence of these discoveries that became fixed in our minds.) The human consciousness, which has now grown to the very size of the planet, makes the psyche of Freud's middle-class world of 1900 look like a special case, limited in time and space. As for Marx, Stalin's rise, long reign, and posthumous fall, the rebellions behind the iron curtain, and the great technological advance in capitalist countries have all sidestepped the events foreseen in the famous dialectic. Continuously extolled by his disciples as the most accurate scientific process, Marx's dialectic, which has become out of touch with facts, has been reduced to a mass of dogma enforced by lies. If rebels against the Communist regime today are not simply "Fascist agitators," then the whole dialectic is a mystification, as Marx himself would have said. The historical process becomes nothing more than a bad alibi for our personal acquiescence. The right of opposition has once again become creative. And it is no longer a question of whether we are going to tolerate the inevitable meaning of history, but of whether we are going to make history.

Orwell's masochistic fantasy prolonged the Stalinist nightmare, refined it, rationalized it, and pushed it to its most logical conclusion. Absolutely everything has conspired to make our intelligentsia confuse this agonized dream with our historical future, clinging to a crazy consistency as if it were an announcement of doom.

But has a temporary "thaw" really been enough to alter our fate? Has a smashed revolution been enough, or even a hushed-up revolt among Russian youth? Are these things sufficient to change a fatal destiny? Has not the trauma brought on by the brief and tragic Hungarian revolution, which was deeply felt throughout Europe, Asia, and in Russia itself, merely created the romantic illusion of renewed freedom, a false alarm dreamed of during a nightmare which, in the long run, is the genuine reality?

We would really have reason to worry if other facts, unrelated

to current events in the East, did not confirm our new-found
optimism. Budapest won its victory—at least morally. Let us
admit that this is not everything. And yet, what had this to do
with the West?

Three vague but obsessive images have been darkening the
future in the minds of most thoughtful people in the West—right
up to the present day. Some kind of economic determinism
seems to have been mercilessly conducting us to the triumph of
the Total Plan, enjoining all life to the service of the state. And
some kind of historical determinism makes us foresee the "decline of the West," and considers inevitable the grinding of
Europe between political blocs. Finally, some kind of technological determinism announces the reign of robots.

But an examination of realities in process does not confirm
these paralyzing predictions. In fact, it dispels them and reveals
a general tendency toward the reawakening of the values of freedom. Therefore, let us look more closely at these fatalistic illusions.

First: "The Soviet Union is the future." The Soviet Union was
the paradise of the working class, the United States the last
bastion of capitalist exploitation, doomed to cyclical depressions
and the ever-increasing impoverishment of workers. The Soviet
Union, consequently, represented the future, while the United
States was condemned by the "movement of history." Such was
the religion of the progressivists. Now for the facts.

No one is unaware that the American worker is the richest in
the world, the Soviet worker one of the poorest. This concrete
argument does not worry the Marxists, but it does throw them
into an acute dialectical crisis. They accuse it of being grossly
materialistic, besides being in bad faith. More delicately, Bert-
rand de Jouvenel, comparing the economies of the United States
and the Soviet Union, has shown that the Communist enterprise
has produced nothing that distinguishes it essentially from capitalist enterprise in its historical development. After forty years,

it has caught up with the stage of capitalist exploitation, which has been largely left behind by the United States. Marx observed two phases in industrial development: one, distinguished by "the accumulation of capital" and "the exploitation of the worker," had capitalism for its historical agent; the other, defined by the worker's profiting from the fruits of his labor, would be the work of communism. But an examination of facts and figures leads us to the following conclusion: it is the capitalist economy of the United States that has passed into the second phase, and it is the Communist economy of the Soviet Union that remains in the first.

"That doesn't prevent the Soviet Union from representing the future!" our historical maniacs insist. But it is certainly an odd future, racing wildly to rejoin a "past" ritualistically denounced in official toasts. If you overlook the mystifying ceremonies and, instead of reading the publicity folders extolling the benefits of the "cure," simply check the results, you see that the real progress has been in the West, and servitude and iron law in the East. A working class that was better informed rather than indoctrinated, if given a choice of emigration, would pick America *en masse*. Indeed, that is just what the Hungarian refugees in Austria who were free to speak have done.

It is equally striking that in the eyes of these Hungarians the future, if it does not lie in the Soviet Union, is not in Europe either. . . . We can imagine a few of the reasons why. But what are they worth?

Second fatalistic illusion: "Europe is doomed." Dethroned by two wars and ruined by division into twenty-five sovereign states —states incapable of proving they are sovereign—Europe seems given over by history to an ignominious reapportionment: the east to Russia, the west to America, the middle neutralized. The decline of Europe seems irreversible.

The movement for federal union was launched immediately after the war by the Congress of Montreux and the Hague Con-

ference. It has already produced the Council of Europe, the
Common Market and Euratom. It would be very strange if it
could be stopped there. The Constituent Assembly is its next
step. A Federal Authority should emerge from such a congregation, for everything demands it and the necessity is written
plainly in the facts, even if it has not yet reached the retarded
minds of nationalists.

Not one European state can defend itself alone. Not one can
declare war without raising its hand to ask permission—which
is refused. Not one can live in economic autonomy. Not one,
then, is independent. But together they all can be, and they are
beginning to realize it. Three hundred and thirty million inhabitants to the west of the iron curtain, plus one hundred million
more retrieved from behind it, would make a force superior to
the Russians and Americans combined. Of course, I am speaking only of numbers, not of quality.

The lugubrious prophecies of a Spengler or the fascinating
speculations of a Toynbee, inspired by the mythical idea of
evolution—climbing, culminating, crumbling, declining, fate-
fully dying—are clearly old-fashioned in the light of a Europe
again moving to the head of progress. Actually, it is another
prophecy that is coming true. Proudhon, a participant in the
revolution of 1848, said, "The twentieth century will inaugurate
the era of federations, or human history will again spend 1,000
years in purgatory." And indeed, we have arrived at the federal
era—it is no longer hypothetical. History once more depends
upon what we do, and not on any imaginary curve, a traceable
evolution, or a dialectical process whose strings a party knows
too well. Let us stop looking for a meaning to history, which is
an alibi for rejecting our vocation; let us rather learn how to
direct it.

Third fatalistic illusion: "We're moving toward the reign of
robots." Machines are invading our lives; we are going to be en-

slaved by them. They have already enchained our bodies, dictating our actions and the rhythm of our days. Before long, electronic brains will be dictating our thoughts through the radio. Good-by, idle nature; good-by, endless meditation; mechanical monotony is going to dominate our disciplined existences. It will be the end of freedom, of the right to hesitate, to err. The experts, those sorcerer's apprentices, have unleashed unknown forces on the world. It's too hot or too cold for the season; crazy accidents and madmen are increasing; planes are crashing —believe me, it's the bomb. It's going to destroy nine-tenths of humanity. One day it will knock the earth right out of orbit.

I have heard these words every single day from somebody. Who has not? Curiously enough, everything is false in such language; it is only a way of talking abusively.

Machines are invading our lives? If only they were! For they are extremely expensive. A Chevrolet never rolled into my court-yard spontaneously, intending to invade me. Nor has a washing machine. On the contrary, what difficulties I encounter, in my part of the country, trying to *obtain* a telephone!

Do you speak of the thralldom of the telephone? Have you ever seen one make a call by itself? It is always *someone* who uses it. When it rings in your house, you don't know who it is, so you answer. You are not a slave of the telephone but of your own curiosity.

You think the reign of machines will isolate you from nature? It is just the opposite. Express trains, planes, scooters, and little cars convey crowds of city dwellers to beaches, mountains, forests. It is nature, it seems to me, that has the right to complain about an excess of machines, not man.

You mention the sorcerer's apprentice. And what journalist hasn't mentioned him, thinking of the bomb? But the bomb is nothing without orders from a president or a general. The bomb isn't dangerous—man is. As for electronic brains (in a metaphorical sense), they can do nothing that wasn't prescribed for them.

If they work for us, so much the better. But if you tell me that they are going to think for you, then you deserve it. In the story, the sorcerer's apprentice sets loose unknown powers. But our experts do exactly the opposite: they domesticate energies revealed by their calculations. What is let loose upon the world, once again, is man.

In reality, there is only one group of men who have the right to curse machines: not the middle class, not the intellectuals, but the nineteenth-century workers and those who labor on assembly lines. They alone have been physically, and perhaps even morally, subjected to the tyranny of mechanical rhythms. They alone have been transformed into "living cogs in a dead machine," in Marx's dreadful but correct words. But then, it is precisely the robots that will deliver them from their chains.

Eloquently perpetuated by Bernanos, an unparalleled misunderstanding is attached to the synthetic word "robot." Just what is it? It is not, as millions believe, an automatic man out of science fiction. It is even less a man-made mechanical slave. It is a machine, nothing more, nothing less. It is a tool, conceived by man, to take his place in monotonous, exhausting, or hazardous work. There could be nothing more inoffensive. On the other hand, the invention of the knife, so rarely criticized, has provoked the destruction of several million human lives.

It is here appropriate to recall the time lag I mentioned before. The evil that Karl Marx and Proudhon reviled, the evil that was then ignored, was the semi-automatization of industrial production. Since there was no possibility of returning to the past, the remedy was sought in total automatization, freeing the worker not only from his struggle with excessively difficult or dangerous materials, but also from the inhuman monotony imposed by the machine. The remedy, then, was the robot, the recent use of which has been called automation. It is really odd that Western thought, discovering the peril a hundred years late, directs its wrath against the remedy.

Far from increasing the evil so long deplored by those who have never suffered from it, automation can begin to deliver the worker from mechanical servitude. But the intermediate results will go much further. They are incalculable.

Workerless factories, producing night and day under the simple surveillance of a skeleton crew, mean (wherever they exist) the suppression of the proletarian class. Generally, in the future, such factories will make superfluous the dialectical process of the revolution in giving power into the hands of workers. Hence the continued development of technology, not the Communist Party, will be the agent for transcending the conflicts created by technology itself.

How shall we foresee and measure the scope of the changes initiated by this technological liberation? What shall we do with all the leisure time that will be opened up? And what about all the related problems of the education of children, adults, and technicians? This is the problem of cultural resources, on which demands will be made on a rapidly enlarged scale. Beyond all the enormous questions that I leave to economists and sociologists, beyond the classical problem of full employment and the length of the work week, man is now confronted with how to use time. But this implies nothing less than the problem of freedom, the problem of the meaning of our lives . . .

To the philosophers of the decline of the West, of the decline of culture, of the necessity of impending tyrannies, I make this simple proposal. Drop these terrible subjects for a while, be complacent, and consider the novelty of our epoch; this is excellent training for disciplined thought and for overcoming dizzy spells! I propose a cloture on fifty years of pessimistic ruminations. For a long time they were justified, but today they are in danger of surviving their predicted calamities. I propose a new role for the intelligence: to create freedom while searching for it, agreeing to face up to its risks and testing them first in the imagination. I propose a renewed idea of progress, giving up our illusions but also going beyond our skepticism. Such progress does not mean an increase of consumer goods or the elimination of our evils, for every conceivable solution would put an end to our freedom. On the contrary, I imagine true progress to involve *the extension of human risk*.

Although there is much more to be said, it is not my business to draw conclusions, but merely to open doors.

14 The Future of Christianity

Many pious souls who are very attached to their Christian beliefs are troubled by my optimism; they feel that I am perhaps too "secular." "If peace," they say to me, "should finally become a real thing in the world, and if prosperity should become universal, leisure common, and health guaranteed by the welfare state; if science, technology, and psychoanalysis should arrive by the end of the century at a point where they resolve our great moral and material problems, the individual and collective difficulties that have tormented mankind for thousands of years; if progress, in the Western meaning of the word, actually achieves its objectives —and this is conceivable—won't religion in general and Christianity in particular become superfluous? Won't the concern inspired by perpetual need be appeased? Will salvation, pardon, grace, and the prayer of intercession have any meaning to human beings who are satisfied?"

It would be far too easy to reply that the promises made by progress will never be wholly kept. For the fact is, they have more chance of being kept, at least partially, than ever before. And even if they were never kept at all, the principal question remains: Is it true that religious concern depends upon material dissatisfaction and upon our social and psychological needs?

Must we really believe that religious interest will wane as our material contentment increases?

Let me say right off that any religion that feels it must fear the final success of progress is hardly worth defending. For it clearly considers itself as a remedy, and no remedy is better than health; as a kind of archaic, medieval tranquilizer making it easier for us to swallow our inevitable misery—but no anodyne is preferable to genuine peace; and ultimately as the complement to a deficiency—which will have no reason to survive, once plenitude has been gained.

Besides, on the hypothesis that progress should succeed, and our earthly needs be fulfilled, it is not merely a remedial religion that would be threatened with extinction because of falling into disuse, but equally or even more, scientific research and technological development—even the very idea of progress.

Actually, I discern at least two mistakes lurking behind this apprehension about the future of Christianity. They involve both the function of religion and the very nature of man.

The function of religion is not to compensate for our evils, or to make us forget them, but to direct our entire being toward the truth, and to affirm a truth that transcends us. And the function of Christianity, in which it is distinguished from all other religions, is to lead man to incarnate the truth. Since truth transforms man "through the renewal of his understanding,"[19] it leads him to transform the world and not to conform to it. The secularizing ambitions of science and technology, and also Marxism, and all the doctrines of progress, are direct and legitimate conclusions that Western thinkers—whether believers or unbelievers —have drawn from the Christian attitude before the world.

On the one hand, man's nature differs from that of the beast because he "cannot live by bread alone." This biblical verse expresses neither a wish nor a reproof; it is a simple statement of fact. That is the way man is, incapable of being satisfied or of

19 Rom. 12:2. See Chapter 10, "The Challenge of Marxism."

living contentedly when his physical needs alone are satisfied. (If this were not so, the inhabitants of our modern prisons would be happier than two-thirds of the human race, who are underfed but free.) "Man infinitely goes beyond man," Pascal said, long before Nietzsche. Man's nature is to pass beyond Nature.

From this I conclude that a religion which fears the success of progress would not be genuine Christianity in any event, and the man who feels spiritually "appeased" by such material success would no longer be a real man.

Some will doubtless say I am wrong, and refer to the sinister futures foreseen by George Orwell and Aldous Huxley. They describe psychophysical conditions so marvelously *successful* that the concern for truth and unending research have completely disappeared and men have become nothing more than a sort of sophisticated cattle. In short, these writers take for granted a built-in check of progress, effected by currently imaginable methods of science and technology at the service of propaganda. Logically speaking, such a process is unthinkable: if technology triumphed over man, it would negate itself with the same stroke, for the closer it came to its absolute limits, the weaker the sources of its energy would become. In practice, both writers foresee the intervention of a human group which would remain outside the process and would push the necessary button for the asymptote to join the axis, despite the laws of mechanics.

For a short while the Nazis and Stalinists looked as if they were about to succeed in this tele-commanded suicide of those areas of mankind subjected to their totally hypnotic police-state power. Their rapid failure, however—after twelve years in one case, twenty-five in the other, mere seconds in the historical continuum—gives us a certain reassurance in regard to the chances of contemporary man. No one believes in these madmen any longer except a handful of intellectuals who were once fashionable in free-world capitals. In the whole world they have perhaps two hundred thousand readers, almost all middle class;

few disciples, and no martyrs. They have nothing in common with the primitive Church. The true danger is not there.

But if we acknowledge that the phenomenon of the "death of God" is limited to certain groups that are quite restricted, though for a time they were intellectually influential; and that the impending triumphs of a scientifically organized life will not eliminate religious concern from the immense majority of mankind; if we acknowledge, moreover, that the leisure time gained through technology will, on the contrary, cause the diffusion of culture and consequently of metaphysical concerns throughout the entire human race, quite another problem presents itself to Christianity: not atheism, not indifference—but the problem of *other religions*.

The world's cultures are destined to interpenetrate each other more and more. The ancient religions of Asia, varieties of black magic, modern versions of gnosticism, and superficial or ingeniously imagined syncretisms will inevitably gain larger audiences in the West. What will become of Christianity in this fantastic competition? Its fundamental and dogmatic claims to represent the unique and universal gospel, incarnated once and for all, may appear exorbitant, even untenable. Just what are Christianity's chances in meeting such a challenge?

We certainly cannot speculate on its chances as if Christianity were a party, or a nation, or an ideology, or a civilization, for it is very different from all of them. Karl Barth would simply limit himself to saying that, since Christianity is the Word of God delivered to man, its future depends upon God alone and should not preoccupy the Church. And more than one Christian will invoke the promises made to the Church to convict me of lack of faith, if not of vain curiosity bordering on blasphemy.

But while it is true that Christianity is essentially different, it is existentially linked to realities which are both historical and "worldly" in the Pauline meaning of the word. Accordingly, it simply cannot refuse to answer the questions the present world now poses to it, and which Reformation Europe, still shut in upon itself, ignorant of other religions and lumping them all under the name of paganism, did not present. For the Reformation, indeed, all these other religions were simply paganism, the synonym for scandalous error and the unenlightened soul.

Historical Christianity is *also* a party, or even a group of parties; it is *also* an ideology, and it is linked to a certain civilization which it has unquestionably transformed, but not without slipping into that civilization's forms of thought and organizational structures, which were established long before the arrival of Christ. Christianity's chances for the future depend, therefore, also upon the chances of those confessions which compose it and on the chances of Western civilization in the world. But this dependence should be understood in two distinct ways. Christianity can triumph or perish, along with its separate denominations and with Western civilization, if it remains vitally bound up with both of them. But it can also overcome its present-day disunity, more or less detach itself from specifically Western trends of thought, and thus survive them; it can save its soul by renouncing its traditional forms, and then perhaps it can gain the world.

This, at any rate, is what I would like to try to imagine now in a fashion as precise as the art of historical and social conjecture permits. This is hardly a matter of exact science, but it is far from being a utopian daydream. Utopia is only the projection of an ahistorical future based on our desires and fears: it is a compensating image that does not teach us anything about a *possible* future, but simply describes, in reverse fashion, our partial vision of the present, emptied of all the connections and necessary interrelations that determine its actual existence. That is why I once defined Utopia as "a system without a future."

Christianity is a party (or, rather, a group of parties which sometimes compete and sometimes co-operate) in so far as it presents itself to the world not only as revealed truth, but as a group of organized churches, each possessing its doctrine, its own structure, its own institutional network and effective membership.

The plurality of its denominations has perhaps not retarded or impeded it from spreading throughout Asia and Africa up until now, but it is not very likely that one of the three or four great branches—Catholic, Orthodox, Protestant, or Anglican—will ever be able to impose its authority over the others, winning the non-Christian world for itself. Among the historic confessions, only Catholicism and Protestantism are in a position even to aim at such a goal, if not achieve it.

Catholicism's fundamental aspiration to universality, suggested by its very name, is also to its advantage as an organization which has remained admirably effective after four centuries,[20] and has been imitated by the great sociopolitical movements of our day (including both the Communist Party and other totalitarian regimes). It possesses an equally remarkable intellectual flexibility which has allowed it to adapt itself, in spite of its doctrinal discipline, to milieux as different as Mandarin China, tribal Africa, or the Puritan-tinged culture of the United States. Its preservation of a kind of magic thought and a ritual that works *ex opera operato,* the heritage of ancient and oriental religions (the cult of relics, transubstantiation, the quantitative value of recited prayers, exorcisms, and so on), equally favor its influence over the so-called pagan world, although at the cost of preserving spiritual equivocations in the first generations of converts.

Conversely, it has against it a basic absolutism, less in doctrine than in clerical education and discipline; its centralization in Rome, which is more of an imperial symbol than an apostolic one; its Aristotelian doctrinal attachment; and its long tradition of hostility to the freedom of democratic aspirations, which force

[20] The current organization of the Church of Rome dates from the Council of Trent, 1545–63.

it to enter the century only while moving backward, tardily and grudgingly.

Protestantism's advantage is its tradition of greater receptivity to present developments in both scientific and technological culture:[21] it was the father of the moderate democratic regimes that rule those nations of the world which today are healthiest from the social, civil, economic, and political point of view. It has always favored federalist solutions, allowing a conciliatory evolution, contrary to the Church of Rome which has almost always sided with absolute forms of power, generating revolutions quick to develop totalitarian aims. No totalitarian doctrine has ever been able to develop and blossom in kingdoms and republics stamped with the mark of Calvinism. In contradistinction, the Austrian Hitler, formed by Catholicism—as he insisted—created his movement in Bavaria; Mussolini built up a socialist Rome in opposition to papal Rome; Franco and Salazar have exploited situations typical of the Catholic habitus; and the former seminarian Stalin used the caesaropapism of the czars as his model.

I notice, moreover, that the only monarchies in Europe that have remained stable are Protestant: Sweden, Norway, Denmark, Holland, and Great Britain. And those monarchies have also accommodated themselves to socialism without great difficulty, and to the most concrete realizations of the most open democracy.[22]

Federalist, evolutionary, favoring scientific research, educating citizens who are free because responsible, Protestantism has a much better chance than Catholicism of contributing to the sociopolitical formation of tomorrow's world.

[21] More than eighty per cent of the Nobel Prizes for science from 1901 to 1960 (in physics, chemistry, medicine, and physiology) have been given to countries that are Protestant. And for the years between 1941 and 1960 the rate has been ninety per cent.

[22] See Chapter 12, "The Ecumenical Movement and Federalism."

Conversely, it has against it its tendency to fragmentation, to strict particularism and a moral rigidity which is often more middle-class than evangelical. In a more general way, one should also mention its rationalistic tendency to dispel all sense of mystery, which limits—without rectifying—a fundamentalism surely less defensible than Catholic "magic" and really not any more Christian. If pagan sacralism is the natural temptation of Catholicism, modern secularism is the natural temptation of Protestantism, and no one can deny that both have yielded more than once during the last few centuries.

This rapid analysis indicates, I believe, that Christianity's great chance for survival in the Western as well as the non-Christian world resides in an ecumenical convergence of the virtues found in both the major faiths. Is this convergence merely desirable, or can we uncover some first positive signs of it at the present time? There is no doubt about the first question. A living combination of Protestant federalism and Catholic universality would, by its very nature, protect us somewhat from the anarchic individualism and authoritarian collectivism which are the typical deviations of Christian personalism, that central doctrine common to our two principal faiths.

As for the second question, in earlier chapters I have already revealed several indications that encourage a certain optimism. I shall mention them again, adding a few more words. Among Catholics, there has been a renaissance of biblical studies and the growing demand for missals in the vernacular; among Protestants, a renaissance of liturgy and of the meaning of the Church. We should also include the discovery of social realities by members of the Orthodox clergy, who have been subjected to the Soviet challenge; the fusion of Protestant denominations in Europe, the United States, and India; the emphasis laid by Pope John XXIII on the lay apostolate and on episcopal autonomy, and finally, the burgeoning hope for ecumenical unity among all the faiths.

All this has occurred and become increasingly evident during the last thirty or forty years. Indeed, if we compare the rhythm of this phenomenon of convergence with that of the divergence which has dominated the sociohistorical evolution of Christianity for the last sixteen hundred years,[23] it really looks like a sudden mutation, a mutation toward union in diversity, leaving behind the time of fanatical uniformity which had multiplied divisions and hardened them.

Christianity is also an ideology in so far as it is bound to a specific culture that has its historical source in Europe.

Born of an encounter that was fortuitous, according to the historian, or "providential," according to a certain theology—but in any case, neither rational nor necessary—Christianity is made up of three anomalous phenomena: Greek philosophy, the Roman Empire, and the revelation of Jesus Christ. First proclaimed in the Jewish Temple, Christianity spread in the Near East (Palestine and Syria, Asia Minor and the Caucasus, Egypt and Ethiopia), then in Europe, where it was organized in structures that copied those of the western Roman Empire. In the course of the sixteen centuries that followed its official recognition by the Emperor Constantine (the Edict of Milan, A.D. 313), its attempts at eastern expansion were arrested in India on the Malabar Coast, crushed in China at the end of the tenth century, and then blocked for a long time by the appearance and triumph of Islam in the Near East. On the other hand, it had established itself and was durably organized in Celto-Germanic Europe before conquering the two Americas and Australia, and taking root in the European colonies of black Africa. Thus a series of accidental and world-wide conjunctions have, during fifteen hundred of its

23 The first schisms resulting from Christian heresies date from the third and fourth centuries: Manichaeism, Arianism, Donatism, Monophysitism, and so forth. They persisted both during and after the Middle Ages—schisms between Rome and Byzantium, Albigensians and Waldensians; Hussites, the antipopes, and finally the Reformation and its aftermath.

nearly two thousand years of existence, turned Christianity into the supreme religion of Europe and its conquests.

Now, on the threshold of a new world, a world suddenly almost unified by the marvels of our technology and the diffusion of our values, one wonders whether this strict adherence of Christianity to European culture represents a hope for the future or a fault from the very beginning.

From the worldly point of view, it is unquestionably a piece of luck. For the same complex—the Greco-Roman, Judaic, and "barbarian"—from which Christianity took its forms and structures has also created both science and technology. Today, most of mankind has adopted our sciences and technology, as well as the moral, economic, social, and political values that arose from the secular aspects of this cultural complex. To a certain degree— greater than most people believe—Christianity sustained, catalyzed, and qualified the entire context of this development in a decisive fashion. Our civilization, if it is not Christian, is at least Christianized from its very outset; it is a civilization that much of mankind seeks to make its own, with unequal success.

Avid for our immediately useful products, and unconscious of how firmly tied these products are to our moral and religious values, the peoples of the world, who have only recently achieved a Western type of independence, are actually subjected to the spiritual field of force brought to them by our machines. If ever a religion had the opportunity, by means of its context, to impose itself on the thought, daily rhythm, and even the feeling of people ignorant of its dogmas, or who even deny them, it is this Christianity clearly stamped "Western." No other great religion, whether Hinduism, Buddhism, or Islam, has ever had such vehicles—such means of intellectual penetration—as the idea of progress, equal rights, respect for the human person, social legislation, the sciences of matter and life, technology, and the spirit of research at any cost.

Naturally, I am not suggesting that all these vehicles of West-

ern culture act as an army of missionaries conducting men to
baptism, or even to faith; I merely mean that they unconsciously
orient both the leaders and the masses of Africa and Asia to a
general attitude toward life, society, and nature, of which Western Christianity alone can explain the historical genesis, and of
whose good ethical and spiritual use it alone holds the secret.
Nor am I saying that it is enough for an Asian or an African to
demand equal rights for all, whatever his caste or tribe; for him
to accept simultaneously the Pauline or evangelical conception
of society and the brotherhood of mankind—whether Jew or
Greek, slave or free. But I insist, along with Henri de Man and
many other sociologists, who happen to be agnostics, that the revolutionary phenomenon is unthinkable in areas of Asia and
Africa that have not fallen under Christian influences.[24] Born of
Christianized Europe, of a soil long tilled by a Christianity more
or less faithfully and legitimately interpreted and applied, our
Western civilization, which the whole world is striving to adopt,
creates new conditions and problems wherever it penetrates. The
indigenous religions of other cultures simply cannot cope with
these conditions and problems. What is needed is a conception of
life either derived from Christianity or Christian in itself: this is
a new aspect of Christian opportunity.

Nevertheless, even if one admits that *in fact* the extension of
Western civilization prepares and calls for a corresponding extension of Christianity, it does not necessarily follow that this call
will be listened to, or that this civilization is the only good one.
It may be the most effective, or even the best that exists, without
being the best possible. In its daily contacts with varying human

24 The Malabar Coast (Christianized since the seventh century) gave birth to
the social movements in India. And it is there that the only Communist state on
the subcontinent, Kerala, came into existence. Gandhi himself, it is well known,
was strongly influenced by Christian ideas. In Japan, the success of the Socialist
Party owes a great deal to the evangelist Kagawa. In Africa, it is leaders educated in Europe and become Christians who head the progressive parties in most
recently liberated states.

conditions, it may also reveal its weaknesses and its gaps. Finally, it may destroy the high spiritual and cultural values born of Hinduism, Buddhism, and Islam without substituting for them the values of Christianity, which may be forgotten in transit.

Let me sum up. A modern machine can never convert a man to Christianity. But set it down and put it to work in the middle of a Buddhist or animistic community, and it will rapidly disturb traditional equilibrium. If the material progress brought by the machine is to become a real human good, the Christian conception of the world (which shaped the civilization that produced the machine) must be expressed in a technological context. Otherwise it runs the risk of creating more evil than good.

My basic conclusion is this: Western civilization can prepare the way for Christianity in the people who adopt it, if these people understand the intimate links the Christian conception of life possesses, both of origin and in terms of ends sought, with Western civilization. It is first necessary for united Christians themselves to become aware of these connections; then they should explain them to the world. This is the complete missionary program asked of today's Christians, a program whose scope and world-wide urgency most Christians are far from recognizing.

But this does not exhaust the questions posed to us by the Western imprint of Christianity, in so far as it is a sociohistorical phenomenon.

If, on the one hand, it is a matter of showing non-Christian peoples, fascinated and too easily convinced by Western progress, that this progress would not be real and remains unthinkable apart from a Christian conception of the world; on the other hand, it is no less necessary to show Christians that their religion's truth transcends the historical forms assumed by Christianity in the West.

For the value of the universal truth of the gospel of Jesus Christ to be made apparent, the "Christian message" must dissociate itself from its accidental links with the conditions and customs of the peoples who lived around the Mediterranean when Christian doctrine was formed—just as, later on, the Nordic people adopted this doctrine and accommodated it to their ways.

I shall limit myself to three examples of this necessary dissociation.

1. The medieval Church had linked Christian truth with Ptolemaic cosmology, with Aristotelian philosophy, with the tripartite social hierarchy of clergy, nobility, and third estate (itself of Indo-European origin, to be compared with the castes in India), and with the Romano-German monarchical regime. Little by little it had to dissociate itself from these historical forms, as it was successively challenged by science, the Reformation, and evolution toward increased social equality. Let us note that a Galileo, a Luther, and a Rousseau claimed, as their own, principles actually *more Christian* than those current in the Church, in whose name they were condemned. They contributed, consequently, to drawing Western thought into the original and ultimate universality of Christianity. It is in the prolongation of this "permanent reformation" of the Christian message, in this effort to sift it more carefully from its circumstantial attachments to cultural forms—to thought, life, or social organizations that have become antiquated or too regional—that the worldly chances of Christianity are to be found. Theologians and Western Christian thinkers have not delayed in undertaking the immense and challenging task for religion which the unification of the world represents in this second half of the twentieth century. The work of a Maritain and of a Karl Barth to recall the churches to the essential matter of their own message, and the labor of a Paul Tillich, of a Bultmann, of a Teilhard de Chardin, of a Louis Massignon, to liberate the Christian message from what could injure its authentic communication with the spiritual values of other traditions—these two apparently contradictory efforts actually converge toward the same end: it is the Truth alone

that must be communicated, and therefore must be made communicable.

2. In so far as communal worship remains an essential part of Christianity, it is evident that its traditional symbols, borrowed from Mediterranean civilization, must be translated into the terms of corresponding realities in other civilizations. The sacred vestments of Christian priests are copies of those worn by priests in imperial Rome, and of the kings and "sacred" personages of the Middle Ages. Why should the surplice or the cassock be worn in the twentieth century? They were, respectively, the ceremonial dress and working garb of twelfth-century Europe. Must we not seek out corresponding vestments for today that will have symbolic worth not only in the West, but in the East and in Africa? But this is of only secondary significance. The use of bread and wine in communion is much more important. The grapevine is typical of Greco-Romano-Semitic culture in the Mediterranean, but Asia and black Africa know nothing of it. What use can the Christian missionary make of the numerous parables about grapevines in the gospel, or about drunkenness in Genesis? Islam is also familiar with wine, but forbids it, and it is from this prohibition that the eleventh- and twelfth-century mystics drew their esoteric lyricism. . . . I shall content myself with pointing out certain difficulties that appear only on the fringe of the present epoch—but ones which we must consider.

3. The need for a single language capable of translating Christ's universal message resulted in the eastern Church's preservation of ecclesiastical Slavonic or Coptic, while the western Church stopped with liturgical Latin; but nobody understands these languages any longer except the priests! Will not the future require a new, living, universal language? English would probably be the most convenient. Or should the liturgy be recited in the language of each country, as in the Protestant formula? In any case, it is clear that this linguistic translation will imply many others: ethical, psychological, philosophical, and even social.

Analogous comments could be made on other specifically European traits which were borrowed by Christianity over the ages but are not essential to it, such as middle-class—if not Victorian—morality. These are the things that endanger Christianity's opportunity all over the world, stifling its power to be assimilated as a truth for all time and all the faces of mankind.

It seems certain, therefore, that the ecumenical movement cannot stop at a first level of success, which a federal union of all Christian faiths would represent. This union in its turn will at least have to enter into a dialogue with the two other great religions descended from Abraham: that is, Judaism and Islam. And tomorrow's Christian thinkers will have to search together with Buddhist and Hindu thinkers as well, to see if there is a way of translating the great spiritual concepts of grace, faith, the Person, and above all love, which are the fundamentals of Christianity, and which Oriental traditions seem to exclude. All this must be undertaken, not in a spirit of condescending mutual tolerance, nor of theological laxness, nor simply for the sake of peace, but rather in the spirit of genuine catholicity which is inclusive of all truth.

As a result of this immense, this planetary effort, which is certainly not unprecedented—think of the Jesuits in sixteenth-century China—and was prefigured in the first calling of the apostles, "Go and teach all nations," no living religion appears to possess the promise of a world future comparable to that of Christianity.

More easily translated than any other into all cultural contexts; alone in its concern to discover the ways and means of universal communication and original inspiration, and—because of this —now predestined moderator of scientific civilization; the religion of Christ is also, above all, the only one that has been able to sum up its entire law in the commandment of love—love of God, love of self, love of neighbor. So far as I can see, this is the only conceivable rule for a society of men which wants not merely to live in peace, but to be open to the action of the Spirit of Truth.

KANSAS SCHOOL OF RELIGION
University of Kansas
1300 Oread Avenue
LAWRENCE, KANSAS

Date Due

NOV. 4 1969			

Demco 293-5